Amen

ISLAM AND CATHOLIC THEOLOGY
VOLUME 1

Series Editors

Editorial Board

Amen

Jews, Christians, and Muslims
Keep Faith with God

PATRICK J. RYAN, SJ

The Catholic University of America Press

Washington, D.C.

Library of Congress Cataloging-in-Publication Data
Names: Ryan, Patrick J., 1939– author.
Title: Amen : Jews, Christians, and Muslims keep faith with God / Patrick J. Ryan, SJ.
Description: Washington, D.C. : The Catholic University of America Press, 2018. |
Series: Islam and Catholic Theology ; Volume 1 | Includes bibliographical references and index.
Identifiers: LCCN 2018022373 | ISBN 9780813231242 (pbk. : alk. paper)
Subjects: LCSH: Abrahamic religions. | Theology, Doctrinal. | Christianity. |
Judaism—Doctrines. | Islam—Doctrines.
Classification: LCC BL80.3 .R93 2018 | DDC 201/.4—dc23
LC record available at https://lccn.loc.gov/2018022373

In memory of
Cardinal Avery Robert Dulles, SJ
and
Professor Wilfred Cantwell Smith,
faithful teachers

and for
Edward Nutsugah
and
Mary Ryan O'Reilly,
faithful to the end

and for
D.,
still struggling

"And yet, when the Son of Man comes,
will he find faith on earth?"
(Luke 18:8)

CONTENTS

Acknowledgments   ix   /   List of Abbreviations   xiii
Preface   xv

Introduction: A Long Letter Begun   1

1 Faith as a Response to Covenant   19

2 Abraham: A Father in Faith   44

3 Faith and Culture: Rejection, Accommodation,
   and Integration   78

4 Prophetic Faith, Repentance, and the Development
   of Tradition   120

5 Faith Facing Death: Hopes and Fears   156

6 Circling around God: The Faith of Pilgrims   179

7 Naming the God with Whom We Keep Faith   204

Conclusion. A Long Letter Ended   231

Selected Bibliography   237   /   Index   251

ACKNOWLEDGMENTS

I begin with thanksgiving, acknowledging precious mentors, most of whom have gone before us marked with the sign of faith. Among these I mention Jesuits who have taught me: Ronald Sams, Stephen Duffy, John Boyd, Herbert Musurillo, William Noon, Avery (later Cardinal) Dulles, Joseph Fitzmyer, and, still among the living, Edward Mally. Secondly, I remember with great gratitude the scholarly and personal example at Harvard of the late Wilfred Cantwell Smith, Annemarie Schimmel (my dissertation director), Ilse Lichtenstadter, George Makdisi, and Muhsin Mahdi. I also wish to thank Prof. John Carman, still very much alive and a continuing source of wisdom. I remember as well with deep gratitude the late Kevin Starr, prolific historian of California and one-time senior tutor at Eliot House of Harvard College (1970–73). Along with his wife, Sheila, and the master of Eliot House at that time, the late Alan Heimert, Kevin made me feel at home in 02138, the most opinionated zip code in the world.

Among my colleagues at the University of Ghana at Legon I especially treasure the memories of the late John Koster, SVD, Paul Ansah, Kwesi Dickson, and John Hunwick. Two scholars first known at Legon remain friends and mentors to the present day: Canon John Samuel Pobee and Lamin Sanneh, the latter now a professor at Yale University. I also wish to thank my many students over the years, especially Muslim students at the University of Ghana, the University of Cape Coast, and Fordham University, as well as Jesuit students at Hekima College in Nairobi, Kenya, and at Arrupe College in Harare, Zimbabwe. Over the years since 1964, friends in Africa have formed me in ways they little suspected, especially my fellow Jesuits in Nigeria and Ghana: the late Eamon Taylor and Isidore Bonabom, and—among the liv-

ix

ing—Donald Hinfey, George Quickley, Chukwuyenum Afiawari, Gerald Aman, John Ghansah, Samuel Okwuidegbe, and Tyolumun Kinga-Upaa. I must also mention lay friends in Africa of long standing: the late Dr. Anthony 'Supo Akingbade and Cosmas Edmundson, along with such living friends as Ebrima Ousman Camara, Samuel and Anna Quarshie, Emmanuel Attigah, Stella Ansah, David Ackon, Samuel Atarah, Prosper Adotey, Joseph Kwame Attah, Pius Kodjo Buame, Anthony Akande, George Atta-Boateng, and Dolapo Fakeye. In New York City I still miss the presence of the late Hans and Lotte Lichtblau, who made me a West Sider; I continue to rejoice with friends made at Holy Trinity Catholic Church, especially the two Thomases, Leonard and Sandi, and Colleen Glazer.

During various sojourns at Fordham University I have benefited from the companionship and scholarly encouragement of many Jesuits, especially the late Raymond Adams and Gerard Reedy, as well as the continuing scholarly and personal cooperation and friendship of Joseph Lienhard, Christopher Cullen, and Thomas Scirghi. Joseph McShane, the president of Fordham University, deserves special thanks for inviting me to take up the Laurence J. McGinley Chair in Religion and Society at Fordham, encouraging me as well in the direction of Jewish-Christian-Muslim trialogue. My current provincial superior and former rector, John Cecero, is gratefully acknowledged as the first person to suggest this academic move. Several of my colleagues at Fordham deserve special thanks for bringing me here in the first place (Professors John Entelis and Byron Shafer) and for bringing me back to Fordham more than once. In particular, I wish to thank the university's provost, Prof. Stephen Freedman.

Jewish and Muslim scholars have contributed beyond measure to my understanding of faith in general and of their own faith traditions in particular. I mention in particular my respondents at McGinley lectures at Fordham over the past nine years: Rabbi Daniel Polish (Congregation Shir Chadash), a friend for fifty years, and Professors Amir Hussain (Loyola Marymount University), Magda Teter (Fordham University), Hussein Rashid (Barnard College), Sarit Kattan Gribetz (Fordham University), Mehnaz Afridi (Manhattan College), Claudia Setzer (Manhattan College), Jerusha Tanner Lamptey (Union Theological Seminary), and the late Alan Mintz (Jewish Theological Seminary). John Borelli (Georgetown University) and Jack Miles (University of California, Irvine) have also helped in more ways than I can count, as well as another Jesuit, Richard Clifford (Boston College School of Theology and Ministry).

Some parts of this book (in "A Long Letter Begun") have already appeared in a somewhat different form in two different issues of *Commonweal*; thanks are offered to the editor, Paul Baumann, for permission to reuse and expand them. The original forms of chapters 1–7 were first printed privately as pamphlets by Fordham University, along with Jewish and Muslim responses, and the lectures appeared as well in *Origins: Catholic News Service Documentary Service*. Particular thanks are due to associate editor Mary Esslinger for all her selfless labor. All of these chapters have been considerably reworked and expanded for this publication.

Many attributions are assigned to the old saying that "No man is a hero to his valet," and in my case no adage proves truer. Dr. Anne-Marie Kirmse, OP, the sole research associate of the McGinley Chair since its inception in 1988, has served me as selflessly as she served my predecessor in the chair, Cardinal Dulles. She has tracked down references, explained complicated academic and technical details, suggested improvements, edited out excrescences, proofread with an eagle eye, reminded me where I am supposed to be at every hour of the day and night, and sewn on buttons as necessary. Dr. Kirmse, a Dominican, is a very Ignatian "woman for others." An expert corps of graduate research assistants, marshaled by Sister Anne-Marie, have served the McGinley Chair under the banner of her black and white Dominican cross, especially Dr. Michael Canaris (now at Loyola University in Chicago), Joshua Bishop, Alexander Miller, Vanessa Williams, Christopher Sweeney, Dorothy Chang, Taylor Bartlette, Allen Wilson, Stefano Zordan, Mary Stapleton Smith, Henry Omeike, CSsR, and Jack Pappas. Extraordinary undergraduate student workers have astounded me with the facility of youth to deal with computers and to deal with me: John Frank Hinck, Matthew Windels, Thomas Ginch, B. Patrick Killion, and Christopher Penello. Finally, at the Catholic University of America Press I wish to thank acquisitions editor John Martino for shepherding this manuscript into green pastures. Last but not least I thank my immediate family for their love and support, especially Liam O'Reilly, the loving husband of my late sister, Mary.

For all these friends, living and deceased, I give thanks to God, echoing the words of William Butler Yeats when he gazed on the portraits of his friends in the Municipal Gallery in Dublin:

> Think where man's glory most begins and ends,
> and say my glory was I had such friends

Unless otherwise noted, all quotations from the Hebrew Bible and the New Testament in this book will be taken from *The Harper-Collins Study Bible*. I have constantly compared this translation of the Hebrew Bible with the Jewish Publication Society's translation, *Hebrew-English TANAKH*. Where there are important differences between the translations, I will note them. Certain passages I will translate myself and these will be noted as such. All translations from the Qur'an in this book are my own.

DS	*Enchiridion Symbolorum Definitionum et Declarationum de Rebus Fidei et Morum* (ed. Denzinger)
EI2	*The Encyclopaedia of Islam: New Edition* (ed. Gibb)
EJ2	*Encyclopaedia Judaica*
EQ	*Encyclopaedia of the Qur'an* (ed. McAuliffe)
JPS	*Hebrew-English TANAKH*
FOTC	The Fathers of the Church series
NCE2	*The New Catholic Encyclopedia* (ed. Carson)
NJBC	*The New Jerome Biblical Commentary* (ed. Brown et al.)
NRSV	*The HarperCollins Study Bible (New Revised Standard Version of 1989)* (ed. Attridge)
OED	Oxford English Dictionary

Jews, Christians, and Muslims all finish prayers with the word "Amen." Each of the first four sections of the Book of Psalms ends with a prayer of praise for God to which the faithful Jew is to respond, sometimes even twice, with the word "Amen": "Blessed be the LORD, the God of Israel, from everlasting to everlasting. Amen and Amen" (Ps 41:13). "Amen" is an affirmation of fidelity to God and the quintessential expression of hope that God's glorious presence may "fill the whole earth" (Ps 72:19). All the people of Israel are to respond to God by blessing the LORD, the God of Israel: "Let all the people say 'Amen'" (Ps 106:48).

In the Christian tradition, Jesus himself inverts the order of saying "Amen" and begins many of his most important sayings with a single or a double "Amen," the single "Amen" more typical of the Synoptic Gospels and the double "Amen" unique to John's Gospel. Thus Jesus invites his disciples, then and now, to put their faith in him the way the people of Israel had put their faith in the LORD, the God of Israel. Christians themselves are to respond to the faithful love of God manifest in Jesus with their own "Amen" at the conclusion of prayers, their "Amen" derivative from the "Amen" of Jesus. "For in him every one of God's promises is a 'Yes.' For this reason it is through him that we say the 'Amen,' to the glory of God" (2 Cor 1:20).

Amin in Arabic also ends prayers, and especially the most commonly used prayer in the Muslim world, the first *sura* of the Qur'an. Nevertheless, the *Amin* always uttered at the end of any recitation of that *sura* is not part of the Quranic text. The person who prays that first *sura* or who hears it prayed by others commits himself or herself to its basic expression of faith in the sovereignty of one God alone (Qur'an 1:1–7):

In the name of God, the Merciful One, Filled with Mercy:
Praise belongs to God, Master of the Universe, the Merciful One,
    Filled with Mercy,
Ruler of the Day of Judgment.
It is You we serve, You we beg for help:
Guide us on the straight path,
The path of those whom You have graced, not the path of those who merit
    Your wrath, not the path of those who lose their way.

In Hebrew, and also in Arabic, *Amen* or *Amin* come from cognate consonantal roots (*alep-mem-nun* in Hebrew and *alif-mim-nun* in Arabic). The Septuagint, the Greek version of the Hebrew Bible, continues to use the word *Amen* untranslated but the other verbs related to that root in Hebrew are usually translated with forms of the verb *pisteuein*, and the New Testament follows suit. The basic meaning of "Amen" in all three scriptures is the same, an address to God: "I entrust myself to You; I put my faith in You, I keep faith with You."

In this book I examine faith as it is understood by Jews, Christians, and Muslims. This book is not meant to be a work of systematic theology, an exhaustive treatment of the act of faith. What this book offers is several approaches to faith as a category of human experience open to God, a faithful God who reaches out to grasp the faithful human being at the same time that the faithful human being reaches out to grasp a faithful God. This two-sided faith, divine and human, lies at the center of each of these religious traditions. I examine faith as one might examine a gem, gazing at different facets in turn. I also bring into this study the personal reflections of one who has tried to live a life of faith in the company not only of my fellow Christians but also in the company of Jews and Muslims, friends and companions of mine for many decades. I have also lived in the company of good friends who say they have no faith.

I begin this book with a letter I have been writing in various stages and for a long time, a letter to a friend of very troubled faith, who sometimes even calls himself a person of "non-faith." He finds it difficult to say "Amen." I will return to this letter to my friend again and again throughout this book and also at its conclusion.

Amen

A Long Letter Begun

A few decades ago in Africa I met and became friends with an international public servant and diplomat, whom I shall call D. We have remained friends, mainly by correspondence but also through occasional visits, ever since. Raised a Catholic but a man of very troubled faith, my friend is always trying to come to terms with what it means to be a Christian and a Catholic, always reading works of theology and philosophy, even though his professional interests lie elsewhere. He has in recent years read many things I have written, especially earlier versions of most of the chapters in this book. His response has been generous, but he always comes back to the same critique: "Patrick, that's all well and good, but what does this mean to you? Why do you put your faith in God? What does it all mean to you?"

D., this long letter on faith—a series of meditations worked out over some years—is written for you. It is also, quite obviously, written for me, meant to help me come to some understanding of my own faith. I thank you for challenging me to write it.

The Epistle to the Hebrews, an anonymous hortatory sermon or set of sermons probably written in the late first century CE, aimed to comfort Jewish Christians sometimes disappointed, or at least discouraged, in their adherence to Jesus as Lord and Messiah. They were people caught between their uncomprehending Jew-

ish families and the Gentile Christians who now, generation by generation, gradually came to outnumber them in the early church. They were
people at a loss, a situation known as well by many later people of faith.

The eleventh chapter of the Epistle to the Hebrews begins with a
verse sometimes seen as a definition of faith, a verse I would rather suggest is an evocation of what it means to put one's faith in God, what it
means to keep faith with God. I start with the translation in the New
Revised Standard Version, but I want to delve more deeply into the original Greek and the overtones and undertones with which it resounds:
"Now faith is the assurance of things hoped for, the conviction of
things not seen" (11:1). Faith described as "assurance" and "conviction"
sounds a bit smug to modern ears, even a trifle fanatical: an offer of pie-
in-the-sky-when-you-die-bye-and-bye combined with an annoying certitude about intangible or invisible realities. Such certitude or conviction seems unavailable to outsiders, to the general public. Is that what
this anonymous preacher of the Epistle to the Hebrews is trying to shout
at us down the echoing corridors of so many centuries? I think not.

Let me suggest my own translation, one that attempts to avoid the
typically Greek and Latin reliance on nouns rather than on verbs for
suggesting the meaning of a reality. I propose to translate this verse as
follows: *Faith is the reality that undergirds our hopes, the argument that
convinces us about realities we do not see.*

The Reality That Undergirds Our Hopes

What is the Greek word that lies beneath assurance and "reality that
undergirds"? *Hypostasis* is a word designating something that lies beneath something else as its basic support, its ultimate foundation. This
Greek word is translated root by root into Latin as *substantia*, "substance." I am only interested here in the architectural imagery suggested by the Greek of the Epistle: *hypostasis* as groundwork, as undergird-
ing reality. I take it to mean that faith lays the foundation that prompts
us not to look upward but to look forward, to live in hope for the future
in an ultimate sense. It is a foundation from which we can look for-

ward, not only towards this world but also towards the world to come.

But even if faith as *hypostasis* undergirds our hope, it must be admitted that it sometimes provides a very shaky foundation. In a book that Pope Benedict XVI, then Joseph Ratzinger, published in German in 1968, he recalls the first scene in Paul Claudel's epic drama, *The Satin Slipper*. A Jesuit missionary, brother to the main character of the drama, has barely survived a pirate raid and shipwreck. Lashed to a mast of the sunken ship, the Jesuit now drifts over the raging waters. "I really am fastened to the cross," the Jesuit soliloquizes, "but the cross on which I hang is not fastened to anything else. It drifts on the sea."[1] Ratzinger in 1968 saw the Jesuit's situation as an apt model of faith for many in the modern world: there is certainty, fastened strongly to the mast, but there is also a raging sea of uncertainty heaving just below the floating mast that rides the waves. How could it be otherwise?

My grandmother, a woman of eighty when she died, asked my mother one day when they were alone whether my mother thought there was a life after death. My mother was more than a little shocked by this inquiry from an old Irish woman, legally blind all her life and illiterate as a result, a woman who never had the leisure or the ability, one would have thought, to raise philosophical or theological questions. She assured my grandmother that there was hope for blessed survival. Both of them widows, they knew full well the sorrow of death and separation. My mother's foundation in faith—inherited from her mother—was returned as a gift to her mother when the sea beneath the drifting mast of my grandmother's faith proved too turbulent. I visit their graves now and think of those women of faith.

Faith, then, undergirds what we hope for in the future. There is much that frightens us, especially as we approach the end of life, but there is, not by our own efforts but by God's graciousness, a future for which we can hope. God's graciousness in promising that future—that graciousness often mediated to us through our fellow mortal beings,

---

1. Joseph Cardinal Ratzinger, *Introduction to Christianity*, trans. J. R. Foster, new ed. (San Francisco: Ignatius Press, 2004), 43–44. The German original was first published in 1968 and the English translation first appeared in 1969. Revisions were made in the English translation in 1990 and 2004; more revisions of the English translation are still needed.

people of faith like my mother and my grandmother—gives us reason
to hope. For most of us that future full of hope is inextricably linked
with a personal future, a future with much loved persons surrounding
the One who gives us hope and loves us to the end. Jeremiah put it
well when urging the deportees in the Babylonian Exile to wait in patience for their future redemption: "For surely I know the plans I have
for you, says the LORD, plans for your welfare and not for harm, to give
you a future with hope" (Jer 29:11).

Is this self-deception, D., a mirage in the desert, a well where there is no well?
Perhaps it is, but then again, perhaps not.

"If the person of faith," Ratzinger continues, "can bring his faith to
perfection only on the ocean of nothingness, temptation and doubt, if
he has been allotted the ocean of uncertainty as the only possible lo-
cus for his faith, so too, in reverse, the person with no faith is not to be
understood undialectically as one merely lacking faith."[2] People of no
faith live with as many doubts as do people of faith; only fanatics have
no doubts, no fear of the future. Ratzinger recalls in this context the
story told by Martin Buber about the Enlightenment Jew, a rationalist
with no faith, who went to visit Levi Yitzhak, the rabbi of Berditchev,
to engage the rabbi in philosophical arguments about the basis for his
faith. When he arrived, he found the rabbi walking up and down, ab-
sorbed in a book. Barely acknowledging the guest's arrival, the rabbi
looked up to utter only one sentence: "But perhaps it is true after all."
After a while the rabbi told the Enlightenment Jew that his fellow rabbis had wasted their time trying "to lay God and his Kingdom on the
table before you, and neither can I. But think, my son, perhaps it is
true." The disciple of Enlightenment skepticism left the rabbi's home
haunted by that "perhaps."[3]

"Perhaps it is true after all." People of faith, D., and people of no faith have to
live with doubt, with uncertainty. It is part of the human condition.

2. Ibid., 44–45; here the translation has been corrected with the help of my colleague, Joseph
T. Lienhard, SJ, based on the text in *Einführung in das Christentum* (Munich: Kösel-Verlag, 1968), 9.
3. Ibid., 45–46. For the original German, see Martin Buber, *Werke* (Munich / Heidelberg: Kösel-
Verlag / Verlag Lambert Schneider, 1963), 3:348. The words of the rabbi that so disturbed the Enlightenment Jew are "Vielleicht ist es wahr."

There is a cave in northeastern Ghana, in the Tallensi area not far
from Tongo, where members of different clan lineages traditionally settled their disputes, especially about land, in the invisible presence of a
spirit called Tongnaab. Nowadays the cave is more frequently sought
out by tourists, the idly curious, people with nothing important to
bring to a shrine for adjudication. That was not the way nearly nine
decades ago when the British anthropologist Robert Sutherland Rattray first visited that cave. Petitioners often came from as far away as
southern Ghana to seek out the liminal power and the mystery of what
the southerners called Nana Tongo: Grandfather/Grandmother/Ances-
tor Tongo.

The petitioners were not easily received by the priest of the shrine.
Before they could enter, they had to strip naked and walk backwards
into the cave. The floor of the cave, made up of boulders, proved unsteady. As the daylight from the entrance faded, the naked petitioners became aware of scorpions and other creatures of the darkness
scampering around their feet. Despite their nakedness, they began to
sweat. And then they gradually became aware of a sound, echoing and
re-echoing in the cave like the bellowing of a bull. The priest interpreted the bellowing as the spirit demanding offerings of chicken, sheep,
goats. The terrified petitioners complied: they had real problems, were
unsure of their footing, stripped of all their defenses.[4] Like the Enlightenment Jew haunted by the "perhaps" of the rabbi of Berditchev, like
the Jesuit tied to the mast tossed about by the waves in Claudel's drama, petitioners at Nana Tongo's shrine were thrown off their balance.
Their faith and their hopes for what lay ahead of them was both steady
and unsteady, sure and unsure.

Faith is hard to define, hard to explain: a sense of surety beneath

4. The voice of the god in the cave seems to have been caused by a pierced piece of wood on
a string swung about the head of the priest's assistant, a youth ensconced much further inside the
cave. Such a device, often called a bullroarer, is known in many parts of the world, and is sometimes
called a rhombus. See Robert Sutherland Rattray, *The Tribes of the Ashanti Hinterland* (Oxford: Clarendon Press, 1932), 361–65. In these few pages Rattray describes the ceremony he underwent at that
shrine on May 6, 1928. Kenneth K. A. Anti, a former colleague of mine at the University of Cape Coast
in Ghana, has described in his dissertation the same ceremony he underwent at least a half-century
later, and it is from him (rather than from Rattray) that I learned of the Tongnaab's bullroarer. Also
see Jean Allman and John Parker, *Tongnaab: The History of an African God* (Bloomington: Indiana
University Press, 2005).

which heaves a turbulent sea of doubt. There are many things, many aspects of life and death we have not seen, we may never see, but these are realities we hope to see, realities we hope to hear, realities we hope to touch. Faith gives us a place to stand, to take a stand, even if the place where we stand is itself floating on an ocean of uncertainty. Perhaps it is the only place we have to stand. We crane our necks and listen intently, trying to understand what we hear only indistinctly in the darkness. We reach out towards realities unseen and yet hoped for in the cave. We live in hope that beyond the darkness, beyond the turbulence, the realties we hope for are—and are there. Are we deceived?

Perhaps we are, D., but then again, perhaps not.

The Argument That Convinces Us

Imaging faith as the reality that undergirds our hopes, the shaky foundation—but still a foundation—from which we can catch some inkling (at most) of things hoped for in the future, is only one image of faith of the two offered in this single verse of the Epistle to the Hebrews. Faith is also imagined in less future-oriented terms as "the conviction of things not seen." "Conviction," the NRSV translation of the Greek word *elengchos*, owes much too much of its subjectivity to Martin Luther and his emotional quest to find a merciful God. My own suggestion is that it should be translated in logical and juridical imagery as "the argument that convinces us about realities we do not see."

The Greek term *elengchos* most famously characterized a philosophical argument, the process by which Socrates elicited from his interlocutors, through a line of reasoning that they had not previously followed, a truth that they had not recognized before. The other secular use of the word comes not from philosophical deduction but from the usage of law courts, where the *elengchos* leads to the conviction of the criminal in objective terms, not just the subjective process of convincing the criminal of his own guilt, but also the more interactive process of convincing the judge of the objective facts involved in the case before the tribunal.

Faith, D., can convince us in argument about the realities we do not see. What realities? The two greatest realities: the depths of self, the depths of God.

First and foremost we must begin with the depths of ourselves, the depths of our human experience: the innermost, nonphysical recesses of the human person. Many people live out their lives without ever plumbing those depths, never gaining any insight into who they are. It is from within those depths, first of all, that we as human persons—you and I—experience most profoundly what we know and love, and yet we do not see. From the firm but at the same time unsteady vantage point of my subjectivity and your subjectivity, we can catch some glimpse of the Reality that is the direction towards which our innermost selves, like arrows, are aimed. To what or to whom are our innermost personhoods directed? Simply projections of ourselves? We launch the arrows of mind and heart from the bows of our innermost lives towards a high-flying and finally unattainable bird, a bird that catches the eye as it glints in and with the light of sunrise or sunset, something like the kestrel of Gerard Manley Hopkins's sonnet "The Windhover":

> I caught this morning morning's minion, king-
> > dom of daylight's dauphin, dapple-down-drawn Falcon, in
> > > his riding
> > Of the rolling level underneath him steady air, and striding
> High there, how he rung upon the rein of a wimpling wing
> In his ecstasy! then off, off forth on swing
> > As a skate's heel sweeps smooth on a bow-bend: the hurl and
> > > gliding
> > Rebuffed the big wind. My heart in hiding
> Stirred for a bird,—the achieve of, the mastery of the thing!
>
> Brute beauty and valour and act, oh, air, pride, plume, here
> Buckle! AND the fire that breaks from thee then, a billion
> Times told lovelier, more dangerous, O my chevalier!
>
> No wonder of it: shéer plód makes plough down sillion
> Shine, and blue-bleak embers, ah my dear,
> Fall, gall themselves, and gash gold-vermilion.

Hopkins is seldom very easy, but it is important to parse his words, to savor his imagery of the transcendent. The poet begins by saying that he has glimpsed ("caught") at dawn a high-flying bird, a small falcon or kestrel sometimes called a windhover in Britain because of its seeming to pause in mid-flight. Apart from its action in flight, the windhover is a nondescript, rather small bird, but the poet characterizes it as the morning's darling ("minion," from the French *mignon*) and also the royal heir to the monarchy of the sky, the "king-/dom of daylight's dauphin." More words of French origin appear later in the poem. Dawn is breaking and the sun has not risen above the horizon and yet the clouds are flecked with the colors of the coming sunrise: this is the "dapple-dawn" that draws the windhover into its flight. The exquisite ascent of the windhover at dawn, its dipping and circling effortlessly like an ice skater, captivates the poet: "his riding / Of the rolling underneath him steady air, and striding / High there, how he rung upon the rein of a wimpling wing / In his ecstasy! then off, off forth on swing, / As a skate's heel sweeps smooth on a bow-bend: the hurl and gliding / Rebuffed the big wind." The rush of the poet's language imitates the rising and swooping bird; the bird's flight evokes in the somewhat withdrawn poet a deep admiration for what seems to be ecstatic freedom, rare accomplishment, incredible beauty: "My heart in hiding / Stirred for a bird,—the achieve of; the mastery of the thing!"

In the last six lines of the sonnet the poet reflects on the "brute beauty and valour and act" as well as the "air, pride, plume" of the windhover, addressed as "my chevalier"; this French word for a knight links up with the "minion" and "dauphin" of the first eight lines and the "sillion" (in French, *sillon*, a furrow) later in the poem. In Britain, French was long the language of the monarchy; the windhover awakens this regal memory in the poet. He marvels at how the windhover in its graceful flight catches and refracts the light of the rising sun as it suddenly ascends and then swoops downward: "Buckle! AND the fire that breaks from thee then, a billion / Times told lovelier, more dangerous." Such raw beauty, the poet recognizes, can also be glimpsed in something as earthbound and plodding as an iron plough that shines with use as it cuts open a furrow, or in something as moribund as the smol-dering coals ("blue-bleak embers") in a hearth that burst into flame when stirred up: they "Fall, gall themselves, and gash gold-vermillion." The flight of an otherwise nondescript bird at dawn, the plodding pro-cess of ploughing soil, the stirring up of nearly dead embers in a hearth: in each instance, movement makes each of these very ordinary realities radiate with extraordinary beauty.

Hopkins dedicated this sonnet "To Christ our Lord," but it can also be understood, more generally, as an evocation of the transcendent majesty of God discernible in mundane realities towards which we launch the arrows of knowing and loving from our innermost depths. Through the human capacity for insight into what Hopkins called the "inscape," the innermost selfhood of created realities, the radiance of these mundane things stands revealed. St. Augustine caught a sense of that same radiance that can only be glimpsed from the depths of the human spirit when he described in his *Confessions* how he came first to perceive the "unchangeable light" beyond all merely finite lights:

Advised to return to my own self, I entered, with You as my guide, into my deepest recesses. I was able to do so because You had become my helper. On entering into myself I saw, as it were with the eye of my soul, what was beyond that eye of my soul, beyond my spirit: Your unchangeable light. It was not the ordinary light visible to all flesh, nor was it something greater but still of the same sort, albeit shining more brightly and spreading its light everywhere more intensely. It was not this, but something different, very much different from all those things. It was not simply above my mind like oil floating on water or the sky stretched over the earth. This light was above me because it had made me; I was below it because I was created by it. One who knows the truth knows this light, and one who knows it knows eternity, and love knows it. O eternal truth, true love and beloved eternity: You are my God. I sigh for You day and night. When I first came to know You, You drew me up so that I could see that what I saw fully *existed*, but I did not yet *exist* fully, so that I might see. Meanwhile You overcame the weakness of my vision, sending forth most strongly the beams of your light, and I trembled at once with love and dread, finding myself far away from You in the region of unlikeness.[5]

5. Augustine, *Confessions* 7.10. This is the author's translation. See also Augustine, *Confessions*, trans. Henry Chadwick (Oxford: Oxford University Press, 1992), 123.

The theologian Karl Rahner, famous for his complicated philosophical-theological language, once characterized God as "the incomprehensible term of human transcendence."[6] The word translated as "term" in the original German of Rahner is *Woraufhin*, an adverb of direction (whither, where-to, toward which) used as a substantive to indicate that human interiority never fully comprehends or grasps the boundless Reality towards which it is aimed. The soul—the radical interiority of you or of me—is aimed very high indeed. We can never reach the high-flying windhover with the arrows of heart and mind that we launch, but we can aim in that direction.

God, however, will always fly higher and draw us further upward; in the Latin phrase, *Deus semper maior*—God is always greater. In Augustine's meditative commentary on Psalm 63:7—"You have been my help, and in the shadow of your wings I sing for joy"—he lays a foundation for so describing the absolute transcendence of God:

I rejoice in good deeds, because the shadow of Your wings is over me. Because I am a chick, the kite will carry me away, if You do not protect me.... We are little chicks: let God therefore protect us under the shadow of His wings. What happens when we have grown up? It is good for us even then that He protect us, so that under Him as One greater we would always remain chicks. For He is always greater, no matter how much we may have grown up. Let no one say: let Him protect me while I am little, as if at some time one could arrive at such maturity as to be self-sufficient. Without the protection of God you are nothing. We should always want to be protected by God; then we will be able to be always great in Him, as long as we remain little under Him. "In the shadow of Your wings I will sing for joy."[7]

---

6. Karl Rahner, *Foundations of Christian Faith: An Introduction to the Idea of Christianity*, trans. William V. Dych, SJ (New York: Crossroad, 1982), 454.

7. This is the author's translation of Augustine, *Enarrationes in Psalmos* 63 [Vulgate 62], available online at www.augustinus.it. This meditation of Augustine may in some sense lay the foundation for the condemnation at the Fourth Lateran Council (1215) of Joachim of Fiore, who tended to exaggerate the difference between the divine persons in the Trinity, and in some sense reduce the utter transcendence and mystery of God: "Between the Creator and the creature no similitude can be expressed without implying a greater dissimilitude." See *The Christian Faith in the Doctrinal Documents of the Catholic Church*, ed. Josef Neuner, SJ, and Jacques Dupuis, SJ, rev. ed. (New York: Alba House, 1982), 109. For the Latin original, see *Enchiridion Symbolorum Definitionum et Declarationum de Rebus Fidei et Morum*, ed. H. Denzinger and A. Schönmetzer, SJ, 32nd ed. (Freiburg im Breisgau: Herder, 1963) (hereafter, *DS*), §806.

Only God fully *exists* in Augustine's terminology; Thomas Aquinas called God *ipsum esse subsistens*: "The Being that Exists through and of Itself."[8] We frail human beings *exist* only partially, and for a time. Frail as we are, we still can aim the arrows of our deepest selves towards the always more transcendent horizon, the goal of our deepest being and longing. Sometimes, however, we feel unable to keep our eyes on the windhover; sometimes we lose the vision that draws us up and out of our selves; sometimes we forget that we are chicks under the shadow of his wings.

In those moments of doubt, D., the argument about the realities we do not see no longer seems to convince us. You and I have spent a long time in places where Christians and Muslims live together, sometimes on good terms, and sometimes not. My Muslim friends in West Africa, I discovered as I grew to know them, also struggle with their faith. They and we have a Muslim hero to emulate.

A Muslim's Crisis of Faith

Abu Hamid al-Ghazali (d. 1111), Iranian by birth and the most prominent Sunni Muslim scholar in late eleventh-century Baghdad, felt in the year 1095–96 that he was losing his faith, missing the point of the argument about the realities he could not see. Better known for his forty short volumes of devotional writings ("The Revival of the Disciplines of Piety") written in the last decade of his life, Ghazali originally made his academic reputation as a professor of Islamic law in the Nizamiyya, a mosque university in Baghdad. Ghazali's chief patron in Baghdad, the Iranian *atabeg* ("father-commander") known by the sobriquet Nizam al-Mulk, had been the power behind the throne of two Seljuq

---

8. Thomas Aquinas in the *Summa Theologiae* I, q. 3, a. 4, answers the question, *Utrum in Deo sit idem essentia et esse* ("Whether in God his essence and existence are the same"), with the response that *Deus non solum est sua essentia ... sed etiam suum esse* ("God is not only his essence ... but also his existence"). In other words, God is nothing other than limitless being—being untrammeled by any qualification of being something or other, or any diminishment that would be the result of coming to exist or ceasing to exist. See *Summa Theologiae, Pars Prima*, ed. Pietro Caramello (Turin: Marietti, 1950), 16b–17a. The phrase *ipsum esse subsistens* seems to be a somewhat shortened form of a phrase found later in the same section of the *Summa Theologiae* I, q. 4, a. 2: *Deus est ipsum esse per se subsistens: ex quo oportet quod totam perfectionem essendi in se contineat* ("God is that very Being existing through Itself: because of which It must contain every perfection of Being in Itself").

Turkish emperors and weak Arab caliphs for nearly four decades, until he was dismissed from office in 1092 and assassinated a year later. Did these political turns of fortune upset Ghazali's equilibrium? Or was it the philosophical writing he had been studying in those years?

Whatever caused his crisis, Ghazali narrates its physical components vividly:

> God put a lock upon my tongue so that I was impeded from public teaching.... [My] tongue would not utter a single word: I was completely unable to say anything. As a result that impediment of my speech caused a sadness in my heart accompanied by an inability to digest; food and drink became unpalatable to me so that I could neither swallow broth easily nor digest a mouthful of solid food.[9]

Resolved to give up his teaching position in Baghdad and pursue again the sources of his faith as a Muslim, Ghazali decided to throw his disciples off his path, claiming that he was going off on the pilgrimage to Mecca, "all the while planning secretly to travel to Syria."[10] His faith in crisis, he wanted to return to the first experiences of faith that had motivated Abraham and Muhammad. After two years of obscurity in Damascus, where he often locked himself into the minaret of the Umayyad mosque, Ghazali then departed for Jerusalem where he would often shut himself up in the Dome of the Rock, a locale much associated with the Prophet Muhammad's heavenly ascension. It is most likely that Ghazali shut himself up in the cavern underneath the rock where pious tradition maintained that the spirits of faithful Muslims await the day of resurrection.[11] From Jerusalem he also went to visit the tomb of Abraham in nearby Hebron/al-Khalil before finally departing for Arabia and the pilgrimage sites in and around Mecca.[12] After his pilgrimage Ghazali returned, at the behest of his children, not to Baghdad but to his native Iran where he settled. No longer very attracted to the life of a scholar jurist, he had come to realize that the life of Sufis, Muslim mystics, was more important than any other form of Islamic existence: "All their mo-

9. Al-Ghazali, *Deliverance from Error: An Annotated Translation of* al-Munqidh min al-dalal *and Other Relevant Works of al-Ghazali*, trans. Richard Joseph McCarthy, SJ (Boston: Twayne, 1980), 79.
10. Ibid., 80.
11. See Oleg Grabar, *The Dome of the Rock* (Cambridge, Mass.: Belknap Press of Harvard University Press, 2006), 73–74 and 168–69.
12. Al-Ghazali, *Deliverance from Error*, 80–81.

tions and quiescences, exterior and interior, are learned from the light of the niche of prophecy. And beyond the light of prophecy there is no light on earth from which illumination can be obtained."[13]

When the sources of faith dry up, when we are no longer able to keep our balance on the reality that undergirds our hopes, when we can no longer follow the argument that should convince us about things we do not see, it is time—and more than time—to pray, to go on pilgrimage, to forsake our attachments to the sources of our pride. Ghazali learned that, and left behind a lesson for all people of wavering faith: "In the morning I would have a sincere desire to seek the things of the afterlife but by evening the hosts of passion would assail it and render it lukewarm. Mundane desires began tugging me with their chains to remain as I was, while the herald of faith was crying out: 'Away! Up and away! Only a little is left of your life, and a long journey lies before you!'"[14] The journey of life and the journey of a pilgrim have much in common. Delaying any such journey brings us to no destination, no destiny.

Confessions of a Five-Minute Atheist

I promised, D., finally, to interrogate myself about my own faith. Have I ever hesitated to put my faith in God? Have I ever doubted whether God was really there? I am sure I have many times, in small and even trivial ways. I have not always lived a life worthy of the commitment made for me in baptism, renewed by me in confirmation, renewed and specified again in my vows as a Jesuit, and in my ordination as a priest. But those infidelities still pale in my imagination with the one time I actually gave some thought—very briefly, as it turned out—to the possibility of throwing over the whole life of faith. Looking back on it, it seems to me somewhat comic, but it did not seem very comic at the time.

Although I hate to admit that I was ever unhappy in Africa, where I lived for twenty-six years, I have to confess that my first year as a Jesuit scholastic in Nigeria, more than fifty years ago, was not the easiest, either for me or for the fellow Jesuits with whom I lived, or (to put it more honestly) who had to live with me. In the first few months of that

13. Ibid., 81.
14. Ibid., 79.

academic year, I was carted off three times from the high school where I was teaching to the hospital, suffering from bacillary dysentery; the fourth time, dysentery was complicated by bronchitis and malaria. The doctor dosed me heavily with chloroquine phosphate, and I recovered after a few days in the hospital. What he neglected to mention about chloroquine phosphate was that big doses of it cause dizziness, especially when one stands up quickly. It also increases ocular sensitivity to bright light and difficulty in reading. And, yes—he remembered to tell me a month later—"Sometimes it causes depression."

"Thanks a lot," I replied. "I had a wonderful Christmas."

The rest of the school year progressed fairly normally, once I got used to the challenges of living in Africa. I stopped drinking water unless it had been boiled; I had more soft drinks than I ever want to taste again. At any rate, toward the end of that first academic year, I found myself one hot sunny afternoon using my siesta period to read a memoir by the Irish writer Honor Tracy. In fact, Honor Tracy, as I have since discovered, was not Irish at all. She was English, and her real name was Lilbush Wingfield, but she wrote a great deal about Ireland, where she lived for many years. Most of what she wrote was either fiction or gossip, some of it quite amusing.

On that particular sunny afternoon in May 1965, I had just closed a book of Tracy's when I realized, on reflection, that I really didn't want to be a Jesuit anymore. What I wanted was to move to Ireland and write. I was twenty-five and had both a B.A. and an M.A. in English, plus something called a licentiate in philosophy. What was all that literary training for? Why not call the Jesuits quits right now and launch into a writing career? Why not call the church and God quits as well? A friend has suggested me that maybe I was only having a crisis of vocation, not a crisis of faith. But I remember that May afternoon in Nigeria very vividly: it was a crisis of faith.

What do you do when the past eight years of your life as a Jesuit, the past twenty-five years of your life as a Catholic, suddenly lie in shards around your feet on a sunny afternoon? I stood up and walked into the next room, which was, in fact, my bedroom. I sat on the edge of my bed and stared out the window at an open playing field on the school grounds. I felt empty of faith and hope and love, all at once. A fly buzzed around my head.

In that arid moment, something odd happened. For some reason, words that I'd once had to sing in Latin, at a funeral a few years earlier, came back to me, and hit me profoundly, with a mysterious impact. I've thought many times about the words and their effect on me. But first let me describe the circumstances in which I happened to find my-self singing those words.

I don't like to sing solo. I have a fair enough voice, if you go for a *basso* that is not particularly *profondo*. I had sung in my high-school glee club, and as a Jesuit in formation I sang in choirs. In my second year of philosophical studies I stopped; but soon afterward, a Jesu-it who taught us history of philosophy died suddenly. Jesuits are not used to singing the Divine Office in common, but it was our tradition at that time to precede the funeral Mass with the singing in Latin of the Office of the Dead. The choir director approached me a day before the funeral and asked if I would be willing to sing one of the Latin lessons at matins, as he wanted the lessons sung from within the congregation rather than from the choir loft. Because of my diffidence about singing solo in public, I was reluctant, but finally I agreed.

On the morning of the service, the day of a tremendous ice storm, the community had the eerie experience of welcoming the deceased man's identical twin to the funeral. It was as if the Jesuit had come back from the dead as a layman. The Office of the Dead began in mid-morn-ing, and I waited with some trepidation. When at last I stood to sing, nervousness and a huge surge of adrenaline made me start out too high for my vocal range. I wondered immediately if I would be able to finish from where I had started, but somehow I did, to my own surprise and that of my fellow Jesuits.

And now one question from that reading, sung in Latin on a cold morning in the first days of January 1963, came back to me nearly two and half years later, as I sweltered in the heat and sudden existential anxiety of that May afternoon in Nigeria in 1965. Here is what I remembered, seemingly out of nowhere: *Quid tibi dicam, o custos hominum*? ("What shall I say to you, O Guardian of Humanity?"). As I was to discover many decades later, the quotation was slightly inaccurate—but accurate or otherwise, it was enough to end my five minutes of atheism, my desire to throw the whole damned thing over and launch out on a career as a man of letters.

What did that Latin quotation say to me that afternoon nearly half a century ago? It began, surely, in the notion that God was no mere Big Someone or Something outside of me, the anonymous Ground of Being. Rather, in the words of the great Jewish philosopher Martin Buber, God was a fathomless, transcendent "Thou" with whom, even in my moment of wavering, I was still wrestling. But what of it? What, really, did I hear in the chanted Latin running through my mind that afternoon, which reversed the bleak intuition of the utter emptiness of myself and the mysterious absence of God?

I was not sure; and it would take me a long time, and a long way round, to find out. One piece of an answer came three and half years later, when I read—in *The New Yorker*—a short story by Isaac Bashevis Singer, "A Friend of Kafka." The story's main character, Jacques Kohn, is a somewhat shiftless writer and former actor in the Yiddish theater of Warsaw. In exchange for a "loan" of a zloty, Kohn beguiles the narrator with tales of his somewhat racy life. In the process, he compares his experiences both to the travails of Job and to a very competitive game of chess with an incomparable Master:

Why did Job continue to live and suffer? So that in the end he would have more daughters, more donkeys, more camels? No. The answer is that it was for the game itself. We all play chess with Fate as a partner. He makes a move; we make a move. He tries to checkmate us in three moves; we try to prevent it. We know we can't win, but we're driven to give him a good fight. My opponent is a tough angel. He fights Jacques Kohn with every trick in his bag.[15]

At the conclusion of the story Jacques Kohn sums up what may be called his personal theology, as he thanks the narrator for more zlotys:

15. Isaac Bashevis Singer, "A Friend of Kafka," in *A Friend of Kafka and Other Stories* (New York: Farrar, Straus and Giroux, 1970), 6–7.

"Well, if there is a God, He will reward you. And if there isn't, who is playing all these games with Jacques Kohn?"[16]

I liked Jacques Kohn immediately. Here was a man who understood that God sits across the table from you, engaging you in the game of life. A life of faith is no comfy nap on the lap of a kindly celestial grandparent. No, faith in God is a struggle in the night like Jacob's; it is a chess game with an expert who has many tricks up his supernal sleeve.

That story and its attractively roguish protagonist stayed with me over the years. Meanwhile, as a priest reading the breviary in English, I searched in vain in the Office of the Dead for those words of scripture I had once sung in Latin on that cold morning in January 1963, the words that had come back so suddenly and sharply to me in May 1965. I found nothing. Had I imagined those words? I wondered about it often.

Then, during Lent 2008, I read a delightful book of essays, *Faith of Our Fathers*, by the Irish historian of Christianity at Cambridge University, Eamon Duffy. Duffy shared some of his perspectives on his own faith, and also on the challenge to that faith he experienced decades ago when a good friend, an Anglican priest, died unexpectedly. Despite feeling faithless in confrontation with that death, Duffy continued to go to Mass—and only then, he writes, did he come to realize that "in the face of the Cross, the Mass proclaimed a celebration, an affirmation of the unquenchable life of love."[17]

Duffy expresses regret over the transformation of the Latin Catholic funeral liturgy after the Second Vatican Council, when the once mournful liturgy became a more upbeat Mass of the Resurrection, with the famous dirge *Dies Irae* usually omitted. Not only does Duffy rue this transformation, but he also voices a more recondite nostalgia for the loss of the pre-Vatican II version of the Office of the Dead, famous for its nocturns featuring readings from the Book of Job. The nine readings from Job in the old Office of the Dead, Duffy writes, "explored the whole gamut of human feeling in the face of suffering and death: fear, anger, self-justification, reproach, longing for relief, trust, affirmation."[18]

16. Ibid., 16.
17. Eamon Duffy, *Faith of Our Fathers: Reflections on Catholic Tradition* (London: Continuum, 2004), 7.
18. Ibid., 121.

Shortly before reading that passage in Duffy's book, I had come into possession of a single volume of the Latin breviary of a cousin, a priest, who had died at the age of ninety-nine. Fresh from encountering Duffy's hankering for the pre-Vatican II Office of the Dead, I flipped through my late cousin's breviary. It didn't take long to find the correct version of the Latin words that had come to me forty-three years earlier on that May afternoon in Nigeria. What I had only partially remembered, it turned out, was the Latin Vulgate translation of Job 7:20. The original was *Peccavi, quid faciam tibi o custos hominum*? ("I have sinned; what shall I do for you, O Guardian of Humanity?") The Hebrew original of that verse is better translated in its context: "If I sin, what do I do to you, you watcher of humanity? Why have you made me your target? Why have I become a burden to you? Why do you not pardon my transgression and take away my iniquity? For now I shall lie in the earth; you will seek me, but I shall not be" (Job 7:20–21).

And so the gift of my late cousin's breviary, combined with Eamon Duffy's lament for the old Office of the Dead, helped me discover the connection I had not quite made for many decades. Job, Jacques Kohn, and I turn out to have much in common: we live with a God who is a questioner, a contentious fellow player in the game of life; and God likewise lives with us as questioners and contentious fellow players, if on a more modest scale. Those last words of Jacques Kohn from Singer's story, about the chess game of life, have remained with me for fifty years, as have the partly remembered words of Job in the Office of Dead. Taken together, both remind me that our God is not a mere metaphysical support system. In the game of life, of my life, he sits hunched over across the chessboard from me, figuring out his next move. And I am mulling over mine as well.

God, of course, is a grandmaster, and ours is hardly a contest of equals. Yet—and this is the important thing—we both keep playing. Sometimes I complain about his moves; sometimes he complains about mine; and the game goes on. *What shall I say to you, O Guardian of Humanity?*

CHAPTER 1

Faith as a Response to Covenant

When I was a child, D., my contemporaries and I used to swear to our veracity with a curious phrase: "Cross my heart and hope to die." We also sometimes used that formulary when we had engaged in mischief that we didn't want our parents to know about: those words sealed a conspiracy with a fellow malefactor against snitching. Looking back, it seems obvious to me that we were swearing by the sign of the cross made over our hearts and thus we were using, indeed misusing, covenantal language of a distinctly Christian cast. I remember especially making that pledge with a fellow mischief-maker when an adult claiming to be a plainclothes policeman had confronted us for throwing pebbles at a passing train of the Long Island Railroad. All the rest of that summer afternoon of my fifth year I lived with guilt for the misdeed I had sworn with my fellow criminal never to divulge. That night, in a suitably baptismal setting, the bathtub, I confessed to my mother what had happened and what I had sworn never to divulge. I agreed with her never to throw pebbles again.

Many years later, while I was living in Ghana, a student friend told me the equivalent of such a conspiratorial covenant in his own childhood. He and another boy had stolen some ripe ears of corn from the field of a neighbor which they proceeded to roast over a fire and eat. To seal their conspiracy, the two boys pricked each other's thumbs and sucked a drop of each other's blood. My student and I also recognized that crossing-my-heart-and-hoping-to-die and the sharing of conspiratorial blood both participated in the pattern of covenant-making, in these cases covenants made between equal partners in crime. We confessed to each other many years later three misdeeds in our childhood: the original mischief each had committed, the conspiratorial oath-taking, and finally the breaking of the oath taken. We laughed at ourselves and at our common human nature, faithful and at the same time faithless.

Covenants between Equals

Not every conspiracy is wicked, or even naughty. When two people breathe together in metaphorical terms—*conspirare* in Latin provides the root for "conspiracy"—when they think and love in harmony, they form a third reality that is neither the one nor the other: the bond of their friendship, or perhaps even the bond of their marriage. Indeed, it is that third element that they hold in common that makes possible the bond between them. The Hebrew Bible commemorates this reality in Psalm 133, a "song of ascents" to be sung by pilgrims going up to Jerusalem and its temple for one of the prescribed feasts in the Israelite calendar. "How very good and pleasant it is when kindred live together in unity! It is like the precious oil on the head, running down upon the beard, on the beard of Aaron, running down over the collar of his robes" (Ps 133:1–2). The pilgrims singing this psalm as they approach the temple enter in some sense into the priestly kinship of Aaron and the sons of Levi, servants of the temple worship in Jerusalem.

Not every brother equally loves his brother, as the Genesis stories of Cain and Abel, Jacob and Esau demonstrate. Sometimes a brotherhood that is not consanguineous stands out as a better example of a covenant between equals. No greater example of such a bond of love between people can be found in the Hebrew Bible than in the account of the covenant of friendship struck between Jonathan and David, two unrelated men who had every natural and political reason to be rivals.[1] Their

1. For a different interpretation of the covenant between Jonathan and David, see Tom Horner, *Jonathan Loved David: Homosexuality in Biblical Times* (Philadelphia: Westminster, 1978), 26–39. The *Pirke Avot*, the best known tractate in the Mishnah, datable to the first centuries CE, gives the covenanted love of Jonathan and David as the prime example of "a loving relationship ... which

friendship proved in the long run fraught with tragedy. Jonathan had in some sense broken with his father, Saul, and conspired with David, in whom he recognized the future of monarchy in the United Kingdom of Israel and Judah. It is possible that Jonathan had also recognized that neither he nor his father deserved the kingship any more, both having disobeyed the LORD in matters great or small (1 Sm 13–15). But still, Saul was Jonathan's father, and a loyal son could not renounce that relationship easily.

When the youthful David overcame the Philistine Goliath and brought his head into Saul's court, we are told that "the soul of Jonathan was bound to the soul of David, and Jonathan loved him as his own soul" (1 Sm 18:1). The narrator goes on to recount how he "made a covenant with David, because he loved him as his own soul" (1 Sm 18:3). Jonathan acted out this covenant by giving David his royal clothing, armor, sword, bow, and belt. Jonathan's love for David, combined paradoxically with his filial devotion to his father, finally led to Jonathan's death along with Saul on the battlefield. Foreseeing what would happen to him in the struggle between his father and David, Jonathan begged David to remain faithful to their mutual covenant and to extend that covenant fidelity to Jonathan's family: "If I am still alive, show me the faithful love of the LORD; but if I die, never cut off your faithful love from my house, even if the LORD were to cut off every one of the enemies of David from the face of the earth" (1 Sm 20:14–15). David could not completely keep that covenant; the Philistines, the quintessential enemies of Israel with whom David had gone into alliance, killed both Saul and Jonathan. David mourned father and son, but his mourning for the latter underlined the seriousness of their mutual covenant: "Jonathan lies slain upon your high places. I am distressed for you, my brother Jonathan: greatly beloved were you to me; your love to me was wonderful, passing the love of women" (2 Sm 1:25–26).

David's mourning for Jonathan was compounded further when Jon-

---

does not depend on something," contrasting it with the incestuous love of Amnon for Tamar (2 Sm 13). *Pirke Avot* notes that such a loving relationship "which does not depend upon something will never come to an end." See *Torah from Our Sages: Pirke Avot*, trans. Jacob Neusner (Dallas: Rossell Books, 1984), 164.

athan's brother Ishbosheth (Ishbaal) was murdered by David's soldiers against their commander's precise wishes; David had the murderers executed for their crime (2 Sm 4:1–12). David sought out Mephibosheth (Meribaal), the son of Jonathan, in order to "show him kindness for Jonathan's sake" (2 Sm 9:1). Even when Mephibosheth proved somewhat vacillating in his loyalty to David during the rebellion of Absalom, David accepted his disavowal of treason. "The king spared Mephibosheth, the son of Saul's son Jonathan, because of the oath of the LORD that was between them, between David and Jonathan the son of Saul" (2 Sm 21:7). The Song of Solomon declares that "love is strong as death" (Song 8:6). The covenantal love of Jonathan and David survived Jonathan's death, proving stronger still.

A covenant between equals, such as that of David and Jonathan, has been characterized as a parity covenant, and it lies at the basis of all true friendship. Greek and Roman philosophy characterized true friendship as something based not on the self-interest of either friend but on their common commitment to a third reality: virtue. Thus Aristotle in the fourth century BCE defined "complete friendship" as "the friendship of good people who are alike in virtue. For each alike wishes good things to the other, insofar as he is good, and each is intrinsically good."[2] Cicero, three centuries later, concurred: "Friendship is nothing other than shared sentiment about all realities divine and human, combined with good will and generous love .... There are, moreover, those who make the supreme good depend on virtue, and they do well [to say this]. But the very virtue they make [the supreme good] gives birth to and sustains friendship. Friendship cannot be attained in any way without virtue."[3]

The fidelity that equal spouses and equal friends pledge to each other sets the stage for understanding the fidelity between unequal partners in a relationship, such as the fidelity that binds God to human beings and human beings to God. In ancient times, such a relationship

2. Aristotle, *Nicomachean Ethics*, trans. C. D. C. Reeve (Indianapolis, Ind.: Hackett, 2014), 1156b (139).

3. Cicero, *De Amicitia* 20, as found in M. Tulli Ciceronis, *De re publica, De legibus, Cato maior de senectute, Laelius de amicitia*, ed. J. G. F. Powell (Oxford: Clarendon, 2006), 328; author's translation.

was also called a covenant, very like the unequal covenants or treaties struck between imperial sovereigns and their vassals in the Middle East in the second millennium BCE. Such suzerainty covenants, as these international treaties were called, provided the ancient Israelites with an image—defective, perhaps, but still quite vivid—for the relationship between the LORD and Israel. That imagery continues as a theme in the Christian and Muslim traditions as well, but each of these faith traditions puts different emphases on the divine and human partners in the covenantal relationship and the faith that binds those partners.

Understanding the bilateral nature of faith as a response to a pact or covenant offered by God, the unequal divine-human reciprocity that is God's fidelity to humankind and humankind's fidelity to God, can help us glimpse something of the unique closeness of the interrelated faith traditions of Jews, Christians, and Muslims. Faith as a concept can designate both the action of the divine partner in such a covenant (a faithful God) and the action of the human partner or partners swearing fidelity to a covenant (a faithful person, faithful people). Such divine-human bonding the Hebrew Bible calls covenant (*berit*), the New Testament develops as a new covenant (*kaine diatheke*) and the Qur'an calls *mithaq* or *'ahd*. As each of these three traditions of faith developed historically, the inequality of the human and divine partners in such covenants could develop into something akin to the equality of a parity covenant, a partnership in love, a relationship of deep and even passionate friendship with God. It is the compassion of God—the mystery of what has been called divine condescension or graciousness—that alone makes such a development possible.

Faith and the Suzerainty Covenants in the Hebrew Bible

Neither the five Books of the Torah nor the whole of the Hebrew Bible exhaust all that the Jewish tradition for more than three millennia has thought about covenant and faith. In an attempt to describe Israel's relationship to its LORD, the Torah borrows imagery from the legal instrument in the international law of ancient times already alluded to, the suzerainty covenant. In 1954 the biblical archeologist George E. Mendenhall outlined six principal elements found in ancient Hittite covenants that closely parallel divine-human covenants found in the Hebrew Bible,[4] especially the covenant struck at Shechem by Joshua (Jos 24:2–27):

1. The covenant begins by naming the divine Suzerain: "Thus says the LORD, the God of Israel" (24:2a).

2. The historical prologue follows, detailing the previous benefactions of the divine Suzerain to the vassal, from the time of Abraham to the entry of Joshua and the people into the land of Israel (24:2b–13).

3. Stipulations imposed by the divine Suzerain follow (24:14–22), beginning with the most comprehensive: "Now therefore, revere the LORD, and serve him in sincerity and in faithfulness" (24:14a).

4. Provisions are made for the preservation of the covenant document: "Joshua wrote these words in the book of the law of God; and he took a large stone, and set it up there under the oak in the sanctuary of the LORD" (24:26).

5. Where the Hittite suzerainty covenants would list gods who witnessed the pact, Joshua pointed only to the stone placed under the oak as the witness to what God's vassals had committed themselves: "'See, this stone shall be a witness against us; for it has heard all the words of the LORD that he spoke to us; therefore it shall be a witness against you, if you deal falsely with your God'" (24:27).

6. The curses and blessings typical as a sixth major element in a Hittite covenant do not occur in the text of the Shechem covenant renewal, but they do occur at the conclusion of the renewed covenant in the Book of Deuteronomy (Dt 27).

The suzerainty covenants of the Hebrew Bible make grander claims than do the suzerain-vassal treaties of the ancient Near East, given the

---

4. George E. Mendenhall, *Law and Covenant in Israel and the Ancient Near East* (Pittsburgh: Biblical Colloquium, 1955). This booklet reprints "Law and Covenant in Israel and the Ancient Near East, Part I," *The Biblical Archaeologist* 17, no. 2 (May 1954): 26–46, and "Law and Covenant in Israel and the Ancient Near East, Part II," *The Biblical Archaeologist* 17, no. 3 (September 1954): 49–76.

transcendent majesty of God and the specially chosen status of Israel. The loyalty of Israel as vassal to God responds to the prior choice
of Israel by God. This preeminent loyalty of God is most dramatically
portrayed in the account of the renewal of the covenant of Sinai after
Israel's sin of worshiping the golden calf. God's self-naming in the pre-
amble to this renewed covenant features what has been called in later
Jewish tradition the thirteen attributes of God's mercy, showing God
to be more merciful and more loyal to the divinely initiated covenant
than might be expected of any worldly suzerain dealing with a vassal:
"The LORD, the LORD, a God merciful and gracious, slow to anger, and
abounding in steadfast love and faithfulness, keeping steadfast love for
the thousandth generation, forgiving iniquity and transgression and
sin, yet by no means clearing the guilty, but visiting the iniquity of the
parents upon the children and the children's children, to the third and
the fourth generation" (Ex 34:6–7).[5]

The attributes of the LORD in this passage translated as "abounding in steadfast love and faithfulness" (*rab-hesed we-'emet*) point to
the core of God's preeminent loyalty to the covenant struck at Sinai.
Hesed and *'emet* in combination are an example of what classical rhet-
oricians called hendiadys: one single meaning intended by two words
in combination.[6] Thus the phrase may be translated as loving fidelity
or faithful love.[7] The graciousness of God is demonstrated in God's extending a covenant to humankind. God's unceasing fidelity to that covenant—God's "truth" in the sense of God remaining true to the divine
promises—is what this hendiadys denotes.

Israel's faith, then, is expressed most perfectly as the human response to the prior initiative of a faithful and loving God, God's *hesed
we-'emet*. The Ten Commandments are important not so much because

5. In the text as quoted the rabbis count twelve attributes, but they tend to take out of context
the word "remit" (*we-naqeh*) as a thirteenth attribute, ignoring the "not" (*lo'*) that follows in verse
7b. See Nahum M. Sarna, *The JPS Torah Commentary: The Traditional Hebrew Text with the new JPS
Translation Commentary* (Philadelphia: Jewish Publication Society, 1991), 216.

6. See Nelson Glueck, *Hesed in the Bible* (Cincinnati, Ohio: Hebrew Union College Press, 1967), 55.

7. John's Gospel echoes this phrase when it asserts that the Word made flesh reflects the Fa-
ther's glory as an only Son, "full of grace and truth" (in the Greek, *pleres charitos kai aletheias*).
See Pheme Perkins, "The Gospel According to John," in *The New Jerome Biblical Commentary*, ed.
Raymond E. Brown, SS, Joseph A. Fitzmyer, SJ, Roland E. Murphy, O. Carm. (Englewood Cliffs, N.J.:
Prentice Hall, 1990) (hereafter, *NJBC*), 951b (section 61:25).

of the originality of their content, not that different from many other moral codes, but because of the insistence in the Book of Exodus that they are the commands of God. Human obedience to those words of command defines an Israelite as a person of faith and Israel as a whole as a community of faith covenanted with God.[8] The noun "faith" (in Hebrew, *'emuna*) occurs less frequently in the Hebrew Bible than forms of the verb with the same tri-consonantal root (*alep-mem-nun*). Faith is less a thing than a relationship, divine and human. God's faith or fidelity is absolute; human faith or fidelity is sometimes fallible. One of the principal connotations of this tri-consonantal root for faith suggests security of attachment to, or solidity of firm connection with, a source of strength and nourishment, as in the attachment of an infant to a nursing mother, or the attachment of a nursing mother to her child.[9]

Apt examples of this motif of faith as attachment or connection can be found throughout the Hebrew Bible, most famously in the account of God showing Abraham the stars as a promise of the extent of his progeny: "And he [Abraham] put his faith in the LORD; and [the LORD] accounted [that faith] to him as righteousness" (Gn 15:6).[10] In a notoriously difficult passage in the prophet Isaiah, playing on the different significations of this same tri-consonantal root, God speaks to the pusillanimous king of Judah, Ahaz, when that king was confronted with the threat of the Syro-Ephraimite invasion of Judah in 735 BCE: "If you do not stand firm in faith, you shall not stand at all" (Is 7:9). More literally, the Hebrew text can be translated by this seeming tautology: "If you are not firmly placed, you will not be firmly placed." The dynamic possibility of human beings keeping faith with God—attaching

8. See Moshe Weinfeld, "What Makes the Ten Commandments Different?," *Bible Review* 7, no. 2 (April 1991): 35–41.

9. *A Hebrew and English Lexicon of the Old Testament with an Appendix Containing the Biblical Aramaic based on the Lexicon of William Gesenius*, ed. Francis Brown, S. R. Driver, and Charles A. Briggs, trans. Edward Robinson (Boston: Houghton Mifflin, 1907), 52–54.

10. This is my own rendering from the very sparing Hebrew text. The NRSV translates it as follows: "And he [Abraham] believed the LORD; and the LORD reckoned it to him as righteousness." *The HarperCollins Study Bible (New Revised Standard Version of 1989)*, ed. Harold W. Attridge (San Francisco: HarperOne, 2006). The JPS translates this verse somewhat differently: "And because he [Abraham] put his trust in the LORD, He reckoned it to his merit." The latter translation has the advantage over the former that it eliminates the word "believe," so weakened in modern parlance, and substitutes a word with a more emotive content, "trusted." Neither the NRSV nor the JPS translation quite catches the dynamism of the triliteral root and its covenantal significance.

themselves entirely to God, connecting firmly to a divine Suzerain who extends a covenant to them—provides the Hebrew Bible with its central narrative. The Jewish scriptures, although they contain many other types of sacred literature, center on the revealed account of the LORD's everlasting fidelity to the people of Israel and the people of Israel's very human mixture of fidelity and infidelity to the LORD.

Israelite faith, then, is not a set of beliefs, as many Jewish authors have insisted.[11] First and foremost Israelite faith is a bilateral, reciprocal relationship between God and human beings, and with the people of Israel in particular, a relationship in which the steadfast love and faithfulness (*hesed we-'emet*) of the LORD elicit and even demand from mortal creatures, as individuals and especially as the community of Israel, the finite response of faith or fidelity. The covenant that the LORD offers to Israel is often imaged as an adoption by God or even a marriage offered by God; in a traditional society in the ancient Near East, a covenant of adoption or marriage offered the possibility of "ingrafting non-kin or distant kin into the lineage."[12] The covenant imagery surrounding marriage will come in for further reflection below.

The Hebrew word *Amen*—repeated after each of the twelve curses the people of Israel call down on themselves if they fail to keep the covenant as delineated in Deuteronomy—symbolizes that response most dramatically (Dt 27:15–26). The last of these twelve curses sums up all the rest: "'Cursed be anyone who does not uphold the words of this law by observing them.' All the people shall say, Amen!'" (Dt 27:26). To uphold the commandments of the LORD by observing them lies at the heart of Israel's faith. Although *Amen* is often translated loosely as "So be it!," it means something much stronger, expressing an oath of fidelity: "I put my faith in this," or rather, and much more importantly, "I pledge my fidelity to You."

11. Israel Abrahams, Jacob Haberman, and Charles Manekin, "Belief," in *Encyclopaedia Judaica*, rev. ed. (Detroit: Macmillan Reference USA / Keter Publishing House Ltd.), 2007 (hereafter, *EJ2*), 3:290–94.

12. Frank Moore Cross, *From Epic to Canon: History and Literature in Ancient Israel* (Baltimore, Md.: Johns Hopkins University Press, 1998), 8. My attention was drawn to this book by a citation in Jon D. Levenson, *Inheriting Abraham: The Legacy of the Patriarch in Judaism, Christianity, and Islam* (Princeton, N.J.: Princeton University Press, 2012), 194 and 232n56.

Faith and Covenant in the New Testament

If the teaching about the covenant given by God to Israel and Israel's sometimes faithful and sometimes faithless responses to the covenant given are in some sense the central theme of the Hebrew Bible, the New Testament centers on faith (*pistis*) in God mediated by Jesus, the source of a new covenant. It is impossible to understand the New Testament, the written account of that new covenant, without understanding it as a document written in Greek chiefly by Jewish Christians of the first century CE.[13] For such Jewish Christians covenant and faith were related terms in the same cultural complex.

In his 1994 monograph on Christian faith, Avery Dulles, SJ, notes that the noun *pistis* (faith) occurs 243 times in the New Testament and forms of the verb *pisteuein* (to keep faith, etc.) also occur 243 times.[14] The Jewish Christians from whom most of the New Testament derives came to terms in different ways with the Pharisee, Sadducee, Qumran, and Hellenistic Jewish interpretations of the tradition of Israel which they had inherited as the faith of their ancestors. As Messianic (or Christian) Jews they were convinced that the death and resurrection of Jesus of Nazareth had inaugurated the new covenant proclaimed by Jeremiah (Jer 31:31–33):

The days are surely coming, says the LORD, when I will make a new covenant with the house of Israel and the house of Judah. It will not be like the covenant that I made with their ancestors when I took them by the hand to bring them out of the land of Egypt—a covenant that they broke, though I was their husband, says the LORD. But this is the covenant that I will make with the house of Israel after those days, says the LORD: I will put my law [*Torah*] within them, and I will write it on their hearts; and I will be their God, and they shall be my people.

Their Jewish-Christian interpretation of this prophetic text was not the interpretation accepted by non-Christian Jews, then or now.[15] Never-

---

13. Luke, the author of the third Gospel and the Acts of the Apostles, was probably a Gentile by origin, but this cannot be definitively proven. See Joseph A. Fitzmyer, SJ, *The Gospel According to Luke (I–IX)*, Anchor Bible 28 (Garden City, N.Y.: Doubleday, 1981), 1:41–47.

14. Avery Dulles, SJ, *The Assurance of Things Hoped For: A Theology of Christian Faith* (Oxford: Oxford University Press, 1994), 3; see also 10–17.

15. For Jeremiah in the seventh century BCE this passage probably meant a hope for a renewal

theless, the way these first Jewish Christians understood this text influences everything they thought about faith and covenant.

In the accounts of Jesus in the Gospels of Mark, Matthew, and Luke (the Synoptics), faith is first and foremost faith in God, a commitment of oneself to God, but this faith or commitment is understood to be mediated by Jesus, even when one or another word denoting faith is expressed without an object: "All things are possible for the one who keeps faith" (Mk 9:23).[16] Usage of the phrase "keep faith" without an object suggests something akin to a covenant between Jesus and those who sought his aid. In the Synoptic Gospels (unlike John's Gospel) Jesus is not the object of faith, but he is, as Dulles notes, "the awakener or catalyst of faith."[17]

The preaching of Jesus in Mark's Gospel begins with a call to repentance and discipleship: "The opportune moment is fulfilled; the reign of God has drawn near; change your inmost being and put your faith in the Good Proclamation" (Mk 1:15).[18] Although the phrase "put your faith in" in that verse is normally translated in English as "believe in," the covenantal—indeed new-covenantal—sense of this inaugural proclamation of what Jesus and the Gospel writer intend needs more emphasis. Note the stress on *metanoia*, a radical change of mind or interior disposition consistent with the first Christians' understanding of Jeremiah's "new covenant" and the Torah the LORD would put "within them," writing it "on their hearts."

The interiority of this new covenant suggested in the text of Jeremiah is clearly symbolized in Mark's account of the way Jesus not only healed but forgave the sins of a paralyzed man in Capernaum. When friends of the paralytic had managed to lower the man into the presence of Jesus by opening the roof of the crowded house where Jesus was preaching, Mark tells us that "Jesus saw their faith" (Mk 2:5), not

---

of the Mosaic or even the Abrahamic covenant for both the Northern and Southern Kingdoms in the era of Josiah (640–609 BCE).

16. Author's translation.

17. In the Synoptic Gospels, according to Dulles, "the term 'faith' is often used absolutely, without any object being mentioned.... Except in the undoubtedly secondary passage, Matthew 18:6, the Synoptic sayings (as contrasted with the Johannine) never present Jesus as explicitly calling for faith in himself" (*Assurance*, 11).

18. Author's translation.

only the faith of the paralytic but also the faith of his litter-bearers. Looking at the paralytic, Jesus at first ignored his physical plight and concentrated instead on the man's inner being: "Your sins are dismissed" (Mk 2:6).[19] Hostile onlookers silently questioned the right of Jesus to assume the divine prerogative of forgiving sins, but Jesus "perceived in his spirit" (Mk 2:8) what they had not expressed openly. He demonstrated his power to forgive sins by also healing the man of his paralysis. A passage like this epitomizes the New Testament concept that a new covenant of divine forgiveness inaugurated by Jesus can be established in the inner being of human beings and written on human hearts.

Peculiar to the Synoptic Gospels is the way certain radical sayings of Jesus are prefaced by the word "Amen," a word normally found at the end of prayers: "Amen, I tell you."[20] This usage occurs thirteen times in Mark, thirty-one times in Matthew and six times in Luke. John Meier, a contemporary scholar of what can be said about Jesus as a historical figure, remarks on the peculiarity of this usage: "Jesus claimed to know directly, intuitively, and without the usual organs that mediate authority, what the will of God was in any given situation—a claim summed up in his solemn affirmation 'Amen, I say to you.' This form of speech ('Amen' not as a response but as an introduction to a new statement) was characteristic of Jesus and does not seem to have been common before his time."[21]

In John's Gospel that peculiar phrase is doubled for greater emphasis and is used twenty-five times: "Amen, amen, I tell you." Normally I would leave the Hebrew and Aramaic words in the Greek New Testament untranslated, but I would prefer, if translating "Amen," to indicate that an "Amen" placed before a statement underlines what follows, laying great emphasis on the teaching, implicitly insisting: "Put your faith in this." The frequent repetition of this introductory phrase points to the growing New Testament tendency to refer to Jesus as the one who inaugurates a new covenant, one centered on a transforma-

---

19. Author's translation.

20. Felix Just, SJ, "'Amen, Amen' sayings in the Fourth Gospel," available at Catholic.resources .org.

21. John P. Meier, "Jesus," in *NJBC*, 1321b. See also John P. Meier, *A Marginal Jew*, 2: *Mentor, Message, and Miracles* (Garden City, N.Y.: Doubleday, 1994), 367–69.

tion and internalization of the Torah: "Amen, I tell you, until heaven and earth pass away, not one *yod*, not one fraction of a letter, will pass away from the Torah until all of it is accomplished" (Mt 5:18).[22] There seems to have been differences of opinion within the early church as to what the phrase, "all of it is accomplished," may have signified. Some Christian Jews continued in strict Torah observance; other Christian Jews and their Gentile Christian associates may have only looked to the Torah for ethical guidance, neglecting the details of *halakha*. Still others may have considered the more intensive and interiorized fulfilment of the Torah—not only not killing your brother, but not calling him "You fool" (Mt 5:22)—accomplished or fulfilled the Torah. All of these early Christians felt that they were accomplishing or fulfilling the Torah in different senses.[23] The variety of these early Christian responses to the fulfilment or accomplishing of the Torah may well reflect earlier developments within Second Temple Judaism. In the Wisdom of Jesus ben Sirach (Ecclesiasticus), a work dating to the late third and early second centuries BCE, much emphasis is placed on the possibility of human repentance for sin and the forgiving and generous nature of God: "To those who repent [the Lord] grants a return and he encourages those who are losing hope.... How great is the mercy of the Lord, and his forgiveness for those who return to him!" (Sir 17:24, 29).

Paul refers to Jesus himself as our "Amen" to God and God's "Amen" to us, our pledge of fidelity to the Suzerain who extends a covenant to us and the Suzerain's pledge of fidelity to us: "For in him every one of God's promises is a 'Yes.' For this reason it is through him that we say the 'Amen,' to the glory of God" (2 Cor 1:20). This sentence of Paul may also correspond to the curious clause in Greek found in Paul's Epistle to the Galatians and elsewhere[24] that can be translated literally as follows: "The human being is not set at rights with God by deeds according to the Torah but rather through *the fidelity of Jesus Christ*" (Gal 2:16).[25] Not many modern translators and commentators on Paul admit the possi-

22. Author's translation.
23. See Raymond E. Brown, SS, "Not Jewish Christianity and Gentile Christianity but Types of Jewish/Gentile Christianity," *Catholic Biblical Quarterly* 45 (1983): 74–79.
24. Gal 2:16, 2:20, 3:22; Rom 3:22, 3:26; Phil 3:9.
25. Author's translation.

bility of this italicized phrase being a subjective genitive ("the faith/fi-delity of Jesus Christ') rather than an objective genitive ("faith in Jesus Christ"). A few modern scholars, however, still defend this interpreta-tion.[26] I find it intriguing as an assertion that Jesus in his fidelity keeps the covenant with God perfectly. It fits very well, moreover, with the no-tion that a faithful God calls human beings into this covenant: "God is faithful through whom you have been called into the companionship of his son, the Messiah Jesus, our Lord" (1 Cor 1:9).[27] By baptism into Jesus—incorporation by the graciousness of God into the company of Jesus—we are enabled, despite our many lapses, to keep faith with God.

John's Gospel, one of the last works in the New Testament to reach its completion, rivals the work of Paul in its usage of forms of the verb "to keep faith" (*pisteuein*), but it never uses the noun "faith" (*pistis*), which occurs 142 times in the corpus attributed to Paul. In the fourth Gospel, "keeping faith" is something one does or does not do, not an abstract concept. Forms of the verb *pisteuein* in John can occur (a) with the preposition *eis* and the accusative, meaning quite literally "to put faith into," (b) with the dative (an indirect object), meaning "to have faith in," (c) with a dependent clause introduced by *hoti* meaning "to have faith that," and (d) with no object at all, direct or indirect, simply meaning to "keep faith."[28]

The Book of Revelation, a work apparently emanating from the circle of the Beloved Disciple, the unique witness in John's Gospel (Jn 21:24), characterizes Jesus at one point as the quintessence of faith: "To the Angel of the Assembly in Laodicea, write [the following]: 'Thus says the *Amen*, the witness both faithful and loyal, 'the Beginning of God's Cre-ation'" (Rv 3:14).[29] As the New Testament meditates more at length on the early church's experience of Jesus, it begins to understand Jesus as

26. For modern advocates of the subjective genitive sense, see George Howard, "On the 'Faith of Christ,'" *Harvard Theological Review* 60 (1967): 459–65, and Luke Timothy Johnson, "Rom 3:21–26 and the Faith of Jesus," *Catholic Biblical Quarterly* 44 (1982): 77–90; for a strong contrary view see Joseph A. Fitzmyer, SJ, "Letter to the Galatians," in *NJBC*, 785a.

27. Author's translation.

28. Dulles, *Assurance*, 14.

29. Author's translation. This usage of "Amen" hints at the poetic account of creation in the Book of Proverbs, where Wisdom is said to have been with God as "a confidant" (JPS translation) or "master worker" (in Hebrew, *'amûn*, from Prv 8:30) before anything else came to be. See NRSV notes to Rv 3:14 and Prv 8:30.

a pre-existent expression of God's selfhood, the eternal Word and Light of God who pitched a tent in the midst of humanity (Jn 1:1–18). The fidelity or faith of Jesus—one with us and one with God—introduces all of humanity into an eternal covenant with God. For the Messianic Jews who attached themselves to the following of Jesus, the bilateral nature of that covenant relationship was in some sense transcended in a divine-human unilateral covenant: God and humanity united in Jesus the Messiah.

Faith and Covenant in the Qur'an

If covenant is the central term of the Hebrew Bible in its elaboration of the relationship between a faithful God and sometimes faithful and sometimes faithless Israel, and if keeping of faith lies at the core of the New Testament's account of the new and interior covenant consummated in the union of God and humanity in Jesus, faith in God alone expressed by various transformations of the tri-consonantal Arabic root *alif-mim-nun* takes center stage in the Qur'an.[30] In a basic derivate from that Arabic root, *amana* signifies trustworthiness, the good faith necessary for conducting ordinary business between human beings: "If you are on a journey and cannot find someone to write for you, then a handshake [will do]. If one of you entrusts another [with something], let the one trusted return the thing entrusted to [the owner] and let [the trustee] reverence God his Lord" (Qur'an 2:283). Even before Muhammad experienced divine revelation, he had proven his trustworthiness in managing the business affairs of the older widow whom he eventually married, Khadija. As such Muhammad was called *al-Amin*, the trustee or trustworthy one.[31] The Qur'an borrows imagery from this human world of trust in business to suggest the reality of a covenant or trust offered by God to humankind, humankind not always ready to bear the burden of God's trust faithfully. "We did, indeed, offer the

30. See Jane I. Smith, "Faith," in *Encyclopaedia of the Qur'an*, ed. Jane Dammen McAuliffe (Leiden: Brill, 2001) (hereafter, *EQ*).
31. See Claude Cahen, "Amin," in *The Encyclopaedia of Islam: New Edition*, ed. Hamilton Gibb et al. (Leiden: Brill, 1960–2009) (hereafter, *EI2*).

trust to the heavens and the earth and the mountains, but they refused to take it up; they were afraid of it. But the human being bore it. Indeed, he was wicked, ignorant!" (Qur'an 33:72). Although covenantal language is not as central to the Qur'an as it is to the Hebrew Bible or even the New Testament, the words *mithaq* and *'ahd* used in the Qur'an denote pacts made between human partners as well as covenants made between God and human beings.[32]

Mithaq derives from a root (W-TH-Q) meaning "binding." The third form of the verb derived from that tri-consonantal root, *wāthaqa*, meaning "extending a covenant," occurs only once in a late passage of the Qur'an. The related third form of the verbal noun, *mithaq*, is used in the Qur'an twenty-five times all told, occurring twenty-two times in Medinan passages. The Surah of the Banquet (Qur'an 5) uses this sort of covenantal language five times in a short passage addressed to the Muslim community at the end of Muhammad's lifetime: "Remember God's graciousness toward you and his covenant [*mithaqahu*] with which he bound you [*wathaqahum*], when you said 'We hear and obey.' Keep God in mind: God is truly aware of what is in your hearts" (Qur'an 5:7). A few verses later the Qur'an reminds Muslims of the sins of past covenanted populations, starting with the Jews, singling them out for blame over what seems to be neglect of the Law (Qur'an 5:12–13):

God had undertaken a covenant [*mithaqa*] with the Children of Israel: "We raised twelve chiefs among you." God said, "I am with you. If you conduct worship and pay the purification tax and put your faith in my messengers and support them and give God a generous loan, I will absolve you of your sins and I will have you enter the Garden under which rivers flow. Moreover, anyone among you who repudiates this [covenant] after that wanders off an even path." And because of their violation of their covenant [*mithaqahum*] We cursed them and hardened their hearts because they distorted the words from their context and they forgot some of what they had been reminded about. You [Muhammad] will always find treachery among them, except for a few. Pardon them nonetheless and overlook [their treachery]. God truly loves those who act kindly.

32. Another word, *bara'atun*, used twice in the Qur'an (9:1, 54:43) to signify the revocation of a covenant, would seem in linguistic terms to be a cognate of the Hebrew *berit*, meaning "covenant." On this topic, and the more general subject of covenant in the Qur'an, see Gerhard Böwering, SJ, "Covenant," in *EQ*.

In this same context the Qur'an does not let Christians off the hook very easily either. "We [also] undertook a covenant [*mithaqa*] with some of those who say 'We are Christians,' but they forgot part of what they were charged to remember, and we have roused among them enmities and hatred until the Day of the Resurrection when God will point out to them what they were doing" (Qur'an 5:12–14). The schismatic divisions of Christians at the time of Quranic revelation, especially in the geographical area best known to Muhammad and the burgeoning Muslim community, undoubtedly underlies this Quranic critique of Christians' infidelity to their covenant.

The other noun used for covenant in the Qur'an, *'ahd*, as well as the related verbs *'ahida* and *'āhida*, refer principally to God's covenants with humankind but are also used for purely human compacts. Adam is the first human being—and a very fallible one at that—to be invited to enter into covenant with God: "We offered a covenant [*'ahidna*] to Adam before, but he forgot and we found no firmness in him" (Qur'an 20:115). Abraham proved a more constant vassal, although the same could not be said of all his progeny (Qur'an 2:124–25):

When his Lord tested Abraham with his commandments and he fulfilled them, [God] said, "Truly I have appointed you to be a leader for humankind." [Abraham asked] "And among my descendants [also]?" [God] said "My covenant ['ahdi] does not extend to sinners." And when we [God] designated the house [the Ka'ba in Mecca] as a refuge for humankind and a place of sanctuary, we [God] said: "Take as your locale of worship the place where Abraham stood. We extended a covenant ['ahidna] to Abraham and Ishmael: Cleanse my house for those who will walk around it, those who dwell there and those who bow down there in prostration.

Words for "faith" and "faithful" play a much more central role in the Qur'an than do words for "covenant" like *mithaq* and *'ahd*. *Iman* (faith), the verbal noun of the fourth form of that tri-consonantal root, '-M-N, occurs forty-five times in the Qur'an; the active participle of that form of the verb, *mu'min* (faithful), often used as a substantive, in singular and plural, masculine and feminine variants occurs 230 times. Other variations on the active verb *āmana*, meaning either to afford security to someone or to put one's faith in someone, occur in the Qur'an 518 times,[33] somewhat more than all the combined occurrences of forms of *pistis* (faith) and *pisteuein* (to keep faith) in the New Testament.

One usage of the active participle *mu'min* in the Qur'an that proves Wilfred Cantwell Smith's insistence that the word should not be translated as "believer" comes in the enumeration of thirteen attributes[34] or praise-names of God as something of a concluding doxology of Qur'an 59, a passage not entirely unlike the earlier mentioned thirteen attributes of mercy in the Hebrew Bible (Qur'an 59:23–24):

> He is God (There is no deity but he!) who is the Ruler, the Holy One, the Source of Peace, the Faithful One [*al-mu'min*], the Guarantor of Faith [*al-muhaymin*], the August One, the Compelling One, the Overwhelming One (Exalted be God above anything they may associate with him). He is God, the Maker, the Creator, the Shaper. To him belong the best of names! Everything in the heavens and on earth exalts him, and he is the August One, the Wise One.

Not only is the name "the Faithful One" (*al-mu'min*) ascribed to God in this passage significant for establishing a Quranic sense of God as the suzerain in a covenant, but the next attribute, *al-muhaymin*, which I have rendered as "the Guarantor of Faith," derives from the verb *haimana* which has as its most basic meaning, "to say 'amen.'"[35] God as the Guarantor of Faith says "Amen" to those who pledge their faith, who say their "Amen" to God. The word "Amen" (in Arabic, either *amīn* or *āmīn*) never occurs in the Qur'an, but, as mentioned above, Muslims conclude the recitation of the opening sura of the Qur'an, their most frequently uttered prayer, with a communal *Amin*. This usage also characterizes the conclusion of an individual Muslim's prayer of petition (*du'a'*).[36] A Syrian legal scholar and mystic of the thirteenth century CE, al-Nawawi, has left to posterity not only a legal corpus but also a much used book

33. See Hanna E. Kassis, *A Concordance of the Qur'an* (Berkeley: University of California Press, 1983), 147–64.

34. The number thirteen is reached by only counting once each occurrence of *Allah* and *al-'aziz* in these two verses.

35. Hans Wehr, *A Dictionary of Modern Written Arabic*, ed. J. Milton Cowan (Ithaca, N.Y.: Cornell University Press, 1966), 1044a.

36. J. Pedersen, "Amin," in *EI2*, 1:436b.

of devotions in which he wrote of the uniqueness of *Amin* in Muslim practice: "It is an approved custom that the *Amin* of those led in worship shall be said with that of the *imam*, neither before nor after. And this is the only place in the prayer-rite where the word of the worshipper is united with that of the *imam*, for in the other utterances he shall follow after the *imam*."[37]

This mutual pledge of faith between God and humanity, implicit in at least some of the attributes or names of God, is most vividly depicted in a Quranic passage that recounts what later Muslim mystics called the *Yawm Alastu* (the Day of "Am I not?"). This section of the Qur'an occurs just after a passage in which God rebukes the people of Israel for their infidelity to "the covenant of the Book" (*mithaq al-kitab*). Precisely at this point the Qur'an turns Muhammad's attention to another covenant, one in which all of humanity is invited to respond to God (Qur'an 7:172–73):

When your Lord took from the children of Adam—from their loins—their offspring, and made them bear witness for themselves [to what God said]: "Am I not your Lord?," they said, "Yes, we have borne witness," lest you say on the day of resurrection, "Indeed, we were ignorant about this," or [lest] you say, "It was only our forefathers who alleged that there were partners [in the Godhead] in times past, before we were their offspring after them. Will you destroy us because of what those liars did?"[38]

Annemarie Schimmel wrote of this "primordial covenant" that it has "impressed the religious conscience of the Muslims, and especially the Muslim mystics, more than any other idea. Here is the starting point for their understanding of free will and predestination, of election and acceptance, of God's eternal power and man's loving response and promise."[39] The primordial covenant of *Yawm Alastu* (the Day of "Am I not?") attested to in the Qur'an is offered to all of humanity without exception.

37. As quoted in Constance Padwick, *Muslim Devotions: A Study of Prayer-Manuals in Common Use* (London: SPCK, 1961), 109.

38. The first *your* in this passage is singular and refers to Muhammad; the second *your* is plural and refers to humanity.

39. Annemarie Schimmel, *Mystical Dimensions of Islam* (Chapel Hill: University of North Carolina Press, 1975), 24.

For Muslims Islam is the religion of nature (*fitra*). A saying is attributed to Muhammad that "every infant is born according to *fitra*;
i.e., [God's] kind or way of creating; 'on God's plan' ... then his parents
make him a Jew or a Christian or a Magian."[40] This saying has many
levels of significance in the Islamic tradition, not excluding one concerned with questions of inheritance by a child orphaned before he or
she has reached the age of discretion. This saying can be very narrowly interpreted to mean that Islam is the only faith that all humankind
should profess. But if one reflects on this saying in the context of the
primordial covenant offered to all of humanity on the day of *Yawm
Alastu*, it might be suggested that this apparently exclusivist saying
about newborn infants actually opens a path towards interreligious
understanding. Each one of us—whatever our present faith commitment or community—was taken by God from the loins of the children
of Adam and given a fundamental choice: to accept God or to reject
God. I would suggest that what unites not only Jews, Christians, and
Muslims, but all of humanity seeking the deepest meaning of life is
that all of us, obscurely but somehow realistically, have entered into
existence, or continue to enter into existence, responding to the Lordship of God with this enthusiastic, indeed joyful declaration of the
Yawm Alastu: "Yes, we have borne witness." The Jewish, Christian, and
Muslim traditions of faith have all sometimes defined who is and who
is not a faithful witness to God in very narrow terms. Passages like this
Quranic account of the *Yawm Alastu* can offer all men and women of
faith reasons for hope that somehow God can and will respond gen-
erously to all the different ways we frail mortals bear witness to God's
Lordship.

Concluding Reflections

Does the relationship of covenantal faith between God and humankind
always remain a suzerainty covenant, an unequal relationship between a merely human vassal and a supremely exalted God? I suggest-

---

40. As quoted in Duncan Black Macdonald, "Fitra," *EI2*, 2:931b–932a.

ed earlier that the inequality of the divine and human partners in such covenants can sometimes evolve into a something more like a parity covenant, a partnership of love, even passionate love, but such an evolution is not achieved by human efforts but by divine compassion, divine graciousness. In a traditional society, the love expressed in a marriage covenant may still suggest a certain amount of suzerain-vassal imagery, but love has a way of equalizing spouses.

The Song of Solomon, originally perhaps a series of wedding songs, came to be understood in the tradition of Israel as songs symbolizing the love of Israel for the LORD, and the love of the LORD for Israel. Israel, the bride, in a dreamlike sequence seeks the LORD who seems to be absent: "I sought him whom my soul loves; I sought him, but found him not; I called him, but he gave no answer. 'I will rise now and go about the city, in the streets and in the squares; I will seek him whom my soul loves'" (Song 3:1b–2a). Such love and longing for God, at the same time both omnipresent and mysteriously absent, can be found as well in the poetry of Judah Halevi, the great Andalusian Jewish poet and pilgrim of the twelfth century. He gave up his life in Spain to pursue his desire to go on pilgrimage to Zion, to behold the face of the God of the covenant in the Land of Promise. But he recognized from the very beginning of his pilgrimage that God was within him as he traveled in search of God and that God was also in search of him. "Where can I find You, Lord?—Your place is high and hidden, But where can I not find You, Lord?—Your glory fills the world! ... I longed to be near You, I called You sincerely, went out to seek You, and found You *me* seeking!"[41]

In the Christian mystical tradition, the covenantal relationship between God and the soul is more than once imaged as a spiritual marriage, a marriage with many ups and downs. It was not only female mystics who were attracted to such imagery. Emboldened by the bridal imagery of the Song of Solomon, John of the Cross meditated on this love in his own poetic work, "The Spiritual Canticle." "Seeking my

41. I quote here from the translation in Raymond Scheindlin, *The Song of the Distant Dove: Judah Halevi's Pilgrimage* (New York: Oxford University Press, 2008), 43.

Love, / I will head for the mountains and for watersides, / I will not gather flowers, / Nor fear wild beasts; / I will go beyond strong men and frontiers."[42] In his commentary on these lines, John recognizes that neither his own soul, nor any devout person's inner self, can find God unless God first discloses the divine love for the seeker:

The soul is aware that neither her sighs and prayers nor the help of good intermediaries ... are sufficient for her to find her Beloved. Since the desire in which she seeks Him is authentic and her love intense, she does not want to leave any possible means untried. The soul that truly loves God is not slothful in doing all that she can do to find the Son of God, her Beloved.[43]

The priority of God in such a covenantal relationship remains, but the majesty of God is muted in love.

In the Qur'an God is not only the majestic Lord of those who keep faith but also their protecting friend (*wali*). As friend, God elicits from human beings the capacity only God can give them for closeness, for friendship. "For those who are God's friends there is no fear for them; they are not sad—those who keep faith, those who focus on God" (Qur'an 10:62–63). The friends of God in the tradition of Islam live out their covenant with God without obsequious fear. Rabi'a al-'Adawiyya, a freedwoman of Basra in Iraq who died around the year 800 CE, exercised the greatest freedom in her friendship with God. Farid al-din 'Attar, a thirteenth-century Persian anthologist of mystical adages, attributed this human-divine exchange to Rabi'a: "'O Lord, if tomorrow you put me in hell, I will cry out, "You have befriended me. Is this how one treats friends?"' A voice called out: 'Rabi'a, do not think ill of Us. Be assured that We will bring you into the circle of Our friends, so you may converse with Us.'"[44] This was the holy woman of whom it was said that she ran through Basra carrying a torch and a bucket of water: "I am going to burn paradise and douse hell-fire, so that both veils may be lifted from those on the quest and they will become sincere of pur-

---

42. *The Collected Works of John of the Cross*, trans. Kieran Kavanaugh, OCD, and Otilio Rodriguez, OCD (Washington, D.C.: Institute of Carmelite Studies, 1979), 427.

43. Ibid., 428.

44. "Rabi'a: Her Words and Life in 'Attar's *Memorial of the Friends of God*,'" trans. Paul Losensky with Michael Sells in *Early Islamic Mysticism*, trans. and ed. Michael A. Sells, Classics of Western Spirituality (Mahwah, N.J.: Paulist Press, 1996), 169.

pose."[45] For Rabi'a, the bond of friendship with God had gone beyond fear of punishment and hope for reward.

The philosopher Martin Buber wrote that "the primary word *I-Thou* can only be spoken with the whole being."[46] Faith is the ultimate form of *I-Thou* in the Jewish, Christian, and Muslim traditions. The *I* of God discloses the divine selfhood to the *Thou* of the human being, establishing a bond that exceeds all human imagining, a covenant that is only God's to offer. Likewise, the *I* of the human being responds to the *Thou* of a self-disclosing God, a God who offers human beings the possibility of entering into such a covenant. God speaks the divine *Amen* to you and to me in covenant, enabling us to speak our *Amen* to God in return. In an age when human beings sometimes find themselves resentful of a God too majestic, it is encouraging to see that some men and women of faith in all three monotheistic traditions in past centuries have preceded us as pioneers along the path of seeking God in a covenant of loving fidelity and faithful love.

How are the divine-human covenants celebrated by Jews, Christians, and Muslims related to each other? The relationship between Israel's ancient covenant with the LORD (variously specified as Abrahamic, patriarchal, Mosaic, Davidic) and the "new covenant" (1 Cor 11:25, Lk 22:20) inaugurated by and in Jesus has been a source of controversy between Jews and Christians for many centuries. Does the covenant inaugurated by and in Jesus replace the former covenant? Is faith or fidelity to God in covenant utterly different for Christians from faith or fidelity to God in covenant for Jews? Jeremiah first spoke of "a new covenant" (Jer 31:31), but Jeremiah's "new covenant" was fundamentally a renewal and greater interiorization of the covenant made with Abraham, the patriarchs, Moses and David, not a different covenant.

The anonymous author of the Epistle to the Hebrews asserts that Jeremiah's new covenant, fulfilled in Jesus, abolishes the former covenant: "In speaking of 'a new covenant,' [God] has made the first one obsolete. And what is obsolete and growing old will soon disappear"

45. Ibid., 151.
46. Martin Buber, *I and Thou*, trans. Ronald Gregor Smith, 2nd ed. (New York: Charles Scribner's Sons, 1958), 3.

(Heb 8:13). But Paul, in the Epistle to the Romans, takes a very different point of view. Paul criticizes his fellow Jews but still insists on their continued covenant relationship with God: "God has not rejected his people whom he foreknew" (Rom 11:7). Paul wants his Gentile disciples to recognize that their own entry into the Christian mystery became possible only because most of Paul's fellow Jews had not yet recognized Jesus as Lord and Messiah (Rom 11:28–31):

As regards the gospel they [the Jews] are enemies of God for your [Gentile] sake; but as regards election they [the Jews] are beloved, for the sake of their ancestors; for the gifts and the calling of God are irrevocable. Just as you [the Gentiles] were once disobedient to God but have now received mercy because of their [the Jews'] disobedience, so they [the Jews] have now been disobedient in order that, by the mercy shown to you [the Gentiles], they [the Jews] too may now receive mercy.[47]

There have been, as mentioned above, great differences between Jews and Christians and also among Jews of various sorts and among Christians of various sorts about the relationship between the cove-

47. On this complex subject, and especially on the Christian viewpoint sometimes called "supersessionism," a theology maintaining that the covenant struck in Jesus supersedes the covenant made with Israel of old, see Eugene Korn, "Covenantal Possibilities in a Post-Polemical Age: A Jewish View," *Studies in Christian-Jewish Relations* 6 (2011), esp. 2–3. Korn refers in this article to the controversy that arose in 2002 after a Consultation of the National Council of Synagogues with delegates of the Catholic Bishops' Committee for Ecumenical and Interreligious Affairs issued a joint statement called "Reflections on Covenant and Mission." That document instanced a "deepening Catholic appreciation of the eternal covenant between God and the Jewish people, together with a recognition of a divinely-given mission to Jews to witness to God's faithful love" and drew the conclusion "that campaigns that target Jews for conversion to Christianity are no longer theologically acceptable in the Catholic Church." Later in the document the Catholic delegates quoted a statement made a year earlier by Cardinal Walter Kasper in which he stated that "the faithful response of the Jewish people to God's irrevocable covenant . . . is salvific for them, because God is faithful to his promises." Among those who reacted negatively to this 2002 document was Cardinal Avery Dulles, SJ, in an article entitled "Covenant and Mission," *America* 187 (October 21, 2002): 8–11. On December 10, 2015, however, the Roman Pontifical Council on Religious Relations with Jews issued a lengthy teaching document that may be construed as agreeing in general terms with the opinions expressed by the Catholic participants in the 2002 Consultation criticized by Dulles. That 2015 teaching document declares, among other things, that "the Church is therefore obliged to view evangelization to Jews, who believe in the one God, in a different manner from that to people of other religions and world views. In concrete terms this means that the Catholic Church neither conducts nor supports any specific institutional mission work directed towards Jews." This does not mean that Catholics cannot or should not receive into the church individual Jews who wish to undergo Christian catechesis or baptism. The 2015 document is very clear about this: "Christians are nonetheless called to bear witness to their faith in Jesus Christ also to Jews, although they should do so in a humble and sensitive manner, acknowledging that Jews are bearers of God's Word, and particularly in view of the great tragedy of the Shoah."

nant struck with Abraham, the patriarchs, Moses, and David and the new covenant made in the dying and rising of Jesus. Are the covenant made with the ancestors of Israel and the new covenant inaugurated in Jesus in some sense really one covenant?[48] The faithful responses of Jews and Christians to the covenant offered by God are variously evaluated.[49]

Most Jews and Christians, however, since the earthly career of Muhammad, have found it difficult to recognize in what sense there is a covenant offered by God in the Islamic tradition to peoples outside the Jewish and Christian communities. Without denying the absolutely unique covenantal bond between faithful Jews and faithful Christians, no one who has lived among Muslims and grown to know them as friends can feel comfortable with a characterization of Muslims as infidels, people outside any covenant offered by God. That has been my experience over the past five decades or more, and I know other Christians and Jews who feel and think the same way. In the chapter that follows we shall return to the covenant in faith made with Abraham and how Jews, Christians, and Muslims define themselves as children of Abraham.

48. See David E. Holwerda, *Jesus and Israel: One Covenant or Two* (Grand Rapids, Mich.: Eerdmans, 1995). In this book Holwerda argues for the oneness of the Jewish and Christian covenant quite controversially, writing that "the deeper reality of Israel and the Davidic kingdom has been disclosed through Jesus Christ. Consequently the claims of Judaism that Israel in its land as such functions as 'Jacob's ladder pointing to Jerusalem on high' [Abraham Joshua Heschel, *Israel: An Echo of Eternity* (New York: Farrar, Straus and Giroux, 1969), 222] is contested by the New Testament's application of Jacob's ladder to Jesus as the Son of Man (John 1:51)" (Holwerda, *Jesus and Israel*, 183).

49. Eugene B. Korn and John T. Pawlikowski express this well in their joint introduction to the collection they edited, *Two Faiths, One Covenant? Jewish and Christian Identity in the Presence of the Other* (Lanham, Md.: Rowman and Littlefield, 2005), 1: "Both Judaism and Christianity are faiths that lay claim to the same biblical covenant initiated by God with Abraham and his descendants. Thus, there is an inseparable connection between the election of Israel and that of the Church, between the old and the new covenant. This biblical covenant, it seems, is at the root of each tradition's understanding of its identity."

CHAPTER 2

Abraham: A Father in Faith

I don't know if you have ever visited the Holy Land, D. The one time I went there, I thought Galilee very beautiful. Much of what I saw in Jerusalem, however, and especially in the Old City of Jerusalem, seemed terribly touristic. The winding streets were replete with souvenir shops selling dreadful T-shirts saying things like, "My grandmother visited Israel and all I got was this lousy T-shirt." The churches, especially in the Old City, struck me as over-decorated, in a nineteenth-century fashion, with the notable exception of the Romanesque Church of St. Anne. The noise and the ecclesiastical chaos in the Church of the Holy Sepulcher simply appalled me.

During that visit to the Holy Land, a Jesuit friend of mine who was teaching at the University of Bethlehem took me to see a site that few tourists or pilgrims ever visit: the Greek Orthodox Monastery of Mar Saba. Located in the Kidron Valley east of Jerusalem, the monastery could only be reached at that time by taking a bus from Bethlehem which delivered us at a deserted spot where the rough road simply petered out. From there we had to hike for what seemed a very long time under the pitiless sun of June in Israel-Palestine. Having come from the rainy season in West Africa, I had not brought a hat but my Jesuit friend had a Palestinian keffiyeh at the ready to protect my head.

St. John of Damascus (676–749) is entombed at the Monastery of Mar Saba. Before he became a monk in midlife, John of Damascus had grown to adulthood in a Christian family of Damascus, a family whose members had long served first the government of Byzantine Greek Syria and subsequently the Muslim Arab rulers of the newly constituted Umayyad caliphate. For reasons unknown—some speculate declining job possibilities for Christian civil servants as Arab Muslims developed managerial skills—John withdrew to the Monastery of Mar Saba in the Palestinian wilderness in his middle years; there he lived the rest of his very long life. John's knowledge of the Qur'an and early Islamic history seems somewhat skewed by the standards of historiography today, but the details of the new religious tradition of his imperial masters may have concerned him less than the theological controversies that were tearing about the Byzantine Christian world in the early eighth century. Iconoclasts, people who blamed all the troubles of the shrinking Byzantine world on the fact that they venerated images, came to power with the Byzantine emperor Leo the Isaurian (r. 717–41). John's spirited defense of images might have led to martyrdom in the Byzantine Empire gone iconoclastic, but John's presence in territories ruled by the Muslim Umayyad caliphate guaranteed his safety until he died at a very advanced age.

Journeying to Mar Saba that June morning I thought of another, and much earlier traveler than either John of Damascus or myself and my Jesuit friend. The patriarch Abraham, according to biblical tradition, passed through these same hills and valleys at a much earlier era when they would have been sufficiently well watered and verdant to make it possible for him to graze his flocks. Was Abraham, like John of Damascus many centuries later, withdrawing from circumstances in Ur of the Chaldeans or Haran that made him want to seek the freedom to worship one God alone?

Jews, Christians, and Muslims all look to Abraham as the first person to put his faith in God. Is this common opinion a bond of unity among the three traditions of faith, or is it rather a barrier? Both opinions can be argued; both sides of this question deserve careful examination and reflection. The one narrative about Abraham revered in all three faith traditions—the willingness of Abraham to offer his son in sacrifice—may well provide the basis for a profound, if deeply nuanced, understanding of the depths of Abrahamic faith.

In the early evening of Sunday, June 8, 2014, Pope Francis, accompanied by Ecumenical Patriarch Bartholomew and a retinue of Catholic and Orthodox clergy, gathered in the Vatican Gardens in Rome for a prayer meeting with two religiously mixed delegations from Israel and Palestine. Heading those delegations were two people not usually identified with prayer, and especially with prayer in public: President Shimon Peres of Israel and President Mahmoud Abbas of Palestine. In their respective addresses to the small gathering, each of the two presidents emphasized his particular concern in the search for peace between Israel and Palestine. Peres noted the presence with him in his delegation to the meeting in Vatican Gardens of "Jewish, Christian and Druze leaders" from Israel; he also mentioned the city of Jerusalem five times in the course of his remarks.[1] Abbas, heading an interreligious delegation from Palestine, singled out among the peoples of Palestine "Muslims, Christians and Samaritans"; he in turn mentioned the city of Jerusalem eight times.[2] Pope Francis, who had just traveled to Jordan, Palestine, and Israel—including Jerusalem—in the company of his Argentinian friends, Rabbi Abraham Skorka and Shaykh 'Umar 'Abboud, spoke about peace in the Holy Land and never mentioned the city of Jerusalem at all.

Neither Peres nor Abbas made any mention of Abraham or of the assertion often repeated that Judaism, Christianity, and Islam are "Abrahamic religions." Without using that phrase, Pope Francis twice made mention of Abraham that evening: "Your presence, dear Presidents, is a great sign of brotherhood which you offer as children of Abraham." In his prayer at the conclusion of his address, Pope Francis addressed God: "Lord, God of Abraham, God of the Prophets, God of Love, you created us and you call us to live as brothers and sisters."[3]

While he was in Jerusalem a little less than two weeks earlier, Pope Francis had met, among others, with the Grand Mufti, the chief legal expert of the Muslim community in Israel and Palestine. In his address to the Grand Mufti, the pope reflected on the model that Abraham provides for uprooted people, for people on pilgrimage—a description that could be used for both Israelis and Palestinians over the past century:

1. "Address of His Excellency Shimon Peres, the President of Israel, Vatican Gardens, Sunday, 8 June 2014," available at www.vatican.va.

2. "Address of His Excellency Mahmoud Abbas, President of Palestine, Vatican Gardens, Sunday, 8 June 2014," available at www.vatican.va.

3. "Invocation for Peace: Words of Pope Francis, Vatican Gardens, Sunday, 8 June 2014," available at www.vatican.va.

At this moment I think of Abraham, who lived as a pilgrim in these lands. Muslims, Christians and Jews see in him, albeit in different ways, a father in faith and a great example to be imitated. He became a pilgrim, leaving his own people and his own house in order to embark on that spiritual adventure to which God called him. A pilgrim is a person who makes himself poor and sets forth on a journey. Pilgrims set out intently towards a great and longed-for destination, and they live in the hope of a promise received.... This was how Abraham lived, and this should be our spiritual attitude.... Nor can we forget that the pilgrimage of Abraham was also a summons to righteousness: God wanted him to witness his way of acting and to imitate him.... Dear brothers, dear friends, from this holy place I make a heartfelt plea to all people and to all communities who look to Abraham: may we respect and love one another as brothers and sisters! May we learn to understand the sufferings of others! May no one abuse the name of God through violence! May we work together for justice and peace! *Salaam!*[4]

Pope John Paul II, just before his Great Jubilee pilgrimage in 2000, had also referred to Abraham as a model: "Together with us, Jews and Muslims also look to the person of Abraham as a model of unconditional submission to the will of God."[5] Pope Benedict XVI, during his 2009 pilgrimage to the Holy Land, spoke at greater length on this theme with an audience of people dedicated to interreligious dialogue:

Faith is always lived within a culture. The history of religion shows that a community of believers proceeds by degrees of faithfulness to God, drawing from and shaping the culture it meets. This same dynamic is found in individual believers from the great monotheistic traditions: attuned to the voice of God, like Abraham we respond to his call and set out seeking the fulfillment of his promises, striving to obey his will, forging a path in our own particular culture.... Abraham's first step in faith—and our steps to or from the synagogue, church, mosque or temple—tread the path of our single human history, unfolding along the way, we might say, to the eternal Jerusalem.[6]

4. "Visit to the Grand Mufti of Jerusalem: Address of Pope Francis, Building of the Great Council on the Esplanade of the Mosques (Jerusalem), Monday, 26 May 2014," available at www.vatican.va.

5. "Commemoration of Abraham, 'Our Father in Faith,' in Paul VI Hall, the Vatican, 23 February 2000," in *John Paul II in the Holy Land: In His Own Words*, ed. Lawrence Boadt, CSP, and Kevin di Camillo (Mahwah, N.J.: Paulist Press, 2005), 49–50. Pope John Paul II had hoped to speak these words in southern Iraq near the site of ancient Ur, but political considerations at the time prevented this part of his pilgrimage. Thus he delivered this address at the Vatican on the eve of his departure for Egypt on February 24, 2000.

6. "Meeting with Organizations for Interreligious Dialogue, Auditorium of Notre Dame Center,

Such generous words about both Jews and Muslims have not always been a part of the Catholic Christian tradition. A prayer that was used on every Feast of Christ the King, which can be dated to the institution of that feast by Pope Pius XI in 1925, consecrated the whole of the human race to the Sacred Heart of Jesus. In the process of that prayer, the authors dealt two blows, one after the other, to anyone working towards a more positive Catholic evaluation of either Islam or Judaism. Islam received the first bashing: "Be Thou King of all those who are still involved in the darkness of idolatry or of Islamism, and refuse not to draw them all into the light and kingdom of God." Note how this sentence lumps together "the darkness of idolatry" with "Islamism," a passage that could be construed as classifying Muslims along with idolaters. Such a nexus sounds suspiciously like the medieval canard that Muslims worshiped an idol named Mahound.[7] The use of the word "Islamism" for Islam, a French term that in recent years has come to denote the rigoristic interpretation of Islam dominant in Saudi Arabia or among the Salafis in different areas of the Middle East, probably only meant the same thing as Islam for the composers of the prayer.[8]

Having trounced Muslims in the hearing of God, the prayer goes on to savage Jews as well: "Turn Thine eyes of mercy towards the children of that race, once Thy Chosen People. Of old they called down upon themselves the blood of the Savior; may it now descend upon them a laver of redemption and of life."[9] From texts like these, in use for nearly four decades before the Second Vatican Council, it is not hard to understand the problem the Council fathers at Vatican II faced when it came to crafting more irenic words about the faith of either Muslims or Jews.

The Council fathers, however, did work out in the 1964 "Dogmatic

---

Jerusalem, 11 May 2009," in *Pope Benedict XVI in the Holy Land*, ed. Yehezdel Landau et al. (New York: Paulist Press, 2011), 65–66.

7. See W. Montgomery Watt, *Muhammad at Medina* (Oxford: Clarendon Press, 1956), 324.

8. The term is too loosely used today, and it is sometimes hard to figure out what people mean by it, other than to say it is a version of Islam that they do not like, if they can be said to like any form of Islam at all.

9. The quotations from this prayer derive from "Consecration of the Human Race to the Sacred Heart of Jesus," as translated in *Liber Devotionum ad Usum Scholasticorum Societatis Jesu*, 5th ed. (Chicago: Loyola Press, 1947), 151–52.

Constitution on the Church" (*Lumen Gentium*) something much more positive about both Judaism and Islam. Relying heavily on Romans 9:4–5, the Council fathers declared that "in the first rank [of those related to the church as the people of God] is that people to whom the covenants and the promises had been given and from whom Christ arose according to the flesh. Through [their divine] election, they are a people most beloved because of their forefathers, for there is no going back on the gifts and the call of God."[10] What *Lumen Gentium* had to say immediately afterwards about Islam also strove to accentuate the positive, but hesitated somewhat when it touched on the subject of Abraham and his relationship to Muslims: "Moreover, the plan of salvation even embraces those who recognize a Creator, first and foremost among them the Musulmans, who profess that they hold the faith of Abraham. Together with us they adore the only one God, the Merciful One Who will come to judge humankind on the last day."[11] The European (especially French, Italian, and Spanish) origins of the term used in Latin to translate "Muslims" in this text (*Musulmanos*) suggest the dominance of continental European input felt in the creation of this text. Furthermore, the phrase about Muslims "who profess that they hold the faith of Abraham" (*fidem Abrahae se tenere profitentes*) seems a trifle grudging, or at least not terribly generous, appearing to cast some doubt on the Muslim claim to the faith of Abraham.

Within a year, however, the Council fathers also completed the brief 1965 "Declaration on the Relation of the Church to Non-Christian Religions" (*Nostra Aetate*). In this document the Council fathers declared, following St. Paul, that Christians have the right to claim Abraham as their ancestor, at least in a spiritual sense: "Looking deeply into the mystery of the Church, this Sacred Synod remembers the link by which the people of the New Covenant are spiritually connected with the root of Abraham."[12] But such a claim by Christians in no way invalidates the fact that Jews retain their identity as God's chosen people, beginning with Abraham and the other patriarchs: "Nonetheless, according

10. Vatican Council II, *Lumen Gentium*, November 21, 1964, n16, available at www.vatican.va.
11. Ibid.
12. Vatican Council II, *Nostra Aetate*, October 28, 1965, n4, available at www.vatican.va.

to the Apostle [Rom 11:28–29], Jews remain for the sake of the patriarchs most dear to God, since God does not go back on the gifts he gave or the call he made."[13]

In the section on Islam, *Nostra Aetate* proved more positive than *Lumen Gentium* regarding the relationship of Muslims to Abraham, but still less confident of that relationship than were Popes John Paul II, Benedict XVI, and Francis in the early twenty-first century. Unlike some Protestant theologians in times past and present, the Council fathers insisted both in *Lumen Gentium* and in *Nostra Aetate* that Muslims worshiped the one and only God. "The Church also looks with esteem on Muslims who adore only one God, the Living and Everlasting One, the Merciful and Almighty One, the Creator of heaven and earth, the One Who has spoken to humankind. [This God] is the One to Whose mysterious decrees they [Muslims] also strive wholeheartedly to submit themselves, just as Abraham—with whom Islamic faith freely identifies itself—submitted himself to God."[14] The assertion that Abraham is one to whom "Islamic faith freely identifies itself" (*ad quem fides islamica libenter sese refert*) falls a little short of accepting the account of Abraham known from the Qur'an and other Islamic sources, but it does go further than *Lumen Gentium* in affirming the Abrahamic identity of Muslims. In the year that had passed since the completion of *Lumen Gentium*, the Council fathers had also created a new Latin word for Muslims—Latinized Arabic in the accusative form: *Muslimos*. Does this small detail hint at the influence exerted at the council by Arabic-speaking bishops and experts?

The more positive evaluations of Islam and its relationship to Abraham in the twenty-first century Holy Land addresses of Popes John Paul II, Benedict XVI, and Francis demonstrate that Catholic Christian reflection on Abraham and his relationship not only to Jews and Christians but also to Muslims continues as a process, and a very complicated process as well. Without endorsing every aspect of the thought on Abraham and Islam enunciated by the French Catholic Islamicist Louis Massignon (1883–1962), there is little doubt that these passages in pa-

13. Ibid.
14. Ibid., n3.

pal addresses and conciliar documents reflect his influence. Massignon identified Abraham as the first in a line of what the Catholic and Orthodox Christian traditions have called apotropaic saints, holy men and women who fend off the results of the sins of others by interceding for them: "More than any other defender of lost causes, Abraham is an intercessor."[15]

Massignon enumerated three intercessory or apotropaic prayers in the Book of Genesis made by Abraham: his prayer for Sodom, his prayer for Ishmael, and his prayer for Isaac. In the first prayer, the one for Sodom (Gn 18:16–33), Abraham bargains with the LORD over how many just people would have to be found to save that city from destruction. Massignon's elaborate understanding of Sodom sees in it much more than one of the cities of the plain; it is "the city of self-love which objects to the visitation of angels, of guests, or strangers, or wishes to abuse them."[16] In the third of the prayers of Abraham, the prayer for Isaac, Massignon meditates on the Genesis account of the binding of Isaac (Gn 22:1–19): "At great cost to himself Abraham carried out to the limit the oath of fidelity which he swore to God when he entered into the covenant of circumcision … he abandoned everything he could think about divinity, even the moral qualification for his acts."[17]

It is in the prayer of Abraham for Ishmael ("O that Ishmael might live in your sight!," Gn 17:18) that Massignon enters into some controversy. He interprets that plea for Ishmael as a prayer for Arabs and for Muslims who trace their Abrahamic inheritance through Ishmael:

God imposed the expatriation or the "hegira" upon his first-born son, Ishmael [Gn 21:14–21]—Abraham consented to this exile in the desert, provided that Ishmael's descendants could survive there, endowed by God for their life in this world with a certain privileged perpetuity which distinguishes that Ishmaelite Arab race with a vocation to the sword, to "iron, wherein is mighty pow-

15. Louis Massignon, "The Three Prayers of Abraham," in *Testimonies and Reflections: Essays of Louis Massignon*, ed. and trans. Herbert Mason (Notre Dame, Ind.: University of Notre Dame Press, 1989), 6. For the original French text, see "Les Trois Prières d'Abraham," in Louis Massignon, *Opera Minora*, ed. Youakim Moubarac (Paris: Presses universitaires de France, 1969), 3:804–16. Although the late Herbert Mason is the translator of most of these works by Massignon, Allan Cutler is the translator of "The Three Prayers of Abraham" included in *Testimonies and Reflections*, 3–20.

16. Massignon, *Testimonies and Reflections*, 10.

17. Ibid., 15.

er" (Qur'an 57:25), which, with the birth of Islam, held sway over all idolaters. Against the latter implacable holy war has been declared so long as they do not confess that there is only one God, the God of Abraham—"the first Muslim."[18]

Most Catholics would be either unfamiliar or uncomfortable with the ideas expressed in Massignon's understanding of the prayer for Ishmael. Nevertheless, his monumental scholarship and his lifelong dedication to difficult and sometimes lost causes made Massignon's memory live on well beyond his death. A prophetic figure, he exercised a long and lasting influence on the church and especially on Catholics engaged in Islamic studies since the papacy of Pope Pius XI.[19]

Others outside the Catholic church in recent years have made much more sweeping generalizations about Abraham and his connection with the so-called Abrahamic religions. Abraham's Path, a pilgrimage/ journey that takes participants through several geographical places identified with Abraham in the Middle East, was originally initiated by people associated with the Program on Negotiation of the Business School at Harvard University. On their website the organizers state that "we value the understanding that Abraham is the father of the three great monotheistic faiths (Judaism, Christianity and Islam) and smaller religious groups, and that he is a cultural figure as well as a religious one."[20] I am not quite sure what the authors mean by describing Abraham as "a cultural figure as well as a religious one," but it may betray a certain not unfamiliar uneasiness with religion at Harvard, at least outside the Divinity School.

In 2012 Jon D. Levenson, a professor of Jewish Studies at Harvard, published an excellent book questioning some of the generalizations about Abraham found in that Abraham's Path website, in the process distinguishing various Jewish, Christian, and Muslim ways of understanding the patriarch. Levenson does grant this much for Abraham's Path: "That the initiative focuses on the figure of Abraham makes em-

---

18. Ibid., 12–13.

19. See Patrick J. Ryan, "The 'Catholic Muslim': The Conversion of Louis Massignon," *Commonweal* 140 (January 25, 2013): 15–18, and Christian S. Krokus, *The Theology of Louis Massignon: Islam, Christ, and the Church* (Washington, D.C.: The Catholic University of America Press, 2017).

20. "Why the Abraham Path," available at www.abrahampath.org/connect/about-us/why-the -abraham-path/.

inent sense."[21] Much more pointedly, however, Levenson takes issue with a bestseller by Bruce Feiler published in 2002 that goes much further down the road of reducing Abraham to a generic culture hero and/or monotheist.[22] Feiler maintains that a primitive Abrahamic monotheism, "the carefully balanced message of the Abraham story—that God cares for all his children," was spoiled by later generations of Jews who narrowed Abraham down to being the progenitor of Jews alone.[23] Christians and Muslims also bear their share in the guilt for narrowing down the significance of Abraham, according to Feiler.[24]

Levenson begins his own work on Abraham by noting the major problem that separates Jews and Christians on one side and Muslims on the other when it comes to understanding Abraham. "However much Judaism and Christianity may diverge, they agree on the canonical status of Genesis."[25] Muslims, on the other hand, do not normally rely on the Hebrew scriptures but on the Qur'an for their accounts of Abraham, although, over the centuries, not a few Muslims have consulted the Hebrew scriptures and the New Testament, without accepting them as unadulterated scriptural sources. It should be noted, however, that extra-biblical Jewish aggadic midrash about Abraham and Quranic stories about Abraham have much more in common than either has with the Abraham stories in the Book of Genesis or the Christian use made of those Genesis stories in the New Testament.

For Jews, Levenson insists that Abraham as portrayed in the Book of Genesis is not the father of an idea—monotheism—but the father of a son, Isaac, and the progenitor through that son of Jacob whose name is changed to Israel and the "Children of Israel" ever afterwards. For Christians, especially under the influence of St. Paul, Abraham is the spiritual progenitor of everyone who puts faith in the LORD as Abraham did, everyone for whom "the LORD reckoned [that act of faith] to him as righteousness" (Gn 15:6).[26] Abraham for Jews and Abraham for

21. Levenson, *Inheriting Abraham*, 173.
22. Bruce Feiler, *Abraham: A Journey to the Heart of Three Faiths* (New York: HarperCollins, 2002).
23. Ibid., 130.
24. Ibid., 152–54 and 174–77.
25. Levenson, *Inheriting Abraham*, 11.
26. The JPS translation renders this verse thus: "And because [Abram] put his trust in the LORD, he reckoned it to his merit."

Christians, and especially St. Paul, are very different from each other, and yet, as Levenson notes, there is a certain closer kinship because both Jews and Christians derive their portraits of Abraham from Genesis. "Judaism and Christianity ... continue the focus in Genesis upon family and descent, even though each in its own way also allows those who cannot trace their lineage to Abraham to enter his family nonetheless and to belong to his covenant."[27] Levenson notes by contrast that the significance of Abraham for Muslims is quite different: "Islam ... disclaims the family dimension altogether and reinterprets covenant in ways that have nothing to do with the adoption metaphor but call instead for a new community made up of moral individuals who have unconditionally submitted to God."[28]

Let me follow the husband of Sarah, Hagar, and eventually Keturah, the father not just of the only sons he begot with Hagar and Sarah, Ishmael and Isaac, but the father as well, according the narrative of Genesis, of the six sons born of Keturah after the death of Sarah. What are the legacies we inherit from this father of many nations? Is the faith of Abraham a bond between Jews, Christians, and Muslims, or is it so ambiguous a connection that it actually constitutes a barrier separating these three communities of faith?

Abraham as the Progenitor of Israel

Much, perhaps too much, has been written about the presentation of Abraham in the Hebrew Bible. I wish to dwell on Abraham not only in the Hebrew scriptures but also, although more briefly, in some of the extra-scriptural or post-scriptural elaborations which sometimes are as well known to Jews as the text of the Torah.

Let us first consider some of the highlights in the Genesis history of Abraham (Gn 12:1–25:11). Certain central themes in scripture are told repeatedly, each time with important variations reflecting the interests of differing narrative schools. There are three accounts of the call of

27. Levenson, *Inheriting Abraham*, 199.
28. Ibid.

the patriarch, called Abram in the first two narratives and Abraham in the third (Gn 12, 15, 17). Each narrative expresses that call as a grant or promissory covenant, a pact in which God takes virtually all the obligations on himself.[29] God assures Abraham, against all odds, that he will take possession of a particular land, Canaan, beget progeny there, and through that progeny become a people who will dwell in the land of Canaan.

The so-called Yahwistic author (J) of Genesis, who uses the Hebrew name for God represented by the unpronounced tetragrammaton (YHWH) for which "The LORD" (*Adonai*) substitutes, seems to be the main source of the first of these call narratives in literary sequence.[30] "Now the LORD said to Abram, 'Go from your country and your kindred and your father's house to the land that I will show you'" (Gn 12:1). The verses that follow take Abram on a great walkabout to and finally in the land he is being shown by the LORD. The territorial or geographical motifs of this chapter predominate. Virtually nothing is said of Abram's progeny. The reader familiar with the whole Hebrew Bible recognizes the later significance of each of the places first visited by Abram. Considered as a whole, this Yahwistic narrative of the call of Abram is totally centered on the Israelite claim to possession of the land of Canaan.

The second major narrative of Abram's call, found in Genesis 15, is usually ascribed to the Yahwist as well, but with possible influences from the so-called Elohist (E), the traditional source that calls God *Elohim*. Precisely because of the importance of the narrative in this chapter for later Israelite identity, it is not insignificant that multiple literary sources are involved; thus the Almighty is addressed as "LORD God" (*YHWH-Elohim*), something of a compound name. The Elohist transformed by the Yahwist, or the Yahwist transformed by the Elohist, pays attention first and foremost to God's promise of abundant progeny to

29. On grant or promissory covenants, see Richard Elliott Friedman, "Torah and Covenant," in *The Oxford Study Bible: Revised English Bible with the Apocrypha*, ed. M. Jack Suggs et al. (New York: Oxford University Press, 1992), 154–63.

30. See Richard Clifford and Roland Murphy, "Genesis," in *NJBC*, 8–43. I presume that the reader is familiar with the source-theory of the authorship of Genesis and much of the rest of the first four books of the Bible.

Abram: "[The LORD] brought [Abram] outside and said, 'Look toward heaven and count the stars, if you are able to count them.' Then he said to him, "So shall your descendants be'" (Gn 15:5). Most dramatically, the LORD "cuts" a covenant with Abram, passing in the form of "a fire pot, and a flaming torch" (Gn 15:17) between the halved animal victims. Just as these symbolic representations of the LORD suggest the pillars of cloud and fire that later accompanied the Israelites by day and by night in the Exodus, the LORD assures Abram that his descendants four centuries later, who will have lived as "strangers in a land not theirs" (Gn 15:13), will eventually return from their sojourn in Egypt to the Land of Promise. This second call narrative in literary sequence promises Abram a vast territory, as much as ever paid tribute to King David several centuries later: "To your descendants I give this land, from the river of Egypt to the great river, the river Euphrates, the land of the Kenites, the Kenizzites, the Kadmonites, the Hittites, the Perizzites, the Rephaim, the Amorites, the Canaanites, the Girgashites, and the Jebusites" (Gn 15:18–21).

The third call narrative, Genesis 17, usually ascribed to the Priestly source (P), pays less attention to land (although it does specify the divine gift of Canaan, in Gn 17:8) and concentrates on progeny, in particular through Sarah (Gn 17:15–22), even though the patriarch pleads for Ishmael, the child he has by then begotten with Hagar (Gn 17:18). Abram's name is changed to Abraham because, for the Priestly source, Abraham will not only be the progenitor of Israel but he will also be "the ancestor of a multitude of nations" (Gn 17:4). In the first instance, this suggests that not only Isaac but also Ishmael and his descendants, later identified with the Bedouins of Sinai and nearby territories (Gn 25:12–18), will father Abrahamic nations. This third call narrative possibly reflects the period of priestly administration of Persian-colonized Judea after the Babylonian Exile, when it had become quite obvious that the descendants of Abraham had survived as a people, some in the Promised Land but many outside it, but their territorial sovereignty and independence had been considerably curtailed. The Priestly author is more concerned with the ritual purity of Abraham's lineage and the marking of that lineage by circumcision (Gn 17:9–14, 23–27). The Israelites are called through Abraham to a life of holiness: "Walk before me and be blameless" (Gn 17:1).

The covenant struck between *YHWH-Elohim* and Abram/Abraham in these three call narratives in the Book of Genesis basically comes down to a grant or promise by the Almighty to give this particular Mesopotamian Bedouin a territory (in particular, Canaan) as new grazing ground for his flocks as well as progeny (in particular Isaac, Sarah's son, although a modified filial inheritance would also be guaranteed for Ishmael, Hagar's son). It is hard to say, from these three complementary narratives, which promise is more basic or original, land or progeny. In any case, for a Bedouin of the ancient Middle East both were essential and intertwined. Without verdant land in which one could pasture flocks, the Bedouin had nothing to give to his progeny. Without progeny the Bedouin had no one to help him drive his flocks to pasture land and to inherit the flocks and the land when the Bedouin himself died. In some sense, it could be said that the diverse human authors of the traditions found in Genesis creatively reinterpreted a generic second-millennium BCE Bedouin predicament as a unique predicament underlying their national and religious identity. Every human predicament is unique for the person who undergoes it. The Book of Genesis assures us that God recognizes this uniqueness and God calls human beings in these predicaments.

The whole of the Torah, the first five books of the Bible, served later generations of Jews as a treasure trove from which they mined elaboration and commentary. An extraordinary Jewish intellectual in the cultivated Hellenistic city of Alexandria in Egypt, Philo (20 BCE–50 CE), evolved his own rather philosophical meditations on the story of Abraham. Philo knew no Hebrew or Aramaic and only visited the nearby homeland of his people once in his lifetime, but he identified himself with the patriarch Abraham, as can be seen in his lengthy disquisition on the Abraham narratives in Genesis. But Philo's approach is distinctly allegorical and philosophical, definitely not territorial. In a document apparently aimed at Gentiles in Alexandria seeking to know more about Jewish monotheism,[31] Philo maintains that the migrations of Abraham "were performed by a wise man; but if we look to the laws of allegory, by a soul devoted to virtue and busied in the search after the true God."[32] In another treatise apparently aimed at Hellenistic Jews rather than Alexandrian Gentiles, Philo compares the migration of Abraham from Ur to Haran to the Promised Land to the various stages through which the mind migrates in the quest for a purer concept of God: "Dwell ... within yourselves, forsaking the land of the Chaldeans, that is, opinion, and migrating to [Haran], the region of the outward sense, which is the corporeal abode of the mind.... Then rouse yourself up and seek to accomplish a migration from hence ... that the eye of the soul, to which God has granted the power of understanding the objects of the intellect, may never be overshadowed by any of those objects appreciable only by the outward senses."[33] With Philo may begin one strand of the tradition of looking to Abraham primarily as a monotheist.

Within Palestine in the first centuries CE aggadic midrash, studied reflection on the narrative portions of the Torah, built up a body of traditional Jewish lore that expands on the biblical narrative and engages the meditation of devout Jews to the present day. The great collection of aggadic midrash on the first book of the Torah that is referred to as *Bereshit Rabbah* (The Great [Commentary on] Genesis), was codified between 100 and 400 CE by Jewish scholars still living in Palestine, but not in Jerusalem, from which the Jews had been banned by the Romans. Typically this verse-by-verse commentary on Genesis, written partly in Hebrew and partly in Aramaic, compares and contrasts a verse from Genesis with a very disparate text from what Jews have called the Writings, including such books of the Hebrew Bible as Psalms and Proverbs. The audience for whom the scholars were writing was probably

---

31. On the different audiences for whom Philo wrote, see Nahum Glatzer's introduction to *The Essential Philo*, trans. C. D. Yonge, ed. Nahum N. Glatzer (New York: Schocken Books, 1971), xi.

32. Ibid., 96. For the Greek of Philo and a slightly different translation, see "On Abraham," in *Philo VI*, trans. F. H. Colson (London / Cambridge, Mass.: William Heinemann / Harvard University Press, 1935), 38–39.

33. Ibid., 181. For the Greek and a slightly different translation, see "On the Migration of Abraham," in *Philo IV*, trans. F. H. Colson and G. H. Whitaker (Cambridge, Mass. / London: Harvard University Press / William Heinemann, 1932), 240–43.

made up of local rabbis exhorting their dispirited congregations to bear up under oppressive foreign domination: the Imperial Roman and later Byzantine hegemonies in Israel. The commentators' own sense of being uprooted deepens their appreciation for what Abram did at God's command when he emigrated first from Ur and then from Haran.

Thus the beginning of the first call narrative of Abraham, "Go from your country and your kindred and your father's house to the land that I will show you" (Gn 12:1), is juxtaposed by the commentators with Psalm 45:10, a verse from a royal wedding psalm with possible significance as well as a celebration of the LORD's espousal with Israel. "Hear, O daughter, consider and incline your ear," the Psalmist exhorts the bride. "Forget your people and your father's house" (Ps 45:10).[34] Abram/Abraham is compared to the bride in his willingness to leave his father's house, no matter the pain involved.

In the meditation on how Abraham nearly sacrificed Isaac (Gn 22:1–19), the commentators of *Bereshit Rabbah* see in the ram that Abraham was commanded to sacrifice the apocalyptic hope of Zechariah for the LORD's eventual triumph over the adversaries of Israel ("The LORD GOD will sound the trumpet and march forth in the whirlwinds of the south" [Zec 9:14b]). They also think of the *shofar*, the ram's horn, the sounding of which ushers in the Jewish New Year:

R[abbi] Judah b[en] R[abbi] Simon interpreted: At the end of ... all generations Israel will fall into the clutches of sin and be victims of persecution; yet eventually they will be redeemed by the ram's horn, as it says, "*And the Lord God will blow the horn*," etc. R[abbi] Hanina b[en] R[abbi] Isaac said: Throughout the year Israel are in sin's clutches and led astray by their troubles, but on New Year they take the *shofar* and blow on it, and eventually they will be redeemed by the ram's horn.[35]

Some of the juxtapositions of verses from the Writings with verses of Genesis seem a trifle farfetched to the modern eye; others seem surprisingly contemporary, even postmodern, in the ways that they reread one ancient text in terms of another, possibly less ancient but still anterior

34. See *Midrash Rabbah: Genesis*, ed. H. Freedman, 3rd ed. (London: Soncino Press, 1983), 1:313.
   35. Ibid., 1:498–99.

to the time of the commentator. So habituated have we become over the last century or so to reading ancient scriptural passages in the light of their putative pre-scriptural sources that it is refreshing to find in this great commentary on Genesis literary parallels to the way in which the ancient Christian writers of the same era read both the Hebrew scriptures and the New Testament. Philo's allegorizing of Genesis and the Palestinian rabbis' meditations on juxtaposed verses of Genesis and the Writings both serve to direct the attention of their contemporaries and ourselves, all of us who struggle to keep faith with a mysterious God, a God who demands of us an uprooting that is sometimes painful.

Abraham as One Justified by Faith

For the preachers and their communities who produced the New Testament, and especially those who surrounded the Beloved Disciple and Paul of Tarsus, the Hebrew Bible accounts of Abraham offered grist for their respective interpretive mills. For many of the sources of the New Testament neither land nor progeny, literally understood, counted for much in their estimate of Abraham and his importance. Already in the New Testament recollections of the preaching of John the Baptist, we receive a hint that for John the Baptist and others looking forward to the reign of God, physical descent from Abraham did not constitute a real claim to share in Abraham's relationship to the Almighty: "Do not presume to say to yourselves, 'We have Abraham as our ancestor'; for I tell you, God is able from these stones to raise up children to Abraham" (Mt 3:9). John's Gospel ascribes to Jesus similar sentiments about his contentious critics who boast of their descent from Abraham: "If you were Abraham's children, you would be doing what Abraham did" (Jn 8:39). But not every New Testament author is equally critical of the religious significance of Abrahamic physical descent; it must always be remembered that the authors of the New Testament were for the most part Jews, even if their first hearers may have been a mixture of Jews and Gentiles who had adhered to the way of Jesus.

Most famously, Paul took up the story of Abraham as early as the fifties of the first century CE and found in it the grounds for his own teaching about justification by faith apart from works of the Law. Both the Epistle to the Galatians and the Epistle to the Romans ground their teaching on this subject on elements in the call narratives of Abraham as preserved in the Book of Genesis. A Jew reading these interpretations of Genesis by Paul might legitimately consider them misunderstandings of the original texts; I would suggest that they are, precisely, different aggadic *midrashim* on these texts, created to express a new and different religious insight from what was first experienced by the authors of Genesis or by later thinkers in the Jewish tradition meditating on these foundational texts.

Levenson points out how differently Jews and Christians have interpreted Genesis 12:3: "And all the families of the earth shall bless themselves by you," as the Jewish Publication Society translation puts it, or "In you all the families of the earth shall be blessed," to use the NRSV translation. Neither translation is made without presuppositions; the first was made under the influence of the great eleventh-century Jewish scholar known as Rashi, who maintains that Abraham was meant to be "a byword of blessing" among all peoples.[36] The second was made under the influence of St. Paul, who saw the verse as evidence that even the Gentiles were included in the blessing of Abraham (Gal 3:6–9).

Paul also reads one verse in the second call narrative, Genesis 15:6, in a way that Jews find peculiar, to put it mildly. Let me quote the Epistle to the Galatians in detail: "Just as Abraham 'believed God, and it was reckoned to him as righteousness' [Gn 15:6], so, you see, those who believe are descendants of Abraham. And the scripture, foreseeing that God would justify the Gentiles by faith, declared the gospel beforehand to Abraham, saying, 'All the Gentiles shall be blessed in you' [Gn 12:3]. For this reason, those who believe are blessed with Abraham who believed" (Gal 3:6–9). What Paul has done in this excerpt is to take two verses respectively from the second call narrative and the first call narrative in the Book of Genesis and load them with meanings that differ from their original sense in the Hebrew text of Genesis as we have

36. Levenson, *Inheriting Abraham*, 31.

it. The first verse cited, Genesis 15:6, states quite simply, after the LORD had promised to give the childless patriarch progeny as countless as the stars: "And he believed the LORD; and the LORD reckoned it to him as righteousness," or "[Abram] put his faith in the LORD, who reckoned it to him as righteousness," to use the Jewish Publication Society translation in contrast with the NRSV. What was the original meaning of this verse? It is hard to say exactly; I can understand why the Italians say that a translator (*traduttore*) is a traitor (*traditore*). The significance of the verse is not terribly clear. It might mean that the LORD God accepted Abram's faith, his profound trust in God's ability to provide him with future progeny. That faith, that trust expressed by Abram, convinced God that Abram was a truly upright person, a person at rights with God, a deeply holy and just man. Is all that meaning found in the word usually translated as "reckoned"?

The second verse cited by Paul, Genesis 12:3, depends for the meaning Paul assigns to it—salvation for Gentiles—on the Septuagintal Greek translation of Genesis: "There will be blessed in you all the tribes of the earth." The Hebrew original, however, can also be understood the way the Jewish Publication Society translates it: "All the families of the earth / Shall bless themselves by you." It is likely that Paul's original hearers and readers, not unlike Philo, only knew the Book of Genesis in the Septuagintal Greek rendering. Paul cites the verse as asserting that "In you [Abram] all nations shall find blessing" (Gal 3:8). But the meaning which Paul had come to read into these texts derives more from his own experience of the action of God in his life, as well as from the experience of the action of God in the lives of his Gentile converts. Paul's meaning did not derive from the text of Genesis in either Hebrew or Greek. The aggadic *midrash* Paul weaves on the first two calls of Abraham in Genesis, not unlike the *midrash* of *Bereshit Rabbah* on Genesis 12:1 or the allegorical interpretation by Philo of the same passage, tells us much more about Paul than it does about the original meaning of the text, if the original meaning of that text can be incontrovertibly established. I think that Paul's interpretation of these texts in Genesis is no more a departure from the Hebrew text than the very different interpretations made by his contemporary Philo and the interpretations woven around the same texts of Genesis by the authors who were probably already starting to work out the *midrashim* of *Bereshit Rabbah* in Paul's lifetime.

Paul tells us in another context that he had been "in my practice of the law a Pharisee, in zeal for religion a persecutor of the church, by the law's standard of righteousness without fault" (Phil 3:5–6). And yet, for all these religious qualifications, Paul came to recognize himself as a sinner. The sin of which he found himself guilty seems to have consisted in his hounding "the Church of God" (Gal 1:13), the earliest followers of Jesus in the Middle Eastern Diaspora in the thirties of the first century CE Luke in the Acts of the Apostles preserves three narratives of Paul's conversion. In this vision Paul heard Jesus asking him a poignant question: "Saul, Saul, why are you persecuting me?" (Acts 9:4; see also 22:7, 26:14).

In the Epistle to the Galatians, Paul is more reticent about the details of his conversion experience, but he does tell his readers that his career as a persecutor came to an end when "in his good pleasure God, who from my birth had set me apart, and who had called me through his grace, chose to reveal his Son in and through me, in order that I might proclaim him among the Gentiles" (Gal 1:15–16). The "in and through" of the Revised English Bible translation translates one preposition in the Greek original of Paul's Epistle: *en*, indicative of an internal experience of Paul, something much more religiously significant than blinding by heavenly light.[37] Paul implicitly compares his call narrative to that of the prophet Jeremiah who also said that he had been chosen before the LORD formed him in his mother's womb to be "a prophet to the nations" (Jer 1:5). Likewise, Second Isaiah's second song of the servant of the LORD begins with the declaration that "The LORD called me before I was born / while I was in my mother's womb he named me" (Is 49:1). A few verses later in that same song the Servant is told by the LORD that he has more than a mission to the tribes of Jacob/Israel: "I

37. Although I normally quote the NRSV, here I use the Revised English Bible translation (New York: Oxford University Press, 1992).

will give you as a light to the nations / That my salvation may reach the end of the earth" (Is 49:6).

To return to Paul's creative reinterpretation of two verses from two of the Abrahamic call narratives, I think it was Paul's experience of Jesus in glory identified with the Jewish Christians he was persecuting that convinced him that he, Paul, was a sinner and that he had a special calling to spread that news to the most notorious sinners of all, Gentiles outside the Law. The Acts of the Apostles notes that Saul/Paul witnessed the execution of Stephen, the first Christian martyr (Acts 7:58), and approved of it (Acts 8:1). Stephen, in Paul's hearing, had replicated the blasphemy ascribed to Jesus (Mk 14:62) when he in his turn also envisioned Jesus as "the Son of Man standing at the right hand of God" (Acts 7:56). That apparent blasphemy—basically a symbolic presentation of the central Christian affirmation that "Jesus is Lord" (1 Cor 12:3)—may have fascinated and disturbed Paul long before his conversion.

The third version of that conversion experience as narrated in the Acts of the Apostles adds to the question, "Saul, Saul, why do you persecute me?" an intriguing additional sentence: "It hurts to kick like this against the goad" (Acts 26:14). I would suggest that the conversion of Paul was gradually building up within him from the time of Stephen's martyrdom until that day on the road to Damascus. The persecutor of the church had been resisting his own instincts of sympathy with these Christians of similar Pharisaic background.

That day on the road to Damascus something happened inside Paul, something that he described as God revealing his Son in and through him, making him a new servant of the LORD or a new Jeremiah sent to proclaim good news to Gentiles. That experience persuaded Paul to read the Septuagintal Greek of the aforementioned texts from Genesis in such a way as to express accurately his new prophetic and apostolic calling rather than to reproduce exactly whatever the original Hebrew texts had said. Paul, like Abram in Genesis 15:6, had put his faith in the LORD—to be more precise, in the Lordship of Jesus—and that act of faith had been reckoned to him as the source of his new righteousness. That faith of Paul, making him righteous in God's sight, could also make such notorious sinners as the Gentiles righteous in God's sight. Through Paul, a new Abraham, all the nations would find blessing. It is not for nothing that the church calls Paul the Apostle of the Gentiles. For Paul, his experience on the road to Damascus linked him at the deepest level with Abram, called to father "a great nation" (Gn 12:2) and also to be one in whom "all the families of the earth will be blessed" (Gn 12:3).

Just as the Jewish tradition elaborated aggadic *midrash* around the Genesis narratives of Abraham, the Christian tradition likewise returned to Abraham, even after the New Testament era. The Syriac tradition ascribes to the fourth-century St. Ephrem (d. 373) a book of genealogies called *The Cave of Treasures*. It is likely that Ephrem's original text was supplemented over the next four centuries and it eventually proved interesting not only to Christians of that era but also to early Muslims. The authors of this work see in Abraham's willingness to sacrifice his son a foreshadowing of the crucifixion of Jesus on Golgotha:

Isaac was thirteen years old when his father took him and went up to the mountain of Yabhos (Jebus) to Melchizedek, the priest of God, the Most High ... , and in that place the Cross of Christ was set up, and on it grew the tree which held the ram that saved Isaac. And that same place is the center of the earth, and the grave of Adam, and the altar of Melchizedek, and Golgotha .... And there David saw the angel bearing the sword of fire. There, too, Abraham took up Isaac his son for a burnt offering, and he saw the Cross, and Christ, and the redemption of our father Adam. The tree (*i.e.* thicket) was a symbol of the Cross of Christ our Lord, and the ram [caught] in its branches was the mystery of the manhood of the Word, the Only One.[38]

Christians have found themselves as challenged as Jews in coming to terms with the willingness of Abraham to sacrifice his son. Rationalists strenuously rejected the ethical implications of the story, but the story lived on to challenge all those who try to set limits on the almightiness and providence of God. Muslims also had to come to terms with the same paradoxical story.

38. *The Book of the Cave of Treasures*, trans. E. A. Wallis Budge (London: Religious Tract Society, 1927), 149–50, available at www.sacred-texts.com/chr/bct/. The pagination follows Budge's 1927 translation. Some spelling has been changed and diacritical signs have been removed.

Abraham as a Pure Monotheist

The first thing that strikes any Jew or Christian studying the Quranic passages about Abraham is the radical difference between Abraham as presented in the Book of Genesis as well as the New Testament and the Quranic Abraham. The call of Abraham to migrate to new pastureland and found a new people through his progeny dominates the Genesis narratives of the Hebrew Bible. But Abraham in the Qur'an in no sense plays the role of the forefather of the people of Israel; in fact, in one of its most famous passages, the Qur'an insists that Abraham was neither a Jew nor a Christian but a *hanif*, a word difficult to translate but probably close to the Syriac word *hanpa* (which resembles the plural form of *hanif* in Arabic, *hunafa'*) said to mean something like "heathen" but with a distinctive sense of an Arab monotheist, neither Jewish nor Christian (Qur'an 3:65, 67–68):[39]

People of the Book: why will you debate about Abraham when the Torah and the Gospel had not been sent down until after him? Can't you understand? ... Abraham was neither a Jew nor a Christian but an Arab monotheist [*hanif*], surrendering [*muslim*] [to God]; nor was he one of those who ascribe partners [to God]. Indeed, those [who are] the people with Abraham are the ones who followed him, and this Prophet and those who keep faith. God is the Friend of those who keep faith.

Denying that Abraham was a Christian seems uncontroversial enough, but it may take some further reflection to demonstrate how even a Jew and a Christian can admit that he was not a Jew, either. The terms "Jew" and "Judaism" in Jewish usage reflect the reality of Israelite faith no earlier than the collapse of the Northern Kingdom of Israel in 721 BCE, and those terms are usually reserved for the population of Judah after the return from Babylon in the late sixth century BCE Abraham took his origins from Mesopotamia and lived about a millennium before the era when "Judaism" developed.

Thus it would, indeed, be ahistorical to call Abraham a Jew. It would

39. See Tor Andrae, *Mohammed: The Man and His Faith*, trans. Theophil Menzel, rev. ed. (San Francisco: Harper Torchbooks, 1960), 108–10.

even be ahistorical to call him an Israelite—a child of Israel, in Hebrew—because he was the grandfather of Jacob or Israel. Abraham was
a native of Mesopotamia and the ancestor of all who worship the LORD
God alone. Much more vivid in the Qur'an are stories of how Abraham
confronted his father and his people about their worship of plural divinities symbolized by idols.[40] Some of these stories are known in extra-biblical Jewish tradition[41] but play no part in the text of the Torah.[42]
Abraham is not the forefather of the people of Israel in the Qur'an but
he is, instead, a prophet of pure monotheism, not only as a theoretical
issue but in practice. Understanding the role of Abraham as a prophet
or messenger of the one and only God is central to the Qur'an. As such,
for Muslims Abraham prefigures or sets the model of prophet and messenger for Muhammad.

The just-quoted passage from the Qur'an describes Abraham as one
who has surrendered himself to God, one who is *muslim*, in the root
sense of the word. The implied context is not ancient Mesopotamia or
the land of Canaan, but the Arabian peninsula and, more precisely Mecca, where the Qur'an portrays Abraham and his son Ishmael undertaking to consecrate the Ka'ba, the central sanctuary of that trading center,
to the worship of one God alone: "And when We [God] appointed the
House [at Mecca] as a refuge for the people and a sanctuary, [We said:]
'Take Abraham's place of worship as your own.' We then contracted
with Abraham and Ishmael that they should purify My House for those
who circumambulate it and those who adhere to it bowing and prostrat-
ing" (Qur'an 2:125).

The Quranic Abraham has little of substance in common with Abraham in the Book of Genesis or Abraham in the New Testament, espe-

40. I prefer this way of putting what is usually referred to as "the worship of idols" or "idol
worship." I have found over many years of living in areas of Africa where not everyone is a Muslim
or a Christian that the religious situation designated by these phrases is one of divided attention
to God, the postulation of other forces in the transcendent realm, somewhat in competition with
God for the attention of worshipers. It is the plurality of divine forces rather than the imaginative
sculpting or depicting of such forces that constitutes the real religious problem for Jews, Christians,
and Muslims.

41. See "Apocalypse of Abraham," ed. and trans. R. Rubinkiewicz, in *The Old Testament
Pseudepigrapha*, ed. James H. Charlesworth (Garden City, N.Y.: Doubleday, 1983), 1:681–705.

42. But note Jos 24:2.

cially in the epistles of Paul, as far as narrative is concerned, but there may be a deeper similarity in the fact that all three scriptures depict Abraham as a human being uniquely in dialogue with one God alone. Even if the human authors of the Hebrew Bible may not have come to a notion of the absolute oneness of God until as late as the era of Second Isaiah (the sixth century BCE), the trajectory of the Genesis narrative about Abraham was headed in that direction. Just as Abraham in Paul's Epistle to the Galatians has much in common with Paul sent to preach to Gentiles justification by faith apart from works of the Law, Abraham in the Qur'an has much in common with Muhammad in seventh-century polytheistic and hostile Arabia, "this Prophet" in the first Quranic quotation cited above, "and those who keep faith" (Qur'an 6:68).

The Quranic Abraham plays the role of the quintessential opponent of the false notion of plurality in the Godhead, a plurality symbolized by plural images or the plurality of the stars, the moon and the sun (Qur'an 6:74–79):

[Recall] when Abraham said to his father, Azar, "Do you take idols as gods? Indeed, I see you and your people in obvious error." Thus we caused Abraham to see the kingdom of the heavens and the earth, so that he might be among those with assurance. When the evening darkened on him, he saw a star. He said, "This is my Lord." But when it set, he said, "O my people, now I am quit of everything you ascribe as a partner [to God]. Indeed, I have directed my eyes towards the One who created the heavens and the earth, as a Gentile monotheist. I am not one of those who ascribe partners [to God]."

In some sense, without making the claim so offensive to Muslims that the Qur'an borrows motifs from the Hebrew Bible or the New Testament, it might be more accurate to say that the monotheism of the Qur'an expresses itself more clearly precisely because Jews and Christians had previously gone through the development from henotheism (the exclusive worship of one god without any theoretical denial of the existence of other gods) to monotheism (the denial of divine reality to anyone or anything but God alone). The post-biblical Jewish tradition, and especially the Book of Jubilees (probably composed more than two centuries before the New Testament), is replete with stories of how Abraham opposed the worship of many gods in Ur and Haran. If Abraham in the Book of Genesis seems to have little pre-call history, the extra-biblical Jewish narratives proved very ready to fill in the gaps.

The Qur'an treasures those stories of Abraham's pure monotheism, his rejection of polytheistic idolatry, which may well have been preserved and shared orally in the Jewish and Christian communities through which Muhammad and his fellow Meccans passed on their trading trips to and from Syria. For Muhammad, these stories known in his general oral environment, were re-presented to him as revelation from God when he began at the age of forty to spend more time in meditation, withdrawn from the hurly-burly of Meccan commercial life. Even before his first experience of revelation, Muhammad and some of his conscientious fellow citizens seem to have criticized the polytheism of the Ka'ba and the dog-eat-dog commercialism of Mecca. That polytheism and that commercialism seem to have been intimately linked: the Ka'ba had for centuries encouraged Arabs from every part of the peninsula to enshrine their local deities in that Meccan shrine and to participate in the *entrepôt*'s commercial life while there. The pre-Islamic polytheistic *hajj* had become something like a business convention in Las Vegas today, with every cultural and religious expression known to the Arabs and their immediate neighbors somehow represented. The monotheism of Muhammad and the moral coterie that surrounded him, especially after he began to share his experiences of revelation in 613 CE, challenged the religio-commercial status quo in Mecca, the commercially attractive packaging of the Ka'ba and its rites that made Mecca an important business hub—a financial mecca, as it were.

The Qur'an did not entirely satiate Muslim fascination with Abraham. Later Muslims, and especially mystics, proved very fond of the man who is called *khalil Allah*, "the friend of God" (Qur'an 4:125). Abraham had also been given that sobriquet in the Hebrew Bible (2 Chr 20:7) and in the New Testament (Jas 2:23). The Andalusian mystic of the late twelfth and early thirteenth century CE, Ibn 'Arabi, delves into that title and finds another meaning in it, Abraham as one permeated by God:

Abraham was called the Intimate [*khalil*] [of God] because he had embraced [*takhallala*] all the Attributes of the Divine Essence. The poet says, "I have penetrated the course of the spirit within me, / And thus was the Intimate [of God] so called." ... It was because Abraham attained to this rank by which he was called the Intimate [of God] that hospitality became a [sacred] act. Ibn Masarrah [an Andalusian mystic and philosopher, d. 931] put him with Michael [the Archangel] as a source of provision, provisions being the food of those provided. Food penetrates to the essence of the one fed, permeating every part: So also with God, although in His case there are no parts but only Divine Stations or names through which His Essence is manifest.[43]

A mysticism that involves not only oneness with God but also very concrete hospitality for strangers—strangers who manifest God in flesh and blood—finds as central a role in Islam as it does in the Jewish and Christian traditions of faith. "Our messengers came to Abraham with good news, saying 'Peace!' and he said 'Peace!' as well. Immediately [Abraham] provided a roasted calf for them" (Qur'an 11:69). Abraham's table—the table of one penetrated by God—welcomes all who come to that table with the greeting of peace from God.

Some Problems with Abraham

There are aspects of the story of Abraham that grate sharply on our modern sensibilities. Twice in Genesis Abram/Abraham passes his wife Sarai/Sarah off as his sister, taken under these false pretenses into the harem of foreign potentates (Gn 12:10–20; 20:1–18). The relationship between the patriarch and his two wives, Sarah and Hagar, poses special difficulties today. The biblical narrative, in a combination of the three major literary traditions in the Pentateuch, makes Sarah seem vindictive and the patriarch feckless. In verses usually ascribed to the Yahwist, Sarah asks her husband to have a child for her with Hagar, her slave-girl, but then the pregnant Hagar is said to look with

---

43. Ibn al‘-Arabi, *The Bezels of Wisdom*, trans. R. W. J. Austin (New York: Paulist Press, 1980), 91, 95.

contempt on her mistress. Sarah deals harshly with Hagar and the slave-girl runs away (Gn 16:3–4). In the wilderness Hagar encounters an angel who tells her that she should submit to the regime of Sarah, but the angel also announces a great future for Hagar's son: "Now you have conceived and shall bear a son; you shall call him Ishmael, for the LORD has given heed to your affliction. He shall be a wild ass of a man, with his hand against everyone, and everyone's hand against him; and he shall live at odds with all his kin" (Gn 16:11–12).

The Elohist's version of the same story locates it after the birth of Isaac. Sarah still seems very cruel, demanding the expulsion of "this slave woman with her son" (Gn 21:10), but Abraham and especially God come off a bit better. When Hagar and Ishmael run out of the water and the provisions Abraham had given them, the hapless mother "lifted up her voice and wept" (Gn 21:16). The Elohist follows up that notice of Hagar's distress by the strange statement that "God heard the voice of the boy" (Gn 21:17). Is the Elohist as impervious to the pain of Hagar as was Sarah? Or is this simply an editorial lapse? Whatever may be the answers to those rhetorical questions, the Elohist goes on to narrate (Gn 21:17–20) how

the angel of God called to Hagar from heaven, and said to her, "What troubles you, Hagar? Do not be afraid; for God has heard the voice of the boy where he is. Come, lift up the boy and hold him fast with your hand, for I will make a great nation of him." Then God opened her eyes, and she saw a well of water. She went, and filled the skin with water, and gave the boy a drink. God was with the boy, and he grew up; he lived in the wilderness, and became an expert with the bow.

The Book of Genesis recognizes in Ishmael the ancestor of the Bedouins of the Sinai and Syrian deserts (Gn 25:12–18), often raiders into Israelite territory. But for all the literary traditions in Genesis, Ishmael is distinctly non-chosen.

The Elohist account of the exiling of Hagar and Ishmael ends with a statement that can easily be ignored, but it is in some way the greatest vindication of Hagar. Ishmael "lived in the wilderness of Paran; and his mother got a wife for him from the land of Egypt" (Gn 21:21). The theologian Delores S. Williams incisively suggests that the maternally arranged betrothal of Ishmael is a manifestation of Hagar's autonomy, as Hagar is "assuming a role ordinarily prescribed for males in most ancient Near Eastern households."[44]

In the New Testament Hagar and Sarah serve St. Paul, quite paradoxically, as images respectively of Torah-observant Jews and Jewish Christians in Galatia—supposedly enslaved to the Law—who are trying to impose their devout legal practice on Paul's Gentile converts. "Now this is an allegory: these women are two covenants. One woman, in fact, is Hagar, from Mount Sinai, bearing children for slavery. Now Hagar is Mount Sinai in Arabia and corresponds to the present Jerusalem, for she is in slavery with her children. But the other woman corresponds to the Jerusalem above; she is free, and she is our mother" (Gal 4:24–26). This Pauline allegory makes it difficult for Christians either to understand or to sympathize with Jewish Torah observance or with Muslim engagement in Shari'a piety.

The only woman named in the Qur'an is Mary, the mother of the Messiah. Hagar, however, may be anonymously remembered in a passage about the settlement of Abraham's family in the vicinity of Mecca. Abraham prays on their behalf: "Our Lord, it is I who have made some of my progeny dwell in a valley without cultivation near your Sacred Dwelling. Our Lord, let them institute the worship there. Make people's hearts incline towards them and give them some fruit so that they may be grateful" (Qur'an 14:37). Despite her Quranic anonymity Hagar remains a strong presence in the Muslim religious imagination through a central rite of the *hajj*, the pilgrimage to Abrahamic sites in and around Mecca. The particular rite within the *hajj* connected with Hagar—the *sa'y*—engages pilgrims in running about five hundred feet (repeated seven times) between points at either end of a colonnaded course. Those points, al-Safa and al-Marwa, mark what once were hills in the barren desert near Mecca. The pilgrims who complete this ritual race are said to imitate Hagar's frantic search for water for her child; at the conclusion of the seventh lap thirsty pilgrims drink from the near-

---

44. Delores S. Williams, *Sisters in the Wilderness: The Challenge of Womanist God-Talk* (Maryknoll, N.Y.: Orbis Books, 2013), 30.

by fountain of Zamzam, imitating Hagar and Ishmael receiving their refreshment from God.[45]

In her Quranic anonymity, Hagar is neither a slave nor a repudiated wife. But later Islamic tradition asserts that she was both a slave and a concubine. One of the earliest attempts at a continuous biography of Muhammad, the *Sirat Rasul Allah* of Muhammad ibn Ishaq (d. 768), ascribes to Muhammad gracious words about Hagar in the advice the Prophet is said to have given before his death to future conquerors of Egypt: "'When you conquer Egypt treat its people well, for they claim our protection and kinship.' I [Ibn Ishaq] asked al-Zuhri [an earlier traditionist] what [Muhammad] meant by making them our kin and he replied that Hagar, the mother of Isma'il, was of their stock."[46] Ibn Hisham (d. 833), a later editor of the text of Ibn Ishaq, comments further on this theme: "[Muhammad] said: 'Show piety in dealing with the protected peoples, those of the settled lands, the black, the crinkly haired, for they have a noble ancestor and marriage ties (with us)' .... By ancestry the prophet referred to the fact that Isma'il's mother came from [the Egyptians] ... Isma'il's mother, Hagar, the mother of the Arabs, came from a town in Egypt facing Farama."[47]

Hagar stands as a witness against the easy male repudiation of wives and concubines in Jewish, Christian, Muslim and other societies, sacred and secular, in times past and even today. Within the Islamic tradition, however, Hagar's importance grew dramatically over the years. By the ninth and tenth centuries, "the Mecca-Ishmael-Hagar tradition rose in prominence and, with it, Hagar's rank as one of Islam's most important female figures, a symbol of Islamic identity."[48] Hagar stands in solidarity, moreover, not only with Muslim women or even with all women, but with all human beings throughout human history, all who have been exploited and disenfranchised anywhere in the world.

45. See Toufic Fahd, "Sa'y," *EI2*, 9:97b and Jacqueline Chabbi, "Zamzam," *EI2*, 11:440a–443b.

46. Muhammad ibn Ishaq, *The Life of Muhammad: A Translation of Ishaq's [sic] Sirat Rasul Allah*, trans. A. Guillaume (Lahore: Pakistan Branch of Oxford University Press, 1955), 4.

47. Ibid., 691.

48. Barbara Freyer Stowasser, *Women in the Qur'an, Traditions, and Interpretation* (Oxford: Oxford University Press, 1994), 49.

Abraham's Obedient Faith

It must be admitted that the Quranic portrait of Abraham lacks so many details of the portrait of Abraham in Genesis that it strikes the Jewish or Christian reader almost as if it were depicting someone else, although extra-Quranic narratives supplement the Qur'an. It features no covenants, no land, no problem with progeny. The one story about Abraham that all three scriptural traditions contain or at least allude to—and the most terrifying—is the narrative concerning Abraham's obedient willingness in faith to offer in sacrifice his only son at God's command. This story may well provide us with the one link that makes it possible for us to talk realistically and fruitfully about Abraham as our father in faith.

The biblical narrative in the Book of Genesis is beautifully crafted. Just as Abraham had originally been commanded by the LORD to leave his country and his kindred and his father's house "to the land that I will show you" (Gn 12:1), so too he is commanded once more to go to the land of Moriah and offer in sacrifice "your son, your only son Isaac, whom you love" (Gn 22:2). When Isaac questions his father as they approach the mountain top as to the whereabouts of "the lamb for a burnt offering" (Gn 22:7), the trembling patriarch assures his son that "God himself will provide the lamb" (Gn 22:8). Isaac is bound and laid on the wood for burnt sacrifice when God's angel intervenes, saving this patriarch from the crime of child-sacrifice known among many populations of the Middle East in ancient times. In so doing God and Abraham provide for a future free of such horrors; a ram is sacrificed instead.

The New Testament alludes directly to this core biblical narrative at least twice. The anonymously written Epistle to the Hebrews meditates directly on the faith this sacrifice demanded: "By faith Abraham, when put to the test, offered up Isaac. He who had received the promises was ready to offer up his only son, of whom he had been told, 'It is through Isaac that descendants will be named after you.' He considered the fact that God is able to raise someone from the dead—and figuratively speaking, he did receive him back" (Heb 11:17–19). The Epistle of James seems to contradict, at least verbally, the Pauline theme of justification by faith apart from works of the Law when it asks a pertinent question: "Was not our ancestor Abraham justified by works when he offered his son Isaac on the altar?" (Jas 2:21). I have said that the New Testament alludes directly to this narrative twice, but most Christians will recognize in the accounts of the passion and death of Jesus and his resurrection "on the third day" (Gn 22:4, Mk 8:31, etc.) a more profound counterpart to the binding of Isaac and his redemption from death by the substitution of a ram.

The account of Abraham's willingness to sacrifice his son never specifies in the text of the Qur'an which son of Abraham is involved; nearly all Muslims take for granted, based on their familiarity with *hadith*, oral reports of Muhammad's teaching and actions, that the only time Abraham had an only son was before the birth of Isaac. The Quranic son, Isma'il, participates much more willingly than Isaac in Genesis. The willingness of both Abraham and his son to offer this sacrifice is the quintessence of *islam* in its root sense, the surrender or submission of oneself to God. Let me quote the relevant passage from the Qur'an (Qur'an 37:102–5):

[Abraham] said: "My son, I have seen in a dream that I must sacrifice you. Look, now, what do you think?" [The son] replied, "Do what you have been commanded. God willing, you will find me among the patient." When they had both surrendered themselves [to God] and [Abraham] had laid his son face down, We [God] called out to him, "O Abraham, you have proved true to the vision." Thus do We [God] reward those who do good.

In the process of such developing monotheism, the story of Abraham develops as well. Some might call these various anecdotal developments types of aggadic *midrash*. It is precisely this sort of development, the stories worked out on the theme of Abraham in the New Testament and the Qur'an, that involves what some would call, across religious lines of division, serious misunderstanding. Others are willing to state without much qualification that Jews and Christians and Muslims are all children of Abraham. Yes and no. Irenical trialogue among Jews and Christians and Muslims would be better served by our frank recognition of the different ways, based on our own historical experiences of faith, we think of Abraham.

The most ancient strains in Israelite thought saw in Abraham not just another Mesopotamian Bedouin looking for grazing land and progeny but the forefather of God's people and the pioneer of their God-given land. Later strains in Jewish thought saw Abraham more as the Jews' forerunner in faith, the first of those marked with the covenant of circumcision (Gn 17:10–14, Sir 44:19–23), the quintessential friend of God (Is 41:8, Wis 7:27). The New Testament abandoned, for the most part, the centrality of biological descent from Abraham and Sarah as well as the territoriality of older Israelite thought about Abraham. Starting from the notions of John the Baptist and Jesus that Abraham's true descendants were those who kept faith with God as he did, the Pauline writings of the New Testament opened up the possibility of descent from Abraham being extended to all of humanity, Jew and Gentile alike, justified by faith apart from works of the Law. The Qur'an, recognizing the monotheism of the People of the Book, looks, however, for something more absolute, a supranational iconoclastic faith in one God who makes demands of all humanity called to surrender itself to God (*islam*).

We Muslims and Christians and Jews may live together more fruitfully and more peacefully if we recognize the polyvalence of Abraham, the polyvalence of great concepts like faith and revelation, community, and the path of righteousness. Once we have learned how we all creatively reinterpret what may seem to be the same stories, how we all work out varying types of *midrashim* on common themes, we may learn to live together in peace.

Is Abraham, then, a bond or a barrier among Jews, Christians, and Muslims? I would suggest that Abraham is a fruitfully ambiguous figure, one whose full significance has to be analogously understood. Abram/Abraham in the Hebrew Bible is in some ways the same, and in some ways very different, from Abraham in the New Testament. Abraham in the Qur'an is in some ways the same as Abraham in the Hebrew Bible and the extra-biblical Jewish tradition and Abraham in the New Testament, and in some ways the Quranic Abraham is quite different.

Perhaps all of us who revere the memory of Abraham and his willingness to sacrifice his only son at God's command need to reflect on the obedient faith of Abraham with Søren Kierkegaard. In his famous prelude to *Fear and Trembling*, Kierkegaard rehearses over and over again other possible narratives of Abraham's willingness to sacrifice his only son. Towards the conclusion of that meditation Kierkegaard insists on the uniqueness of Abraham's faith:

Abraham believed, and he believed for this life. Yea, if his faith had been only for a future life, he surely would have cast everything away in order to hasten out of this world in which he did not belong. But Abraham's faith was not of this sort.... Yes, Abraham believed and did not doubt, he believed the preposterous ... Venerable Father Abraham! Second Father of the human race! Thou who first wast sensible of and didst first bear witness to that prodigious passion which disdains the dreadful conflict with the rage of the elements and with the powers of creation in order to strive with God.[49]

I join Kierkegaard, finally, in his words of apology to Abraham: "Forgive him who would speak in praise of thee, if he does not do it fittingly.... [He] will never forget that in a hundred and thirty years thou didst not get further than faith."[50]

49. Søren Kierkegaard, *Fear and Trembling*, trans. Walter Lowrie (Princeton, N.J.: Princeton University Press, 1941), 34, 35, 37.
50. Ibid., 37.

CHAPTER 3

Faith and Culture:
Rejection, Accommodation,
and Integration

D., like you, I have lived for more than a quarter of a century outside my homeland, principally in Ghana and Nigeria. You have experience not only in Africa but also in Asia. I do not know if you observed this phenomenon in the places where you worked, but several times I remember meeting other expatriates recently arrived in Africa whose first enthusiasm for all things African soon ended in what has been called by anthropologists "culture shock," the rejection in a new cultural setting of everything that was different from the environment in which the expatriates grew up.

An expatriate couple who arrived to teach in Ghana at the same time I did were eating food prepared in the local markets in Accra within two days of their arrival and professing to love everything. By Christmas they returned to their homeland forever, disgusted with everything Ghanaian. I partially outfitted my bungalow on campus a few years later with items purchased from an expatriate woman who came to Ghana with great enthusiasm but constantly fell sick after her arrival with symptoms hard to diagnose.

At other times, and especially among older missionaries who have lived in rural settings in Africa for a long time, I have been delighted to realize that they had taken on some, or even much of the cultural settings in which they had lived. It was not simply acculturation, partial adaptation to the local cultural scene, but something much more radical—what has been called in recent decades inculturation. These missionaries had reached the point where they envisioned the world in a way very different from the vision that would have been typical of people from their original homelands. Such a change of vision made it difficult, if not impossible, for them to return to their homelands; they were expatriated forever.

The human bearers of the Jewish, Christian, and Muslim faith traditions have all experienced culture shock, acculturation, and inculturation at one or another time in their lengthy histories. Those who have rejected their historical and cultural settings, those who have embraced their cultural settings as well as those whose reactions to their cultural settings have been more mixed: all three of these groups have played major roles in the history of monotheistic faith. Understanding the different ways in which people of faith have encountered cultural challenges helps us to understand faith itself and how it motivates us to reach out to God in the concrete situations of our lives.

Over the last few centuries the word "culture" has moved further and further away from its original sense, the cultivation of land. The *Oxford English Dictionary* still gives this agricultural meaning primacy of place.[1] The second meaning of culture suggested in the *OED* is now considered obsolete, denoting worship or reverential homage. By the sixteenth century Thomas More, in his translation of a work by Pico della Mirandola, used "culture" metaphorically to signify the cultivation of the mind. Thomas Hobbes in the seventeenth century, as well as Joseph Addison and Samuel Johnson in the eighteenth century, continued this intellectualist redirection of the term. Along with this transformation of meaning came the sense that "culture" denoted what nineteenth-century Germans called *Kultur*, "high culture," refinement. George Eliot (Mary Ann Evans) in her 1882 novel *Middlemarch* has one figure characterize another as someone pursuing "the vague purpose of what he calls culture, preparation for he knows not what."[2] The Nazi poet and playwright Hanns Johst, in the first scene of his play *Schlaget-*

---

1. See "culture. *n.*" in the *Oxford English Dictionary*, available at www.oed.com (hereafter, *OED*).
2. George Eliot, *Middlemarch* (New York: W. W. Norton, 2000), 52.

er, premiered for Hitler's birthday in 1933, has one crude character tell another, "Whenever I hear of culture ... I release the safety catch of my revolver."[3]

With the development of the social sciences beginning in the second half of the nineteenth century, "culture" came to designate what the *OED* gives as the seventh meaning of the word: "the distinctive ideas, customs, social behavior, products, or way of life of a particular nation, society, people, or period."[4] This broader use of the term reflects the Latin root of the third conjugation verb: *colo, colere, colui, cultus*. From that verb the English language has developed words as varied as colony, agriculture, cultivation, cultus, and cult. In some sense "culture" can be used to designate everything that human beings do with their respective settings in the largest and smallest senses of that word.

Over sixty years have passed since Helmut Richard Niebuhr published *Christ and Culture*, a landmark study of Christian theological typology. The duality, Christ and culture, Niebuhr employed as shorthand for every way Christianity has understood the relationship between Christian faith—especially its theological distillations—and the cultural settings in which these Christian theologies have been elaborated. Those three great types of Christian theological approaches to culture Niebuhr characterized as "*opposition* between Christ and culture,"[5] "fundamental *agreement* between Christ and culture,"[6] and "the church of the center,"[7] the last-named seeking to maintain "the great differences between the two principles" and yet, at the same time, undertaking "to hold them together in some unity."[8]

In this chapter I wish to examine more broadly how the three great monotheistic traditions of faith—Jewish, Christian, and Muslim—have come to terms with the cultural settings in which, in the past and in the present, they have variously thriven, coexisted, or withered. In no small

3. Hanns Johst, *Schlageter*, available at oupacademic.tumblr.com/post/75094913460/misquotation-hanns-johstoh.
4. *OED*.
5. H. Richard Niebuhr, *Christ and Culture*, rev. ed. (San Francisco: HarperCollins, 2001), 40.
6. Ibid., 41.
7. Ibid., 117.
8. Ibid., 41.

way the cultural settings of these three monotheistic traditions have not only been shaped by their cultural settings but have also shaped them. I am not only looking at theological formulations. More importantly, I am interested in praxis: the concrete ways in which Jews, Christians, and Muslims have lived out their faith in times past as well as today. Have people of faith rejected their ambient cultural setting? Have they accommodated with culture? Have they integrated their faith with their culture? I will employ only partially and analogically the three major categories of Christian theological encounter with culture sketched by Niebuhr, especially when dealing with Judaism and Islam.

Faith Rejecting Culture: Contemporary Jewish, Christian, and Muslim Examples

Niebuhr traces a line of development for the Christ-against-culture type in Christian history from certain New Testament writings (most notably the First Epistle of John) to Tertullian in the late second and early third century and through to Leo Tolstoy in the late nineteenth and early twentieth century. Niebuhr rightly characterizes such thinkers and the movements that they have inspired as "Christian withdrawals from and rejection of the institutions of society." He notes, however, the ironic fact that these movements of withdrawal and rejection "have been of very great importance to both church and culture."[9] Is this sort of thing only a phenomenon in the past? Are there examples of such counter-cultural movements—faith rejecting culture—in twentieth- and twenty-first-century Judaism, Christianity, and Islam?

Faith Rejecting Culture in Contemporary Judaism

The most prominent contemporary form of faith rejecting culture in a Jewish setting manifests itself in those minority movements that characterize themselves as *haredim*. External critics of the *haredim* usually call them ultra-orthodox, a pejorative term that the *haredim* them-

---

9. Ibid., 66.

selves reject. *Haredi* Jews represent approximately 8 percent of the Jewish population in Israel, according to a 2010 estimate made by Israel's Central Bureau of Statistics; it has been estimated that about 2 percent of American Jews can be so categorized.[10] Counting exactly how many Israeli Jews and how many American Jews define themselves as *haredim* is problematic, as well as describing their exact relationship to Orthodox Judaism.[11] *Haredim* can be found everywhere in the Jewish world, but Israel and the United States account for most *haredim*. All told, *haredim* may account for about 3 percent of the 13.8 million Jews in the world today, slightly more than 400,000 people. Those figures both in Israel and the United States may be rather fluid, as the rate of child-bearing among the *haredim* in both countries is high. Furthermore, some *haredim* actively recruit other Jews into their ranks.

Why do I characterize the *haredim* as a people of faith rejecting culture? Like Orthodox Jews, the *haredim* strive to lead their lives in strict adherence to *halakha*, Jewish religious law, but they continue in details of lifestyle and occupation to adhere to the customs of an earlier age, most visibly in forms of dress and coiffure, making as few concessions to modernity as possible, tending to live apart from others, including other Jews. The noun *haredim* derives from a triconsonantal Hebrew root, H-R-D, suggestive of fear and trembling. In the final chapter of the Book of Isaiah, a voice less than enthusiastic about the hopes of the prophets Haggai and Zechariah to rebuild the Jerusalem Temple puts more stock in the piety of those Jews who tremble over the word of God: "Hear the word of the Lord, you who tremble at his word" (Is 66:5).[12]

The *haredim* are not a single group but a whole panoply of religious Jews, mainly Ashkenazi (eastern European) in origin but also including some Mizrahi (long-term Middle Eastern) and Sephardi (originally Spanish, later also Middle Eastern) Jews living now in Israel. Within

---

10. See *Statistical Abstract of Israel 2010*, available at www1.cbs.gov.il.

11. Samuel C. Heilman and Fred Skolnik, "Haredim," *EJ2*, 8:348. See also Samuel C. Heilman, *Defenders of the Faith: Inside Ultra-Orthodox Jewry* (New York: Schocken, 1992) and the same author's more recent *Sliding to the Right: The Contest for the Future of American Jewish Orthodoxy* (Berkeley: University of California Press, 2006).

12. The NRSV so translates. The JPS translation prefers constructions with the word *concern* where the NRSV uses *tremble*.

the majority Ashkenazi *haredim*, one can distinguish two categories of such devotees: *hasidim* attached to particular charismatic *rebbes* and yeshiva students who adhere to particular smaller or larger academies and their *roshei yeshiva* or deans. It might even be asserted that loyalty to charismatic personal leadership characterizes nearly all *haredim* subgroups.

The *haredim* of modern times, whether in Israel or in the Diaspora, can be defined as Jews for whom the study of the Torah takes precedence over all mundane concerns, including concern for the nation of Israel. Generally speaking, *haredim* have never entirely reconciled themselves to the secular origins and aims of the Zionist movement. They cite a text from Jeremiah's letter to the exiles in Babylon, as well as a *midrash* (studied interpretation) from the Babylonian Talmud as the basis for their anti-Zionism:

At the outset of the Jews' exile to Babylonia, the prophet Jeremiah ... proclaimed G-d's message to all the exiled ... : "Seek out the welfare of the city to which I have exiled you and pray for it to the Almighty, for through its welfare you will have welfare" [Jer 29:7] ... King Solomon in [the] Song of Songs thrice adjured the "daughters of Jerusalem" not to arouse or bestir the love "until it is ready" [Song 2:7, 3:5, 8:4]. The Talmud explains that we have been foresworn, by three strong oaths, not to ascend to the Holy Land as a group using force, not to rebel against the governments of countries in which we live, and not by our sins to prolong the coming of the moshiach [Messiah]; as is written in Tractate Kesubos 111a.[13]

Needless to say, such a stance by Jews in modern times, in the aftermath of the Shoah and the creation of the state of Israel, is highly controversial, especially for those *haredim* who live in Israel. For many years the *haredim* within Israel have been exempt from service in the Israel Defense Force, but strong political pressure has been exerted in recent times to reverse that exemption. The plan to integrate the *haredim* of draft age into the Israel Defense Force may yet be reversed for political reasons, but the law passed in 2014 envisioned the gradual process to be completed by 2017.[14] By late February 2018, however, the

13. See "Three Strong Oaths," available at www.jewsagainstzionism.com. I have added in brackets editorial clarifications.

14. On the historical origins of this exemption from military service in Israel, see Ruth Levush,

drafting of *haredim* into the Israel Defense Force still threatens to bring down the coalition government in the Knesset.

Faith Rejecting Culture in Contemporary Christianity

Much could be said about Christ-against-culture trends in Protestant circles since the time of Niebuhr, but I will concentrate here on faith rejecting culture in a modern Catholic setting. Much controversy arose after January 24, 2009, when Pope Benedict XVI, in a preliminary effort to reconcile to the Catholic church the followers of the late Archbishop Marcel Lefebvre, lifted the excommunication of the four bishops ordained without papal authorization by Lefebvre in 1988.[15] The seriousness of this excommunication is underlined by the fact that it is one of the five excommunications in Catholic Christianity that can be lifted only by the pope. Even if the four bishops' excommunications were lifted, they (as well as all their allied priests) remained suspended from licit liturgical practice.

It was not only reaction against the vernacular liturgy that characterized the Lefebvrists from the beginning. The Lefebvrists also repudiate much of the Second Vatican Council (1962–65), especially its teaching on episcopal collegiality, religious liberty, ecumenism, and interreligious dialogue. Lefebvre himself, in a "Profession of Faith" he issued on November 21, 1974, on his own behalf and that of his colleagues, had specified that "we refuse and have always refused to follow the Rome of neo-modernist and neo-Protestant tendencies which clearly manifested themselves in the Second Vatican Council."[16]

"Israel: Supreme Court Decision Invalidating the Law on Haredi Military Draft Postponement," available at www.loc.gov/law/help/haredi-military-draft.php. The exemption of the *haredim* from military service paralleled the American practice of exempting seminarians preparing for the ministry from military conscription. For the vote in the Knesset, see Isabel Kershner, "Israel to Phase Out Religious Exemptions," *New York Times*, March 13, 2014, available at www.nytimes.com/2014/03/13.

15. Canon 1382 of the 1983 *Code of Canon Law* specifies that "a bishop who consecrates someone a bishop and the person who receives such a consecration from a bishop without pontifical mandate incur an automatic [*latae sententiae*] excommunication reserved to the Apostolic See." See *The Code of Canon Law: A Text and Commentary*, ed. James A. Corriden, Thomas J. Green, and Donald E. Heintschel (New York: Paulist Press, 1985).

16. See Yves Congar, OP, *Challenge to the Church: The Case of Archbishop Lefebvre*, trans. Paul

The alienation to the present day of Lefebvre's followers in the Priestly Society of Saint Pius X from Vatican II Catholicism cannot be reduced to mere intra-Catholic theological dissonance. A much larger cultural issue is involved. Lefebvre's ideas trace their ancestry to a distinctly Catholic subculture inherited from the late nineteenth and early twentieth century in France, the era of the Third Republic. That subculture, often characterized in theological terms as *intégrisme*, reacted not only against the darker elements in the heritage of the French Revolution, but also against any form of democracy at all, as well as any notion of separation of church and state. Charles Maurras (1868–1952), a lapsed Catholic until he was dying, founded in 1899 a movement and journal called *Action Française*. This movement, not only anti-Semitic in the era of the Dreyfus Affair but also unabashedly monarchist, exercised considerable influence not only in French politics during the Vichy regime but also more generally in the Catholic church in France.[17] Marcel Lefebvre himself had been trained as a priest in a distinctly reactionary seminary in Rome, the *Collège Français*. The rector of that seminary during Lefebvre's years of priestly formation, Père Henri le Floch, adhered to *Action Française*, as did Louis Billot, a French Jesuit theologian based in Rome and a close ally of Père le Floch. Billot had been made a cardinal by Pope Pius X but was eventually deposed from the College of Cardinals by Pope Pius XI precisely because of his connections with *Action Française*.[18]

The desire of Pope Benedict to reconcile the Lefebvrists followed a pattern in recent Catholic history in which attempts have been made to bring back schismatics when their schism centers on views more stringent than those of the papacy. Individual theologians who have embraced positions that may be called less stringent than those of the

Inwood (Huntington, Ind.: Our Sunday Visitor, 1976). Appendix I reproduces Lefebvre's "Profession of Faith," 77–79.

17. For a disturbing account of the Vichy-Lefebvrist nexus, see Ted Morgan, "L'Affaire Touvier: Opening Old Wounds," *New York Times* Sunday Magazine, October 1, 1989, available at www.nytimes.com/1989/10/01/magazine/l-affaire-touvier-opening-old-wounds.html

18. See, in Congar, *Challenge to the Church*, Appendix IV by Francis Whyte, "Action Française and Action Catholique: A brief explanation," 88–90. Whyte succinctly elucidates the connections between Lefebvre and *Action Française*. For a more positive view of Maurras and *Action Française* by a contemporary conservative thinker, see Thomas Molnar, "Charles Maurras, Shaper of an Age," *Modern Age* 41, no. 4 (1999): 337–42.

papacy have been regularly censured. But none of these theologians has fostered a schismatic movement, or at least not yet. Although some German theologians critical of the definition of papal infallibility joined a schismatic movement after the First Vatican Council (1869–70),[19] schism has been a reactionary preserve within Catholicism in the years since the Second Vatican Council.

In the 1940s, nearly two decades before Vatican II, an American schism arose among the followers of Fr. Leonard Feeney, once a New England Province Jesuit. Feeney, a popular religious speaker, writer, and poet, had become in 1943 the spiritual director of the Saint Benedict Center, an independent Catholic student club near Harvard Square. Sharing in the more general Boston Irish-American antipathy to Harvard and the so-called Yankee elite in the late 1940s, Feeney, along with some of his devotees at the Saint Benedict Center, began to criticize the ethos of those Irish-American and other Catholics at Harvard (including members of the Kennedy family) who were striving to assimilate into elite Boston ("Brahmin") society.[20] When prominent Catholic families, who had sent their offspring to Harvard at great expense, discovered that Feeney was urging them to leave Harvard and study with him and his allies at the Saint Benedict Center, there was an uproar. Feeney was eventually dismissed from the Society of Jesus for disobedience when he refused a change of assignment; he was later formally excommunicated by the Catholic church.

Feeney had been teaching a very narrow interpretation of the an-

19. The Bavarian church historian von Döllinger was excommunicated in 1871 for his critique of the definition of papal infallibility at the First Vatican Council. Thereafter he and other theological dissidents identified themselves with the Old Catholic church, a German schismatic group that derived its episcopal succession from the church of Utrecht, an originally Jansenist schism from Roman Catholicism. See the articles "Döllinger," "Old Catholics," and "Holland, Christianity in" in *The Oxford Dictionary of the Christian Church*, ed. F. L. Cross (London: Oxford University Press, 1961).

20. For the Kennedy connection, see Edward M. Kennedy, *True Compass: A Memoir* (New York: Twelve, 2009), 83–85. Robert Kennedy as an undergraduate at Harvard College (class of 1948) had attended at least some of Feeney's evening sessions at the Saint Benedict Center and found himself disturbed by the narrowness and exclusivity of the Catholicism preached by Feeney. He queried his father, Joseph P. Kennedy, about this and his father contacted the archbishop of Boston at the time, Richard Cushing (later Cardinal Cushing), who decided to investigate what was being preached by Feeney. There were probably other queries raised by other Harvard parents and Edward Kennedy's suggestion that his brother Robert may have contributed "an animating impulse of the Second Ecumenical Council of the Vatican" (85) is probably overblown.

cient theological *dictum* that "outside the Church there is no salvation" (*Extra ecclesiam nulla salus*).[21] The papacy's ministry charged with doctrinal orthodoxy, at that time called the Holy Office, in response to an inquiry from the Archdiocese of Boston, considered Feeney's expressed opinions on this doctrine excessively narrow. For Feeney, resentful of Harvard and even of his fellow Jesuits who were graduate students there at the time, "Outside the Saint Benedict Center in Cambridge there is no salvation" gradually became "Outside the Catholic church visibly constituted there is no salvation."[22]

Followers of Fr. Feeney, including some who had converted to Catholicism under his influence, banded together, at first under the aegis of the Saint Benedict Center, but some of them eventually founded a religious congregation of men and women called the Slaves of the Immaculate Heart of Mary. Withdrawing in the 1950s to Harvard, Massachusetts, they lived together with Fr. Feeney a separate communal life as Catholics more Catholic than the pope for more than two decades. Their clerical and religious attire, as well as their liturgical and devotional practice—all minted in the early 1950s—made them distinctive, quite different from the later generation of American Catholics living after the Second Vatican Council. In particular, they eschewed the vernacular liturgy and the other liturgical reforms introduced into mainstream Catholic practice after the Council, as well as anything even slightly redolent of ecumenical or inter-faith dialogue. In many ways they became a cult continuing to live in an American Catholic ghetto

21. For the Latin text of the Holy Office condemnation of this rigorism, see *DS* §§3866–73. The more general understanding today of that Latin *dictum*, first apparently enunciated by the rigorist Cyprian of Carthage in the third century, is that salvation through the grace of Christ is mediated through the church but is available to those who are *de facto* outside the visible church through no fault of their own. See *Catechism of the Catholic Church*, 2nd ed. (Rome: Libreria Editrice Vaticana, 1997), nos. 846–48.

22. I personally knew some of the Jesuits who had studied at Harvard in the late 1940s and early 1950s who were the objects of Feeney's obloquy. One of the original lay founders of the Saint Benedict Center, prior to Feeney's coming there, Avery Dulles, later a Jesuit priest and eventually cardinal, mentions, in a tribute he wrote after Feeney's death in 1978, that he found it hard to understand how Feeney degenerated to the point that he was shouting anti-Semitic diatribes in the Boston Common in the early 1950s. See "Leonard Feeney: In Memoriam," *America* 138 (February 25, 1978): 135–37. For a vivid contemporary account of Feeney's diatribes in the Boston Common in 1951, see Laurence D. Savadove, "Father Feeney, Rebel from Church, Preaches Hate, Own Brand of Dogma to All Comers," available at www.thecrimson.com/article/12/6/.

that no longer existed anywhere but in their own closed community; as such they attracted some adherence from people who felt alienated from Catholicism as it was evolving after the Council.

In the 1970s, however, the Catholic bishop of Worcester, Massachusetts, Bernard Flanagan, made a successful attempt to reconcile the aging Fr. Feeney to the Catholic church, without demanding of him a specific repudiation of his interpretation of the formula, *Extra ecclesiam nulla salus.* Since that time most (but not quite all) of Feeney's surviving disciples have also been reconciled with the Catholic church on the same terms, although some of them continue to live separately from other contemporary Catholics.[23]

At least with conservative schismatics, the Catholic hierarchy on all levels seems to have learned something from the experiences that split the church of Rome from the churches of the East in the fifth century and the eleventh century and from the Protestant churches of the West in the sixteenth century. The attempts by Pope Benedict to reconcile the Lefebvrists in the early twenty-first century followed the pattern of the endeavors made in the era of Pope Paul VI and Pope John Paul II to reconcile the Feeneyites. Time will tell how successful this attempt to reconcile the Lefebvrists will prove, but in the decade or more since Pope Benedict began these efforts, the Lefebvrists have persistently refused to accept central teachings of the Second Vatican Council. Pope Francis has also made many reconciliatory gestures towards the Lefebvrists since 2013; whether these gestures will be accepted by the Lefebvrists or not is still not clear.

Faith Rejecting Culture in Contemporary Islam

The message of the Qur'an received by Muhammad between 610 and 632 was in some sense quite counter-cultural, the culture in question

---

23. See George B. Pepper, *The Boston Heresy Case in View of the Secularization of Religion: A Case Study in the Sociology of Religion* (Lewiston, N.Y.: Edwin Mellen Press, 1988). For insider accounts of these events by followers of Fr. Feeney, see Catherine Goddard Clarke, *The Loyolas and the Cabots: The Story of the Crusade of Saint Benedict Center 1940–1950* (Richmond, N.H.: Saint Benedict Center, 1950) and the more recent work of Gabriel Gibbs, OSB, with Owen J. Murphy Jr., *Harvard to Harvard* (Still River, Mass.: Ravengate Press, 2006).

being what the Qur'an sometimes calls the *jahiliyya* (ignorance) of Muhammad's Arab contemporaries. But *jahiliyya* in the Qur'an was not quite so severe a term as *kufr*, a Quranic term designating the utter ingratitude of those who knowingly repudiate the generosity of God. Twentieth-century Muslim rigorists, however, following the lead of the fourteenth-century teacher, Ibn Taymiyya (d. 1328), reinterpreted *jahiliyya* as something much more sinister. The change from the Quranic use of the term is nowhere more obvious than in a Quranic passage where the more frivolous wives of Muhammad are rebuked for decking themselves out in finery of "the first era of ignorance" (*al-jahiliyyati 'l-'ula*, in 33:33). This is surely an offense far less serious than *kufr*, as most Muslims will recognize, but completely counter-cultural Muslim rigorists find it hard to make this distinction.[24] This may partly explain the extremes of their puritanical attitudes towards Muslim women and girls even today.

In the first Muslim century a rigorist interpretation of Islam emerged among northern Arab nomads who had converted to Islam. They seceded in 657 from the camp of 'Ali, the fourth successor of Muhammad, when he was engaged in struggle to defend his caliphate against Mu'awiya, the governor of Damascus. 'Ali had shown himself willing to negotiate peacefully with Mu'awiya, but some of the northern Arabs who had supported 'Ali seceded from his camp as a result; thus they were later called Kharijites from the Arabic word for secessionists. They considered 'Ali's willingness to negotiate with his opposition as nothing less than total apostasy from Islam. By the end of the seventh century the Kharijites—raging against each other as well as against Sunni Muslims—had split into numerous smaller and smaller rigorist groups, usually taking their names from one or another charismatic leader.[25]

Although Kharijites have not survived as a major sect of Islam,[26] some aspects of their rigorism in defining who is a Muslim and who has rejected God as a *kafir* resurfaced in the fourteenth-century teach-

24. See the editors' brief article "Djahiliyya" in *EI2*, 2:383b–384a.

25. W. Montgomery Watt, *The Formative Period of Islamic Thought* (Edinburgh: University of Edinburgh Press, 1973), 9–37.

26. Only one of these movements survives today, the Ibadiyya, the mildest in their definition of who is a Muslim and who is an infidel. See Tadeusz Lewicki, "al-Ibadiyya," *EI2*, 3:648a–660b.

ings of Ibn Taymiyya[27] and the eighteenth-century doctrine of Ibn 'Abd al-Wahhab,[28] forefather of the dominant school of religious thought in Saudi Arabia. In the twentieth century, moreover, forms of such radical rigorism emanated as well from the Egyptian Sayyid Qutb (1906–66)[29] and the Indo-Pakistani Mawlana Mawdudi (1903–79).[30] These twentieth-century writers, more independent autodidacts in religious and legal questions than traditional scholars, condemned all Muslims who compromised with non-Muslim agenda as agents of *jahiliyya*, an ignorance that they demonized as the equivalent of total rejection of God (*kufr*).[31]

In 1977 the *Takfir wa'l-Hijra* sectarians who had withdrawn into the desert in Egypt to live a pure Muslim life kidnapped and killed a former Minister of Religious Endowments in the government of President Anwar al-Sadat.[32] Similar sectarians assassinated Sadat himself in 1981. Both groups derived at least some of their thought from the writings of Sayyid Qutb, who had been put to death by the Nasser government in Egypt in 1966. Elsewhere in the Muslim world, the school of Islamic disciplines (Dar al-'Ulum) at Deoband in northern India, as well as other madrasas related to it,[33] have proven very narrow in their interpretation of Islam.[34] These schools in Deoband, in the three decades since the Soviet and American-NATO invasions of Afghanistan, have encouraged some of their students (*taliban*), especially those who

27. See Henri Laoust, "Ibn Taymiyya," *EI2*, 3:951a–955a.

28. See Henri Laoust, "Ibn 'Abd al-Wahhab," *EI2*, 3:677b–679a.

29. See J. J. G. Jansen, "Sayyid Kutb," *EI2*, 9:117a–118b.

30. See F. C. R. Robinson, "Mawdudi," *EI2*, 6:872a–874a.

31. "We are also surrounded by *Jahiliyyah* today, which is of the same nature as it was during the first period of Islam, perhaps a little deeper. Our whole environment, people's beliefs and ideas, habits and art, rules and laws—is *Jahiliyyah*, even to the extent that what we consider to be Islamic culture, Islamic sources, Islamic philosophy and Islamic thought are also constructs of *Jahiliyyah*! ... We must also free ourselves from the clutches of *jahili* society, *jahili* concepts, *jahili* traditions and *jahili* leadership. Our mission is not to compromise with the practices of *jahili* society, nor can we be loyal to it. *Jahili* society, because of its *jahili* characteristics, is not worthy to be compromised with. Our aim is first to change ourselves so that we may later change the society." Seyyid Qutb, *Milestones* (Damascus: Dar al-Ilm, n.d.), 20–21.

32. See Maurice Martin and Rose Marie Massad, "'Al-Takfir wal-Hijrah': A Study in Sectarian Protest," in *Arab Culture 1977: Religious Identity and Radical Perspectives*, C.E.M.A.M. Reports 5 (Beirut: Dar al-Mashreq, 1980).

33. See Barbara Daly Metcalf, *Islamic Revival in British India: Deoband, 1860–1900* (Princeton, N.J.: Princeton University Press, 1982).

34. See Wilfred Cantwell Smith, *Modern Islam in India: A Social Analysis*, 2nd ed. (Lahore: Sh. Muhammad Ashraf, 1963), 363–64.

were Afghani refugees, to join the struggle (*jihad*) against these foreign occupations. Although originally quite distinct in their religious orientation, some of these Deobandi *taliban* have joined politically with Jama'at-i-Islami, the Pakistani political disciples of Mawlana Mawdudi.[35]

The religious and political programs of Wahhabis, Sayyid Qutb, Mawlana Mawdudi, and the Taliban in Afghanistan idealize an ahistorical version of the era of Muhammad and the first four caliphs. Such a vision of Islam lacks the cultural and theological depth that might incline it towards a more humane understanding of what Islam has meant for fourteen centuries. Charismatic leaders like the late 'Usama bin Laden encouraged people fired with these ideals to imitate Muhammad's *hijra* from idolatrous Mecca to an abstract Medina in the caves of Tora Bora. Even if the Muslim faith rejecting culture tradition does not exhaust Muslim attitudes towards culture, it has garnered more than a little publicity in the Western media in the past few decades.

Faith Accommodating Culture: Contemporary Jewish, Christian, and Muslim Examples

Niebuhr cites no particular portion of the New Testament as an example of what he calls "the Christ of Culture,"[36] but he does suggest that the New Testament contains references to "believers in the Lord" [who also] "seek to maintain community with all other believers.... So they harmonize Christ with culture, not without excision, of course, from New Testament and social custom, of stubbornly discordant features."[37] The earliest historical example of this phenomenon, according to Niebuhr, would be the Judaizers known in Pauline communities:

Paul's conflict with the Judaizers and later references to Nazarenes and Ebionites indicate that there were groups or movements which were more Jewish than Christian, or which, it might be better to say, sought to maintain loyalty to Jesus Christ without abandoning any important part of current Jewish tradition or giving up the special messianic hopes of the chosen people. Jesus was for

35. Juan Cole, *Engaging the Muslim World* (New York: Palgrave Macmillan, 2009), 171–72.
36. Niebuhr, *Christ and Culture*, 83.
37. Ibid., 83–84.

them not only the promised messiah but the messiah of the promise, as this was understood in their society.[38]

Recent scholarship on Jewish Christianity of the first four centuries, as mentioned in chapter 1, would complicate the somewhat simple characterization of the Judaizers known to Paul and the Ebionites and Nazarenes.[39]

Another variety of the harmonization of Christ with culture Niebuhr notes among those Hellenistic Gentile Christians who became the Gnostics of the second century: "These men—Basilides, Valentinus, the author of *Pistis Sophia*, and their like—are heretics in the eyes of the main body of the Church as well as of radical Christians."[40] Some foretaste of Gnostic doctrines may be referred to polemically in the Johannine and Deutero-Pauline writings of the New Testament. In a much later century of Christian history, a different compromise of Christian faith with prevailing philosophical trends was characterized by Karl Barth as "Culture-Protestantism."[41] Barth used that term to characterize all those thinkers in the eighteenth and nineteenth centuries who extolled a version of Christianity that "commended itself to all those who used their reason but used it in the 'reasonable' manner characteristic of an English culture that found the middle way between all extremes."[42] Such varieties of Judaism, Christianity, and Islam have existed in the past. Do they still exist today? I suggest that there is something like a sliding scale between reasonable accommodation of faith with a cultural setting, on one end of the scale, and wholesale accommodation of faith with culture on the other end.

Faith Accommodating Culture in Contemporary Judaism

Judaism accommodating culture has an ancient history, not entirely savory, in the *hityavnut* (Hellenization) that characterized at least some

38. Ibid., 85.
39. See chapter 1 (above), 41–43.
40. Niebuhr, *Christ and Culture*, 85.
41. Ibid., 84.
42. Ibid., 91.

of the priestly class in Jerusalem in the era of the Seleucid tyrant Antiochus IV Epiphanes (175–164 BCE). The First Book of Maccabees narrates how "certain renegades came out from Israel and misled many, saying, 'Let us go and make a covenant with the Gentiles around us, for since we separated from them many disasters have come upon us'" (1:11). The feast of Hanukkah commemorates the ending of that era of wholesale accommodation of Judaism in the Maccabee insurgency and the renewal of purified Temple worship (1 Mc 4:36–61) and Torah observance that had been neglected by Jews eager to conform to Greek ways.

Even before the destruction of Jerusalem in 70 CE, most Jews were living outside the Promised Land. Although the Hellenistic Jewish philosopher Philo, who lived out his days in Alexandria in Egypt, is often cited as an exemplar of Hellenized Judaism, his Hellenized faith differed dramatically from the degenerate *hityavnut* of the Jerusalem elite before the Maccabee revolution of the second century BCE. Philo remained a Jew but lived out his faith in positive dialectic with the Hellenistic intellectual culture of Alexandria. Although highly philosophical and allegorical in his elaboration of the Jewish tradition, Philo still paid attention to ethical questions. Far from opposing Torah observance, through his allegorical interpretation of Hebrew Bible narratives, he found a way to appeal to Hellenistic Jews to adhere to the regulations of the Torah. Thus he allegorized the migration from Chaldea to Haran of Terah, the father of Abraham (Gn 11:31), as a departure from purely speculative pursuits like astronomy (more akin to astrology at that time) to practical faith oriented towards ethical action: "Why do you take up astronomy and pay such full and minute attention to the higher regions? Mark, my friend, not what is above and beyond your reach but what is close to yourself, or rather make yourself the object of your impartial scrutiny."[43]

With the Roman destruction of the Temple in 70 CE and the denial of entry into Jerusalem or its environs for Jews after 135 CE, Jews began their longest period of exile from what had been the geographical

---

43. Philo, *On Dreams*, as excerpted in *Three Jewish Philosophers*, ed. Hans Lewy, Alexander Altmann, and Isaak Heinemann, 3rd ed. (New Milford, Conn.: Toby Press, 2006), 60.

center of their faith. The survival of Jews and their continuance in To-rah observance was in some sense guaranteed by their confinement to ghettos. With the dawn of the Enlightenment, however, some Jews began to leave the ghetto and enter into the cultural circles of their Christian and even post-Christian European and American neighbors.

What has been called the *Haskala*, the Jewish Enlightenment dating from the eighteenth-century career of Moses Mendelssohn, sometimes resulted in the integration of highly educated Jews into the cultural scene around them. Mendelssohn remained an Orthodox Jew himself, learned in and actively practicing the precepts of the Torah, but willing as well to defend Judaism in terms comprehensible to his non-Jewish intellectual contemporaries. In his most famous work, *Jerusalem or On Religious Power and Judaism*, Mendelssohn calls for tolerance of diversity in religious opinion, maintaining that the faith of Jews could not be summed up, as Maimonides (1135–1204) had done so, in terms of creedal affirmations, but only in terms of ethical commands: "Among all the prescriptions and ordinances of the Mosaic law, there is not a single one which says: *You shall believe or not believe*. They all say: *You shall do or not do*."[44]

Such emphasis on Jewish ethical action tends not only to de-emphasize creedal affirmations but also to de-emphasize so concrete a part of the faith of Jews as Jewish attachment to and longing to return to the land of Israel. Mendelssohn even suggests that the saying of Jesus about rendering to Caesar and to God—words of Jesus (Mk 12:17, Mt 22:21, Lk 20:25) often misunderstood as separating religious and secular concerns[45]—applied as well to Jews in eighteenth-century Bran-

---

44. Moses Mendelssohn, *Jerusalem or On Religious Power and Judaism*, trans. Allan Arkush (Hanover, N.H.: University of New England Press for Brandeis University Press, 1983), 100. The original was published in German in 1783.

45. Jesus left his questioners "utterly amazed" (Mk 12:17) at his ambiguous answer; they had not caught him on the horns of a dilemma. Lawrence Wills in his astute commentary on this passage notes that "the opponents [of Jesus] try to elicit a politically dangerous pronouncement. In 6–7 CE a prophetic leader named Judas ... organized a movement to worship God alone and refuse to pay the tax to Caesar.... The answer [of Jesus] allows for a limited realm in which Roman rule is legitimate, but keeps Jewish practice inviolate from that realm." From "The Gospel According to Mark," in *The Jewish Annotated New Testament: New Revised Standard Version*, ed. Amy-Jill Levine and Marc Zvi Brettler (Oxford: Oxford University Press, 2011), note to Mk 12:13–17. See also C. Clifton Black, revised by Adela Yarbro Collins, "The Gospel According to Mark," in NRSV, note to Mk 12:14: "The *trap* (v. 13) lay in an attempt to force Jesus into disloyalty towards the Romans or towards those Jews who resented the taxes."

denburg. "Give to Caesar and give to God too! ... Even today, no wiser advice than this can be given to the House of Jacob."[46]

Until the twentieth century, Reform Jews tended to separate their Jewish faith from any commitment to a return to Israel, as the 1885 Pittsburgh Platform of Reform Judaism made explicit: "We consider ourselves no longer a nation, but a religious community, and therefore expect neither a return to Palestine, nor a sacrificial worship under the sons of Aaron, nor the restoration of any of the laws concerning the Jewish state."[47] But Reform Jews after 1937 took more and more cognizance of and pride in the emergence of the state of Israel, as later Reform Jewish Platforms make abundantly clear.

Although there are many secularized or less than totally religious Jews in Israel and other parts of the world today, some movements have taken shape in the United States that attempt to construe Judaism in terms that evade much overt God-talk. One such movement, Reconstructionist Judaism, originated with a rabbi born of an Orthodox family in Lithuania but raised and educated in New York City, Mordecai Kaplan (1881–1983). Much affected by his study of the philosophy of John Dewey, Kaplan found himself in controversy with his colleagues at Jewish Theological Seminary, a leading Conservative Jewish institution on the Upper West Side of Manhattan. For Kaplan, "God may ... be defined as the Power that endorses what we believe ought to be, and that guarantees that it will be."[48] Such a definition of God tends to distinguish Kaplan's Reconstructionist Judaism from mainline varieties of Jewish faith.

Another American-originated and even more resolutely secularist revision of the Jewish tradition has been called Humanistic Judaism. Humanistic Jews completely eliminate prayer or any other mention of God from their congregational practice. This movement traces some

46. Mendelssohn, *Jerusalem*, 133. Alan Arkush, the translator of this version of *Jerusalem*, notes that Mendelssohn in another work "weighed the political factors that might favor the successful accomplishment of such an enterprise [the restoration of the Jewish state] in the future" (235n). That other work can be found somewhere (alas, not specified by Arkush) in Moses Mendelssohn, *Gesammelte Schriften Jubiläumsausgabe* (Stuttgart-Bad Cannstatt: Frommann-Holzboog, 1971–).

47. See "The Pittsburgh Platform–1885," available at ccarnet.org/rabbis-speak/platforms/declaration-principles.

48. Mordecai Kaplan, *The Meaning of God in Modern Jewish Religion* (New York: Jewish Reconstructionist Foundation, 1947), 323–24.

of its intellectual roots to late nineteenth-century and early twentieth-century secularist thought. Sherwin Wine, formerly a Reform rabbi, began to enunciate the program of Humanistic Judaism in Michigan in the 1960s. Convinced that scientific rationalism had made the hypothesis of God the Creator superfluous, Wine wrote that "the age of reason is the age without God. While nostalgia preserves him in the vocabulary of the powerful, he has lost his substance."[49]

There is a continuous line of development between the *Haskala* of the eighteenth century, with its rationalist ethics, and these American-originated sub-sects of Judaism, but somewhere along that line of development something very important has dropped out: the centering of Jewish lives on the LORD who spoke to Moses in the burning bush. It is hard to differentiate such Jewish accommodation of faith from a post-Jewish movement like Ethical Culture. Felix Adler (1851–1933), the son of the chief rabbi of Temple Emanu-El in New York City, founded the New York Society for Ethical Culture in 1876. The weekly Sunday meetings of the Society for Ethical Culture help to define it as a definitively non-Jewish venture, and many of its adherents today have never been Jewish.[50] The wholesale accommodation of Jewish faith to the surrounding culture has finally led to the development of a new faith that is no longer, in any visible sense, Jewish.

Faith Accommodating Culture in Contemporary Christianity

The United States has given birth to varieties of Christianity more than a little accommodated to the local political culture, especially the American cultural notion that human beings are endowed with an inalienable right to "the pursuit of happiness."[51] Niebuhr makes reference to

49. Sherwin Wine, *Judaism Beyond God* (n.p.: Ktav Publishing House / Society for Humanistic Judaism / Milan Press, 1995), 32.

50. See Benny Kraut, *From Reform Judaism to Ethical Culture: The Religious Evolution of Felix Adler* (Cincinnati, Ohio: Hebrew Union College Press, 1979).

51. The phrase occurs early in the Declaration of Independence of July 4, 1776: "We hold these truths to be self-evident: That all men are created equal; that they are endowed by their Creator with certain unalienable rights; that among these are life, liberty and the pursuit of happiness."

how Thomas Jefferson "excerpted from the New Testament the sayings of Jesus which commended themselves to him."[52] But the inalienable right to the pursuit of happiness, a phrase introduced into the Declaration of Independence by Jefferson, derived not from the New Testament but, more probably, from philosophers of the eighteenth-century Scottish Enlightenment. It probably meant, according to Garry Wills, "public happiness," which was "a secular and scientific term for men of the Enlightenment, a 'heretical' displacement of man's hopes from the hereafter to those immediate gratifications."[53] In the era since Niebuhr wrote, more than a few Christian movements have arisen in America that interpret the happiness to be pursued less philosophically and more therapeutically as the right to feel good about oneself.

The late Norman Vincent Peale (1898–1993), for decades the pastor of Marble Collegiate Church in New York City, created a movement aimed at what he called "positive thinking," a mixture of comfortable Christianity with popular psychology.[54] A typical passage from *The Power of Positive Thinking* demonstrates how little it has in common with the Gospel:

The happiness habit is developed by simply practicing happy thinking. Make a mental list of happy thoughts and pass them through your mind several times a day. If an unhappiness thought should enter your mind, immediately stop, consciously eject it, and substitute a happiness thought. Every morning before arising, lie relaxed in bed and deliberately drop happy thoughts into your conscious mind. Let a series of pictures pass across your mind of each happy experience you expect to have during the day. Savor their joy. Such thoughts will help cause events to turn out that way.[55]

52. Niebuhr, *Christ and Culture*, 92.

53. Garry Wills, *Inventing America: Jefferson's Declaration of Independence* (Boston: Houghton Mifflin, 2002), 254–55. In the new introduction to this 2002 edition of a book Wills originally published in 1978, Wills admits he may have exaggerated the influence of the Scottish philosophers in the original edition, but he left the text unchanged. "If I were to rewrite it, I would make a more nuanced case for the Scottish influence, but I would still be making that case" (ix).

54. Peale first published *The Power of Positive Thinking* in 1952, and it has been reprinted many times since then. See Norman Vincent Peale, *The Power of Positive Thinking: Special 35th Anniversary Edition* (New York: Simon and Schuster, 1987), described on the dust jacket as "the great inspirational best seller of our time."

55. Ibid., 61.

Peale's prestige began to decline when it became known that a psy-choanalyst who had once worked collaboratively with Peale, Smiley Blanton, did not want to be identified with positive thinking.[56] Peale's alliance with the Republican Party, and especially his parishioner Richard Milhous Nixon, as well as his opposition to the presidential candidacy of John Fitzgerald Kennedy on the basis of Kennedy's Catholicism, also alienated a considerable segment of Americans from positive thinking after 1960. Peale had been one of the few northern Protestant ministers to join an *ad hoc* group called the National Conference of Citizens for Religious Freedom, a group which had as its sole purpose opposing Kennedy's presidential candidacy precisely because he was a Catholic. The Democratic presidential nominee in 1952 and 1956, Adlai Stevenson, who had in those earlier elections been criticized by Peale over his status as a divorced man, memorably said of Peale that "Speaking as a Christian, I find the Apostle Paul appealing and the Apostle Peale appalling." Stevenson seems to have recycled this quip in 1960 when Peale criticized Kennedy's Catholicism.[57]

In the years since the decline of Peale's popularity, other varieties of positive thinking have grown exponentially in Christian settings in the United States, and especially the churches that propagate what has been called the Prosperity Gospel. Several popular American television preachers fit loosely into this category of Christianity accommodated to the American scene, but not all of them are entirely happy with such a characterization. Perhaps the most popular television evangelist of this variety in recent years is Joel Osteen, a Texan and the son of a former Southern Baptist pastor. Without much formal religious training, Joel Osteen succeeded his father in the pastoral direction of the non-denominational Lakewood Church in Houston when his father died in 1999. The Church has since grown dramatically and moved from its original quarters to take over a basketball arena in Houston seating 16,000 people. Services conducted by Joel Osteen can be seen on tele-

56. On the gradual alienation of Blanton from Peale, see Donald Meyer, *The Positive Thinkers: Popular Religious Psychology from Mary Baker Eddy to Norman Vincent Peale to Ronald Reagan*, rev. ed. (Middletown, Conn.: Wesleyan University Press, 1988), esp. 265–68.

57. See Theodore C. Sorensen, *Kennedy* (New York: Harper and Row, 1965), 188–89, and Michael O'Brien, *John F. Kennedy: A Biography* (New York: St. Martin's Press, 2005), 474.

vision on Sunday mornings not only in the United States but also in other parts of the world.[58]

Joel Osteen describes himself as "a life coach, a motivator." He seldom mentions sin or repentance in his preaching and his arena church lacks specifically Christian symbols like the cross. Speaking on *60 Minutes* in 2007 Osteen summed up his message for an ideal television audience member: "I want you to get a bigger vision. There are exciting things in your future. Your future is filled with marked moments of blessing, increase, promotion.... Time and chance are coming together for you."[59] The therapeutic pursuit of happiness, dislodged from the Protestant Christian foundations still visible in the preaching of Norman Vincent Peale, has triumphed in the careers of Osteen and many of his fellow proponents of the Prosperity Gospel. The American Prosperity Gospel exercises a special appeal for people living in parts of the world with mercurial economies, most notably Africa and Latin America. Although most of the leaders of these African and Latin American movements do not consider themselves agents of the American Prosperity Gospel, some of the Anglophone West African Prosperity Gospel preachers seem to have taken on in their broadcast preaching the inflexions of the American South.

It is not only the therapeutic reinterpretation of Christianity that must be included in any account of Christianity acculturated in the American setting. Non-American Christians, and especially non-American Catholics, are always astounded by the patriotism of American Catholics, as well as the patriotism of some other varieties of American Christians, whose church sanctuaries normally feature an American flag prominently among their appointments. Some claim that this custom dates back to the Second World War or even to the American Civil War. Some Catholic sanctuaries counterbalance the American flag in the sanctuary with the Vatican flag. Such a display is inconceivable in European, Asian, African, or Latin American Catholic settings. One possible ex-

58. See Richard Young, *The Rise of Lakewood Church and Joel Osteen* (New Kensington, Penn.: Whitaker House, 2007).

59. Available at www.cbsnews/stories/2007/10/11/60minutes/main_3358652.shtml. See also John Heilpern, "Minister of Finance," *Vanity Fair* (April 2010): 80.

ception to this generalization may be found in Anglican churches in Britain that have become war memorials over the course of the years. Even Church of Ireland (Anglican Communion) church buildings to the present day are replete with tattered regimental banners from the Crimean War or faded Union Jacks of one or another past battle.

Such accommodation of the Gospel to patriotic themes was taken for granted in American ecclesiastical settings for many years, but there has been a reaction in recent decades. Thus, for instance, in 2007 the Catholic Diocese of Richmond, Virginia, specified that "the American flag and any other national or civil flag (e.g. the Vatican flag) have no *permanent* place in the sanctuary, and that instead they be displayed in the vestibule, narthex or commons area." The Diocese of Richmond does, however, allow that "while the *temporary* presence of the flag in the church might be appropriate (e.g. Veterans Day or Memorial Day services), it is better placed elsewhere [than in the sanctuary], in a memorial shrine perhaps." The Diocese of Richmond goes on to note that "a church has been considered almost extraterritorial ... Our churches are places where everyone is welcomed, not just American citizens, a place in which a gospel message that challenges the values of a country may be heard."[60] Needless to say, given the polarities of American politics and religion in recent years, the presence or absence of American flags, as well as their precise placement, has been a controversial issue.

Faith Accommodating Culture in Contemporary Islam

In the Middle Ages, a coterie of Muslims evinced an interest in Greek philosophy (*falsafa*) that accommodated Islam to a Hellenistic cultural matrix. The most famous Muslim philosophers maintained throughout

---

60. "The Display of National Flags in Roman Catholic Churches," Diocese of Richmond-Office of Worship, May 16, 2007, available at www.richmonddiocese.org/worship/guidelines. American Baptists have reached similar conclusions on this question. See the statement by the executive director of the Baptist Joint Committee for Religious Liberty, J. Brent Walker: "Should American flags be in church sanctuaries?," available at www.BJConline.org.

their lives their identity as Muslims, but their esteem for the Qur'an was sometimes attenuated, hinting that it mainly helped the masses to perceive truths that were available to the philosopher through speculation.[61] Abu Nasr al-Farabi (ca. 870–950), a Sunni Muslim and native of Turkestan educated in Baghdad under the tutelage of a Christian master of philosophy, Yuhanna ibn Haylan, eventually served in the court of the Hamdanid rulers of Aleppo, adherents of the esoteric Nusayri ('Alawi) outgrowth of the Shi'i tradition. Straddling these varied religious identities, al-Farabi wrote with deliberate ambiguity that "the idea of the Philosopher, Supreme Ruler, Prince, Legislator, and *Imam* is but a single idea. No matter which one of these words you take, if you proceed to look at what each of them signifies among the majority of those who speak our language, you will finally find that they all finally agree by signifying one and the same idea."[62] Not every nonphilosopher among the Muslims contemporary with or living after al-Farabi would be able to accept this broad declaration. Al-Farabi maintained his serious attachment to the faith of Islam, but sometimes he gave the impression that he considered the practice of philosophy to be the best submission of self to God for the intellectual elite. The external practices of Islamic piety were more important for those not trained in philosophy.

The denunciation of *falsafa* by al-Ghazali (1058–1111)—what he called, in the title of a major work, *The Incoherence of the Philosophers* —did much to reduce the influence of philosophers in the Sunni Muslim world.[63] Ibn Rushd (Averroes, 1126–98), however, valiantly took up the cudgels for philosophy in his critique of al-Ghazali entitled, provocatively, *The Incoherence of the Incoherence*.[64] After 1200, however, the pursuit of *falsafa* mainly flourished in Shi'i Muslim circles.

---

61. Marshall Hodgson sums up the approach of the Muslim philosophers very well: "The Philosophic search is the truest way of honouring and worshipping God; the cults and moral rules and doctrines of ordinary ignorant people are merely imperfect attempts at the true Philosophic way." See *The Venture of Islam: Conscience and History in a World Civilization* (Chicago: University of Chicago Press, 1974), 1:427.

62. "The Attainment of Happiness," in *Alfarabi's Philosophy of Plato and Aristotle*, trans. Muhsin Mahdi, rev. ed. (Ithaca, N.Y.: Cornell University Press, 1969), §58 (47).

63. See W. Montgomery Watt, *Muslim Intellectual: A Study of al-Ghazali* (Edinburgh: University of Edinburgh Press, 1963), 57–65.

64. See Roger Arnaldez, "Ibn Rushd," *EI2*, 3:909b–920a, esp. 915a–916b.

Secularized Muslim-majority countries like Turkey, Albania, and some of the former Soviet republics in central Asia could be cited as modern examples of places where the model of wholesale accommodation of Islam to secular and indeed secularist culture prevailed until recent times. During the years when Mustafa Kemal Atatürk dominated Turkish political life (1920–38), the faith of Muslims was privatized or even reduced to cultural silence. The alphabet was Romanized, cutting the young off from the past of Turkish literature. The Arabic call to worship was effectively prohibited and Western styles of haberdashery— and especially the brimmed hat which made prostration impossible for men—were legislated for all.[65] But even then Turkish cultural identity was linked to the Islamic history of Turkey in ways that the secularizing policies of the Atatürk government could not erase.[66] In the years since Atatürk's death, there has been more and more of an Islamic cultural rebirth in that country, and many contemporary Turks, especially in the major urban centers, are not entirely pleased with the Islamizing tendencies of the current president of Turkey (since 2014), Recep Tayyip Erdogan.

In recent decades the version of Islam propagated in Libya by the late Colonel Mu'ammar Qaddafi (1942–2011) provides the most striking example of Islam that has been modified to fit into its cultural setting. There were in Qaddafi's thought many elements of the Arab nationalist and socialist ideology enunciated more than sixty years ago by Gamal Abdel Nasser, the founder of modern Egypt.[67] When he first seized power in Libya in 1969, Qaddafi attacked all elements of Libyan society that seemed to favor compromise of Islamic values with those of the West. Thus he banned the consumption of alcohol and the licensing of nightclubs, closed down Christian churches, and enforced traditional Islamic criminal penalties.[68] As the 1970s progressed, however, Qaddafi increas-

---

65. For a succinct account of these developments, see Hodgson, *The Venture of Islam*, 3:262–66, esp. 264.

66. For an early recognition of this reality, see Wilfred Cantwell Smith, *Islam in Modern History* (Princeton, N.J.: Princeton University Press, 1977), 161–205.

67. See Gamal Abdel Nasser, *The Philosophy of the Revolution* (Buffalo, N.Y.: Economica Books, 1959).

68. See Lisa Anderson, "Qaddafi's Islam," in *Voices of Resurgent Islam*, ed. John L. Esposito (Oxford: Oxford University Press, 1983), 134.

ingly promoted social and economic policies that differed quite dramatically from standard Sunni Muslim practice.

Between 1975 and 1980 Qaddafi published three slim volumes called collectively *The Green Book*. Given the prominence of Islamic concerns in the first years of Qaddafi's rule, the paucity of references to anything even remotely Islamic in *The Green Book* is quite striking.[69] Unique ideas emanated from Colonel Qaddafi himself, especially on religious matters:

Religion embraces and absorbs tradition. Most material penalties in religion are postponed until the Day of Judgment. The major part of its rules are exhortations, instructions and answers to questions. This law shows proper respect to man. Religion does not acknowledge temporal penalties, except in extreme cases where these are necessary to protect society. Religion embraces tradition, which is an expression of the natural life of the peoples. Thus religion, embracing tradition, is an affirmation of natural law. Non-religious, non-traditional laws are invented by one man for use against another. Therefore they are invalid because they are not built upon the natural source of tradition and religions.[70]

Qaddafi invented his own history of religion, seeming to absorb it into his own personal nationalistic ideology:

Originally, each nation had one religion. This was harmony. In fact, however, differences arose which became a genuine cause of conflict and instability in the life of the peoples throughout the ages. The sound rule is that every nation should have a religion. The contrary to that is abnormal. Such an abnormality creates an unsound situation which becomes a real cause for disputes within a national group. There is no other solution but to be in harmony with the natural rule that each nation has one religion. When the social factor is compatible with the religious factor, harmony is achieved and the life of groups become stable and strong and develops soundly.[71]

On the occasion of the inauguration of the Muslim year 1399 (on December 1, 1978), Qaddafi called for a major change in the Islamic calendar. No longer would it date from the *hijra* (Muhammad's departure from Mecca for Medina in 622) but from Muhammad's death in 632.[72]

69. Ibid., 141–42.
70. Muammar Al Qathafi [sic], *The Green Book* (n.p.: n.d.), 37–38.
71. Ibid., 87–88.
72. Anderson, "Qaddafi's Islam," 144–45.

What was the point of this uniquely Libyan calendar? It eliminated the necessity to refer to the *sunna* or customary practice of Muhammad's lifetime as reported in *hadith* literature. Thus Qaddafi attacked one of the principal sources of Islamic jurisprudence (*fiqh*) and the legal scholars (*fuqaha'*) who practice it

In his last years the singularity of Qaddafi's opinions on Islam was amply demonstrated in lengthy lectures posted on his website. At the end of 2006 Qaddafi suggested that the pilgrimage to Abrahamic sites in Arabia (the *hajj*) should be open to non-Muslim people of monotheistic faith as well as to Muslims. "If the Papal Legate wants to go tomorrow to circle the Ka'aba [*sic*], then that is his right, because the Ka'aba is for all people."[73] By expressing such opinions Qaddafi intended to provoke not only the authorities in Saudi Arabia but also more traditional Muslims critical of his ideas within Libya. "Brother Leader" should not have been confused, as the Western media sometimes did, with those Muslims whom the Western media regularly called fundamentalists in the past or Islamists today. Qaddafi's version of Islam was simply unique and seems to have died with him in the chaos that now envelops Libya.

Faith Integrating Culture: Contemporary Jewish, Christian, and Muslim Examples

Niebuhr at some length distinguishes three varieties of the church of the center that he describes as synthesist, dualist, and conversionist. I will not try to use these three subdivisions of the church of the center to describe the central varieties of contemporary Judaism, Christianity, and Islam. But all three forms of monotheistic faith have centrist traditions, even if those centrist traditions include a fairly broad range of understandings of the faith tradition in question. The distinguishing mark of the centrism of these three traditions is their ability to engage with their cultural settings and to integrate their faith with those

73. "The Meeting of the Brother Leader with the Heads of Churches Present throughout the Great Jamahiriya, the Ambassadors of Friendly Counties, and Political, Religious and Cultural Figures in Libyan Society," March 30, 2006, available at www.gathafi.org.

cultural settings. This centrist integration has been achieved in each case without the total accommodation of the respective faith tradition with its cultural setting, and also without the centrist religious faith tradition so reacting against the cultural milieu as to constitute a faith-based counter-culture.

I will examine only one major cultural and historical problematic posed for all three monotheistic faith traditions in modern times: how centrist Jews, Christians, and Muslims today have faced up to an overwhelming fact of contemporary culture—the encounter, not always amicable, between adherents of these same three major monotheistic traditions. Those Jews, Christians, and Muslims whose faith has rejected culture usually reject inter-faith dialogue as well. Jews, Christians, and Muslims who have accommodated their faith to their cultural settings have sometimes proven more open to inter-faith dialogue, precisely because their own relationship to their particular revealed traditions is so tenuous. Those who wish to integrate their faith in all three monotheistic traditions with their cultural setting, without losing themselves in that cultural setting, still feel a need to come to terms with how other people of faith face up to the same challenge.

Faith Integrating Culture in Contemporary Judaism: The Inter-Faith Challenge

Several eminent Jewish thinkers in modern times have faced up to the religious and cultural pluralism of the world in which we live, and especially the pluralism of monotheistic faith traditions. These thinkers can be found in all the communities of contemporary Judaism. Let me sketch briefly the thought of two modern Jewish thinkers who have attempted to integrate their faith with the fact of religious and cultural diversity. The first has been dead for half a century: the European-Israeli philosopher and student of Hasidic piety, Martin Buber (1878–1965). The other is happily still living, the *emeritus* Chief Rabbi of the United Hebrew Congregations of Great Britain and the Commonwealth, Sir Jonathan Sacks. Neither Buber nor Sacks tried to live their lives in isolation from the pluralistic situations, sometimes quite conflicted, of the modern world. Each of them has spoken to that pluralism in words that have rightly commanded the attention of modern people, not only Jewish but also Christian and Muslim.

Martin Buber only moved to Israel in 1938, but long before that he had been active in the Zionist movement that planned to establish a Jewish home in Palestine. Buber adhered at first to the tradition of what has been called Cultural Zionism, a movement that has not triumphed in the modern state of Israel. Cultural Zionists took seriously the double commitment to immigrant Jews and to long-resident Arabs in Palestine made in the original letter of November 2, 1917, written by Arthur James Balfour, the British Foreign Secretary, to the second Baron Rothschild: "His Majesty's Government view with favour the establishment in Palestine of a national home for the Jewish people, and will use their best endeavours to facilitate the achievement of this object, it being clearly understood that nothing shall be done which may prejudice the civil and religious rights of existing non-Jewish communities in Palestine, or the rights and political status enjoyed by Jews in any other country."[74]

The Cultural Zionists generally, and Martin Buber in particular, took this commitment to Jewish and Arab coexistence in Palestine quite seriously. For Buber and the Cultural Zionists the land of Israel—not the future state as a party to international alliances—was their primary interest. In September 1921, in the wake of early Arab demonstrations against Zionist settlement in what was by then British-mandated Palestine, Buber proposed to the Twelfth Zionist Congress a socialist solution of the Arab question: "Between us and the working Arab nation a deep and enduring solidarity of true, common interests will develop and … in the end must overcome all the conflicts to which the present mad hour has given birth."[75] Buber's proposal was watered down beyond recognition by the Congress to which he had submitted it.

---

74. "Balfour Declaration 1917," *The Avalon Project: Documents in Law, History and Diplomacy*, available at avalon.law.yale.edu/20th_century/balfour.asp.

75. Martin Buber, *A Land of Two Peoples*, ed. Paul Mendes-Flohr (Chicago: University of Chicago Press, 2005), 61.

Buber lived out the rest of his life as a somewhat lonely prophet hoping for Jewish-Arab coexistence. In the process he moved from Cultural Zionism to what has been called Realistic Zionism, reflecting the fact that his ideas developed over those four decades or more until, a few months before his death in 1965, Buber called for "a federative union or rather a confederative one" between Israel and Palestine "so that for each of the two partners the full national autonomy is preserved; neither one should be allowed to injure in any point the national existence of the other."[76] Such a confederation Buber had come to realize could not be effected by politicians, local or international: "In order that so immense a work, an unprecedented work in fact, may succeed, it is indeed necessary that spiritual representatives of the two peoples enter into a true dialogue with one another, a dialogue of shared sincerity and mutual recognition alike."[77] With the outbreak of the Six Day War in 1967 and the consequent Israeli occupation of East Jerusalem, the Old City, and the West Bank, the chances for such Israeli-Palestinian confederation became more and more remote. Buber had died two years earlier; it is hard to imagine, had he lived a few years longer, that he would have died a happy man.

The second Jewish scholar I have singled out as a model of interfaith dialogue, Rabbi Sacks, has written a great deal that touches on this theme, but I wish to quote from a book of his published in 2005, *To Heal a Fractured World*. Early in this work Sacks retells the story once told by a Yale law professor, Stephen Carter. As a boy Carter, an African-American, moved with his family to the Cleveland Park section of Washington, D.C., a white neighborhood. Eleven-year-old Stephen sat with his brothers and sisters on the front steps of their home wondering how they would be received in this new environment. No one greeted them, confirming their suspicion that they were unwelcome. Then, quite suddenly, a white woman, who lived across the street, greeted the children heartily. After entering her own home, she came out again, bringing the children cream cheese and jelly sandwiches and something to drink. Carter learned that the hospitable neighbor was Sara Kestenbaum,

76. Ibid., 304–5.
77. Ibid., 305.

who, Carter eventually found out, was a religious Jew. "In the Jewish tradition," Carter writes, such civility is called "*hesed*—the doing of acts of kindness—which is in turn derived from the understanding that human beings are made in the image of God."[78]

But does that definition limit the love involved only to those linked to God in the covenant of Abraham? Following rabbinical tradition, Sacks insists on a much broader perspective. "*Hesed* is born in the phrase in the second chapter of Genesis, 'It is not good for man to be alone.' … *Hesed* is the redemption of solitude, the bridge we build across the ontological abyss between I and Thou."[79] One can see in these words how deeply Sacks is affected by the most famous book of Martin Buber.[80]

Later in the same book Sacks notes the existence of a narrower sense of *hesed* as the bond of loyalty that exists between God and the chosen people or the loyalty that should prevail between members of that chosen people themselves. He ascribes this narrower notion of *hesed* to the prophetic literature of the Hebrew Bible. In contrast he develops at some length what the later rabbinic tradition calls, borrowing a phrase from the Book of Proverbs (3:17), *darkhei shalom*, the paths of peace. "*Darkhei shalom*," Rabbi Sacks writes, "is essentially *hesed* universalized and applied to those who are not members of our faith."[81] Sacks prefers the rabbinical notion of the *darkhei shalom* to the narrower prophetic notion of peace: "The attempt to bring prophetic peace by human action creates not peace but war."[82] The rabbis in post-Second Temple Judaism "knew that in this not-yet-fully-redeemed world, peace means *living with difference*—with those who have another faith and other texts."[83] In a world of competing religious

78. Stephen Carter, *Civility: Manners, Morals, and the Etiquette of Democracy* (New York: Basic Books, 1998), 71. Carter transliterated the Hebrew word *hesed* as *chesed*. Rabbi Sacks transliterated the same word as *hessed*. For the sake of clarity I am adjusting their texts to demonstrate that they are talking about the same Hebrew word.

79. Jonathan Sacks, *To Heal a Fractured World: The Ethics of Responsibility* (New York: Schocken, 2005), 47.

80. Buber, *I and Thou*.

81. Sacks, *To Heal a Fractured World*, 98.

82. Ibid., 101.

83. Ibid.

absolutisms, Rabbi Sacks prefers the ways of those post-Second Temple rabbis, "the lights of peace (the Sabbath candles)" rather than "the lights of victory (the Hanukkah candles)."[84]

The rabbinical ethic of *darkhei shalom* enunciated by Rabbi Sacks sheds a very gentle light on our modern situation of inter-faith communal living. It integrates a profoundly Jewish faith with the realities of London, New York, and every metropolis where Jews, Christians, and Muslims—as well as men and women of every faith tradition and no faith tradition—must learn to live together in community. Is there hope in this vision for yet another metropolis, Jerusalem? One can only hope that heirs of Buber and Sacks will lead us in that direction.

Faith Integrating Culture in Contemporary Christianity: The Inter-Faith Challenge

Many thinkers in the Catholic and Protestant traditions have theologized about religious pluralism. Pope Benedict XVI was not generally counted among the leaders in this area. Some even assert that Pope Benedict backed away from *Nostra Aetate*. I would suggest, however, that Pope Benedict's attitudes towards inter-faith dialogue and the pluralistic culture in which we live today were developing during the years of his papacy (2005–13).

The media gave much attention in the era of his papacy to criticisms made of Pope Benedict on matters concerning Catholic relations with Jews. But an examination of the pope's writings both before and after his accession to the papacy demonstrates the depth of his reflection on and sympathy with the Jewish tradition.[85] At Christmas in the year 2000, then-Cardinal Ratzinger deplored the past history of anti-Semitism and noted that "our dialogue with Jews is situated on a different level than that in which we engage with other religions. The faith witnessed by the Jewish Bible ... is not merely another religion

84. Ibid., 103.
85. See on this subject the early assessment (July 15, 2005) of Pope Benedict XVI by Rabbi Gary Bretton-Granatoor, Director of Inter-Faith Relations of the Anti-Defamation League: "After 100 Days, It's Clear that New Pope Is a Friend of the Jews," available at www.adl.org.

to us, but is the foundation of our own faith."[86] Speaking in May 2009 at Jerusalem's Memorial to victims of the Shoah, Pope Benedict began with the text from Isaiah that is the source of the Memorial's name, *Yad va-Shem*: "I will give in my house a memorial and a name" (Is 56:5). Of the millions who died in the Nazi era the pope declared that "they lost their lives, but they will never lose their names ... their names are forever fixed in the memory of Almighty God."[87]

Pope Benedict's relations with Muslims have also come in for criticism. His September 2006 lecture at the University of Regensburg on "Faith, Reason and the University" began by quoting with seeming approbation harsh words written by the third-to-last Byzantine emperor, Manuel II Palaiologos, excerpted from a controversial dialogue with an unnamed Persian scholar. The pope's journey two months later to Turkey offered him an opportunity, in that majority-Muslim but decidedly secular state, to express more clearly his "sentiments of esteem for the Muslims and for the Islamic civilization." He also recalled, in a reflective address later delivered in Rome, an unscheduled visit to Istanbul's Blue Mosque while he was in Turkey. "Pausing for a few minutes of recollection in that place of prayer, I addressed the one Lord of Heaven and earth, the Merciful Father of all humanity."[88] A papal moment of prayer in a mosque says more than many irenic words.

The response of Muslim scholars to the pope's Regensburg address led eventually to dialogue with those scholars, and especially the *Common Word* initiative, to be discussed below. By May 2009 the pope, addressing Muslim religious leaders in Jordan, declared that "Muslims and Christians, precisely because of the burden of our common history so often marked with misunderstanding, must today strive to be known as worshippers of God ... mindful of the common origin and dignity of all human persons."[89] Pope Benedict also noted that "the

86. "The Heritage of Abraham: The Gift of Christmas," *L'Osservatore Romano*, December 29, 2000.

87. "Visit to Yad Vashem Memorial: *Address of His Holiness Benedict XVI*," May 11, 2009, available at www.vatican.va.

88. Benedict XVI, "General Audience," December 6, 2006, available at www.vatican.va.

89. "Meeting with Muslim Religious Leaders, Members of the Diplomatic Corps and Rectors of Universities in Jordan: *Address of His Holiness Benedict XVI*," May 9, 2009, available at www .vatican.va.

more recent *Common Word* letter ... echoed a theme consonant with my first encyclical: the unbreakable bond between love of God and love of neighbour, and the fundamental contradiction of resorting to violence or exclusion in the name of God."[90]

Muslim and Jewish responses to Pope Benedict during the eight years of his pontificate were not always positive. Quite a change, however, has occurred since the accession of Jorge Mario Bergoglio to the See of Peter as Pope Francis in March 2013. Very different in personality from Pope Benedict, Bergoglio has also brought to the papacy years of personal experience of inter-faith dialogue with Jews and Muslims in his native Argentina.

Three years before he was elected pope, Bergoglio and Rabbi Abraham Skorka of Buenos Aires published together a book of shared reflections on twenty-nine different issues of concern to people of faith, Jewish and Christian. After the election of Pope Francis the book was hastily translated and published in English.[91] One particular chapter in that book is of special importance for Jewish-Christian mutual understanding. Chapter 24 is entitled "On the Holocaust." Rabbi Skorka starts with the question many Jews ask: "Where was G_d during the Holocaust?" Rabbi Skorka goes on to ask an even better question: "We should ask where people were, both those who took action as well as those who mercilessly and cruelly failed to act."[92]

Bergoglio agreed as well with Rabbi Skorka that the bigger question was "Where was man?" at the time of the Shoah. He went on: "The great powers washed their hands of it, they looked the other way, because they knew much more than what they were saying, just as they washed their hands of the genocide of the Armenians."[93] He continued by saying that "the Shoah ... has a distinctive feature," which differentiates it from the genocide of the Armenians. It was, according to Bergoglio, "an idolatrous construction against the Jewish people. The

90. Ibid.

91. Jorge Mario Bergoglio and Abraham Skorka, *On Heaven and Earth*, trans. Alejandro Bermudez and Howard Goodman (New York: Image, 2013). The Spanish original, *Sobre el cielo y la tierra*, ed. Diego F. Rosemberg, was published in 2010 by Editorial Sudamericana S.A.

92. Ibid., 176–77.

93. Ibid., 177.

pure race, the superior beings, they are idols for the foundation upon which Nazism was built.... Every Jew that they killed was a slap in the face of the living God in the name of idols."[94]

The pope has befriended several Argentinian Muslims as well, and one of them—Shaykh 'Omar Abboud—accompanied the pope and Rabbi Skorka on their joint pilgrimage to Jordan, Palestine, and Israel in May 2014. Abboud, a younger man than either Pope Francis or Rabbi Skorka, testifies that as archbishop of Buenos Aires Bergoglio "showed us and taught us about dialogue.... He brought minorities to the table, to create an unprecedented civic space."[95] Abboud goes on to express his amazement from his many encounters, formal and informal, with Bergoglio in Argentina: "How can a Muslim learn from a Catholic priest? ... I learned the dynamic of Islamic mercy through his words.... From Bergoglio it was a whole lesson in the exercise of mercy, in improving your view of the other by putting yourself in their shoes."[96]

If a picture is worth a thousand words, the picture of Pope Francis, Rabbi Skorka, and Shaykh Abboud embracing beside the Western Wall of the Temple in Jerusalem in May 2014—with none of their faces visible to people other than themselves—speaks more clearly than any statement about what mercy means, and what a realm of mercy might bring to the tense frontiers of Jewish-Christian-Muslim encounter in modern times.

Faith Integrating Culture in Contemporary Islam: The Inter-Faith Challenge

The *Common Word* letter referred to by Pope Benedict was an open letter written to Pope Benedict and twenty-six other heads of churches throughout the world in 2007. The original signatories were 138 prominent Muslim scholars.[97] The actual author of the open letter seems to

94. Ibid., 178.
95. Abboud as quoted in Austen Ivereigh, *The Great Reformer: Francis and the Making of a Radical Pope* (New York: Henry Holt and Company, 2014), 322.
96. Ibid.
97. See "A Common Word between Us and You" (Jordan: The Royal Aal al-Bayt Institute for Islamic Thought, 2009), available at www.acommonword.com.

have been Prince Ghazi ibn Muhammad ibn Talal, first cousin of the present king of Jordan, 'Abd Allah II. The prince wrote the open letter as a follow-up to an earlier open letter, published in 2006, reacting to Pope Benedict's address at Regensburg.

The title of the 2007 open letter derives from a verse in the Qur'an in which God instructs both Muhammad and the Christians of Najran in south Arabia to come to terms on common religious principles (Qur'an 3:64). That divine instruction during the lifetime of Muhammad to seek common religious ground with Christians serves as a model for what the author and his fellow signatories urge on the Christian leaders addressed. The letter seeks ways to coordinate the teaching of the Qur'an and the *hadith* (reports of Muhammad's sayings) with what has been called in the Christian tradition the two great commandments: love of God and love of neighbor (Mk 12:30–31 and parallels). These two commandments derive from the Torah, the first five books of the Hebrew Bible (specifically, Dt 6:4–5 and Lv 19:18).

Even if many would claim that the two great commandments are primarily Jewish and Christian, the *Common Word* letter argues that the same two commandments play a central role both in the Qur'an and in the oral traditions ascribed to Muhammad. Thus Part I of the letter, "Love of God," concludes with a reflection on a quotation from Muhammad on the absoluteness of God not only in the revelation he had received but also in "the prophets that came before me."[98] Part II of the letter, "Love of the Neighbour," draws the parallels between the second of the two great commandments and various passages from the Qur'an and Muhammad's own teaching. "Without giving the neighbour what we ourselves love, we do not truly love God or the neighbour."[99]

The third and final part of the letter comes back to the theme with which the letter began. Although the letter is addressed only to Christian leaders, there are hints in Part III that Jews might also be included in its purview: "The *Two Greatest Commandments* are an area of common ground and a link between the Qur'an, the Torah and the New Testament.... Thus the Unity of God, and love of the neighbour form a

98. Ibid., 23.
99. Ibid., 26.

common ground upon which Islam and Christianity (and Judaism) are
founded."[100] Later in the same section the writers declare that "Muslims, Christians and Jews should be free to each follow what God commanded them."[101]

Alas, the breadth of these quotations from Part III of the letter is
compromised in a section of "Frequently Asked Questions" appended
to the 2009 edition of the letter available online. Responding to a query
as to why Jews are not addressed in the letter, the unknown respondent
notes that "Jewish scriptures are invoked repeatedly and respectfully"
by way of "preparing for a further document specifically addressed
to Jewish scholars." This is fair enough, as far as it goes, but then the
unknown respondent concludes by stating that "this is a Theological
document and the problems between Jews and Muslims are essentially political not Theological."[102] I would venture to suggest, however,
that both Christians and Muslims have to come to terms with the Jewish roots of their respective traditions before there can be any genuine
mutual understanding between Christians and Muslims. Whatever its
limitations, the *Common Word* letter represents an attempt by a broad
conspectus of Muslim scholars to speak for Islam. It begins to face up
to the situation in which humanity lives today, and especially the cultural frontiers where Jews, Christians, and Muslims face each other in
fear and trembling, but also in hope.

Some Muslims in modern times have proven willing to go well
beyond the somewhat circumscribed lines of the *Common Word* documents. Two North African Muslim scholars who have taught outside
the Muslim world at different campuses of the University of Paris—
both of them recently deceased—come particularly to mind: Mohammed Arkoun (1928–2010) and Abdelwahab Meddeb (1946–2014).

The philosopher Mohammed Arkoun, a man very conscious of his
own Berber roots, always insisted that his first language was Berber,
his second French, and his third Arabic. This triple linguistic heritage
gave him a viewpoint somewhat different from many of his Algerian

100. Ibid., 28.
101. Ibid., 31.
102. Ibid., 277.

and French colleagues. He insisted repeatedly that Muslims needed to consider what he called the difference between the thinkable and the unthinkable, the thought and the unthought in their intellectual past, the cumulative contents of the "logosphere" or universe of meaning in which they lived. Arkoun likewise thought that the denizens of the Christian and post-Christian West needed to become aware of the limitations they have set, perhaps unconsciously, on their own intellectual universes.

The modern nation-state has been built and is supported by the creation and reproduction of the glorified national identity.... All the post-colonial states that emerged in the late 1950s ... used the same strategy, with a much more authoritarian, obscurantist, intolerant will-to-power. In Muslim countries, this policy helped to expand the space of the unthinkable and the unthought because a dual censorship has been and still is imposed on intellectual and cultural activities, censorship from above exercised by the state and censorship from below imposed by public opinion, especially on matters related to religion. Many intellectuals came to interiorize this dual control in the name of the Nation, or the religion, adding self-censorship to that already imposed from outside.[103]

Arkoun also held that Islamic intellectual life needed the development of an equivalent to modern scriptural studies in the Jewish and Christian world. "It is unfortunate that philosophical critique of sacred texts—which has been applied to the Hebrew Bible and to the New Testament without thereby engendering negative consequences for the notion of revelation—continues to be rejected by Muslim scholarly opinion.... The reasons for this resistance are political and psychological."[104]

The Tunisian poet and scholar of comparative literature, Abdelwahab Meddeb, was even more provocative than Arkoun in his critique of contemporary Muslim rigoristic thought. Discussing the 2001 Taliban destruction of the monumental sixth-century statues of Buddhas at Bamiyan in Afghanistan, Meddeb railed against the variety of Islam

---

103. See Mohammed Arkoun, *Islam: To Reform or To Subvert* (London: Saqi Essentials, 2006), 13.
104. Mohammed Arkoun, *Rethinking Islam: Common Questions, Uncommon Answers*, ed. and trans. Robert D. Lee (Boulder, Colo.: Westview Press, 1994), 35.

that provoked such vandalism. "From my point of view, all beliefs deserve to be considered: This is a teaching I take from Sufism, notably the Akbarian tradition, elaborated in the framework of Islamic faith by Ibn 'Arabi, the Andalusian master who recommended being *hyle* [Greek for matter, as opposed to form] so that all beliefs can take form within you."[105] The extremely positive attitude Meddeb takes toward the mystical thought of Ibn 'Arabi (1165–1240), which he connects with the later proposal for a universalistic "divine religion" (*din-i-ilahi*) made by the Mughal Emperor Akbar (r. 1556–1605),[106] distinguishes Meddeb from most rigorist Muslims, who repudiate the mystical tradition of Islam in whole or in part, and especially the monistic mysticism of Ibn 'Arabi, and even more so, that of the Emperor Akbar—a mysticism that breaks down the clear distinction between the human and the divine.

Like Arkoun, Meddeb called for the development of a critical study of Islamic sources, and especially the Qur'an:

When it comes to meaning, a fresh interpretation is imperative, one that takes into account the context of its first issuance but also liberates the Text from the constraints imposed by Tradition, whose most reductive and exclusive fundaments have been cultivated and radicalized by some groups. For our part, then, we need to return to that Tradition and seek out the discrepancies and gaps, the overflow of the text that will help us elaborate a meaning that is in step with our century.[107]

Both Arkoun and Meddeb were more at liberty to express such views precisely because they taught in Paris. But there are scholars living in the Muslim world who find inspiration in the writings of these Muslim expatriates or have come to similar conclusions on their own. It can be hoped that their voices will be heard and the much needed internal dialogue of contemporary Muslims advanced.

105. Abdelwahab Meddeb, *The Malady of Islam*, trans. Pierre Joris and Ann Reid (New York: Basic Books, 2002), 129.

106. See Aziz Ahmad, "Din-i Ilahi," *EI2*, 2:296a–297a.

107. Abdelwahab Meddeb, *Islam and the Challenge of Civilization*, trans. Jane Kuntz (New York: Fordham University Press, 2013), 12.

Concluding Reflection

The Jewish, Christian, and Muslim communities of faith over the centuries have created cultures and reacted to cultures they have not created but with which they have had to engage, nonetheless, for better or for worse. In the Book of Genesis we read how Abraham in the heat of the day welcomed three strangers at the entrance of his tent near the oaks of Mamre. Insisting on performing the duties of hospitality, Abraham, together with his wife, Sarah, fed those mysterious guests. The aged couple received as their reward almost unbelievably good news from the LORD, the birth of a son (Gn 18:1–15). The Epistle to the Hebrews in the New Testament alludes to this hospitality: "Do not neglect to show hospitality to strangers, for by doing that some have entertained angels without knowing it" (Heb 13:2). The Qur'an also narrates how Abraham and Sarah received their guests: "'Will you not take something to eat?' [Abraham] said, beginning to fear them. But they said, 'Fear not!' They gave him good news of a knowing son" (Qur'an 51:27–28).

Some Jews, Christians, and Muslims have defined very narrowly whom they would like to see Abraham and Sarah welcome into their tent; they have also defined very narrowly what elements of their surrounding culture they will tolerate in their enclosed communities. Jewish, Christian, and Muslim rejectionists welcome some angels and not others. But at least this much must be admitted: even the rejectionists welcome *some* angels. Narrow as they would like the hospitality of the patriarch and the matriarch to be defined, God and Abraham and Sarah will not feel constrained by their standards. Stringent as such people are in their definition of who is faithful and who is not, the very strangeness of these cultural rejectionists, the social and cultural awkwardness they embrace in modern times, stands as a challenge to those of us who are more at ease in our secular settings.

Some Jews, Christians, and Muslims have so reacted against the most stringent interpretations of their faith traditions as to accommodate themselves almost completely to their secular environments. They almost seem to lose contact with the God in whom their ancestors pledged their faith. Nevertheless, even these Jews, Christians, and Muslims know that they emerge from traditions of faith inherited from the past. The open tent of Abraham and Sarah continues to beckon to them from near the oaks of Mamre, always ready to welcome them back. To be called Jewish or Christian or Muslim may be all that is left of their faith, but that is something, no matter how minimal, and change or deepening of what their respective faith traditions mean to them always remains possible.

Those Jews and Christians and Muslims who have dedicated their lives to integrating their faith in their surrounding cultural settings resemble the patriarch himself when he went out to rescue his nephew Lot and Lot's fellow citizens of Sodom from the hostile tribes who had taken them captive: "[Abram] then brought back all the goods, and also brought back his nephew Lot with his goods, and the women and the people" (Gn 14:16). The king of Sodom was willing to leave all this booty to Abram, but Abram knew he had wealth enough from God: "I have sworn to the LORD, God Most High, maker of heaven and earth, that I will not take a thread or a sandal-thong or anything that is yours, so that you might not say, 'I have made Abram rich'" (Gn 14:22–23). The patriarch eventually prayed for Lot and prayed for Sodom, but his prayer was only partly answered. "So it was that, when God destroyed the cities of the plain, God remembered Abraham, and sent Lot out of the midst of the overthrow, when he overthrew the cities in which Lot had settled" (Gn 19:29). Those who have integrated their faith into their cultural setting finally have to recognize that there are limits even to such integration. The LORD was willing to be bargained down by the patriarch to ten righteous citizens of that city of the plain, but no further (Gn 18:33).

The tent of Abraham and Sarah, concretized in the various past and contemporary traditions of Judaism, Christianity, and Islam described in this chapter, is large and welcoming. Not every guest of Abraham and Sarah will be exactly the same as every other guest, but the tent *is* large and the hospitality abundant. Not only must Jews, Christians, and Muslims recognize each other across religious lines as fellow visitors to the tent of Abraham and Sarah, but different types of Jews, different types of Christians and different types of Muslims have a lot to learn about proper comportment among themselves in the tent. As people of faith we can and must look into the faces of our fellow guests and recognize the image and likeness of God.

CHAPTER 4

Prophetic Faith, Repentance, and the Development of Tradition

From time to time in my life, D., I have found it necessary to apologize, to ask for pardon, to repent. I have no doubt you as a diplomat have had to do so also. It is always a humiliating experience, but it is also a very valuable experience.

As a graduate student decades ago, I hosted two African undergraduates for a summer, a Nigerian and a Gambian, in the apartment adjoining mine at Eliot House, a residential hall at Harvard where I lived as a tutor. An African-American undergraduate friend of all three of us came to visit during the summer and found, to his dismay, that we were not getting along very well. The two Africans, coming from different countries, had no language in common except English. The Gambian student was much visited by his countrymen in the greater Boston area that summer, and when these guests came, they launched into lengthy conversations in their common language, leaving me and the Nigerian student out of the loop. The African-American visitor sensed that a certain coolness had developed between the three of us, two against one.

Before the African-American visitor left at the end of the weekend, he drew me aside and gently took me to task. "You are the priest, you are the oldest. You should make a move." I resented his intervention at first, still feeling aggrieved at the conversational impasse the Nigerian and I had been experiencing. But I decided to apologize anyway to the Gambian; my apology took place over a meal taken at the counter of a nearby diner. It broke the ice. The Gambian also expressed his regrets. I remain a good friend of the Gambian to the present day; both of us mourned the death of the Nigerian three years ago. The Nigerian had given himself over untiringly to medical service to very ordinary people for thirty-five years in a crowded area of Lagos. The Gambian served for several decades under UN auspices the needs of refugees in Africa and Asia. I remain grateful even now that the visiting agent of the reconciliation of the three of us, a youth of twenty-one at the time, took on the prophetic mantle at the end of that weekend and called me to repentance. Suitably enough, he is a United States federal judge today.

Prophetically mandated repentance, turning back from a previous stance and approaching a problem with a new, chastised vision, lies at the foundation of any new and valuable development of our understanding of what transcends us as individuals. The Hebrew word for repentance (*teshuva*) and the Arabic word for the same reality (*tawba*) preserve in their consonantal roots the imagery of turning back; the Greek New Testament word for this inner turning back is *metanoia*, making a change in one's mentality. Repentance not only transforms how we approach the reality of human friendship, but it also revolutionizes how we understand friendship with God. If we are tempted to think we understand God's ways completely, we are mightily deceived. Penance brings us back to first principles, enabling us to see what we have missed, making it possible for us to appraise the depths within familiar reality—familiar reality that we have never completely grasped. There is always more to understand of what is deepest, what is most transcendent. It takes time to develop such understanding; we must turn back, change our mentality, repent.

On March 12, 2000, the first Sunday of Lent in the year that completed the second millennium, Pope John Paul II celebrated a liturgy in St. Peter's Basilica for what was called "A Day of Pardon." There were some in the Vatican at the time who opposed the events planned for the liturgy of that day. There were also some outside the Vatican who criticized the liturgy for its focus on seeking God's forgiveness. They would have preferred something more like an apology to human beings, past and present, who had suffered at the hands of church officialdom. Such personal apology to human victims was and is no doubt in order. But the focus of the prayer in the liturgy of that Sunday—as should be the focus of prayer in all liturgy—was on God, who alone can forgive sins. In the petitions for that liturgy seven prelates of the Roman Curia introduced prayers by the pope.

• The first prayer was introduced by Cardinal Bernardin Gantin, the Béninois who was then the dean of the College of Cardinals. It asked for the forgiveness of sins in general, praying that "in an authentic 'purification of memory' we will be committed to the path of true conversion." Purification of memory, returning to the sources of pain inflicted and apologizing for psychological and spiritual harm done, plays a central role in resolving all human conflict and making it possible to move forward.

• The leader of the second prayer was Cardinal Joseph Ratzinger (later Pope Benedict XVI), the German head at that time of the Congregation for the Doctrine of the Faith, a papal ministry once called the Supreme Sacred Congregation of the Roman and Universal Inquisition. This body is traditionally charged with enforcing theological orthodoxy. Cardinal Ratzinger, widely believed at that time to have opposed the idea of this Day of Pardon, began the prayer for the forgiveness of sins committed "in the Service of Truth" with the admission that "even men of the Church, in the name of faith and morals, have sometimes used methods not in keeping with the Gospel." In Rome one cannot forget the trial and condemnation of the hermeticist and polymath Giordano Bruno, handed over to the secular arm and burned to death in the Campo de' Fiori in 1600, or the 1633 trial and subsequent house arrest of Galileo Galilei for the supposed heresy of claiming that the universe was not geocentric and the earth not immovable. More recent censures of twentieth-century Catholic theologians supplied "men of the Church" in the Congregation for the Doctrine of the Faith with many more reasons to repent.

• Cardinal Roger Etchegaray, a French-Basque prelate long identified with the Pontifical Council on Justice and Peace, began the third prayer, one centered on ecumenical themes. He prayed for pardon for sins that "have rent the unity of the Body of Christ and wounded fraternal charity" among Christians. The fifth centenary of the 1517 Lutheran Reformation offered one opportunity for Catholics and Lutherans alike to ask for pardon, as do frequent meetings in recent years between the pope, the patriarch of Constantinople, and the heads of other Eastern Christian churches.

• The Australian cardinal prefect of the Pontifical Council for Christian Unity and the Council on Religious Relations with Jews, Cardinal Edward Cassidy, prayed for the forgiveness of sins "against the People of Israel," acknowledging "sins committed by not a few [Christians] against the people of the Covenant and the blessings." In the wake of the Shoah, this prayer of repentance—derived from the paragraph on Jews in the Second Vatican Council's *Nostra Aetate*—continues a modern Catholic tradition starkly different from earlier church attitudes.

• The fifth prayer, introduced by a future cardinal, the Japanese Archbishop Stephen Fumio Hamao, president of the Pontifical Council for the Pastoral Care of Migrants and Itinerants, begged forgiveness from God for "sins committed in actions against love, peace, the rights of peoples, and respect for cultures and religions." The prayer specified sins caused by "the desire to dominate others," including in its scope "enmity towards members of other religions and towards the weakest groups in society, such as immigrants and itinerants." This prayer seemed to be addressed to the often unacknowledged sins involved in colonialism and various forms of cultural insensitivity in the church's missionary past.

• The sixth prayer was introduced by the president of the Pontifical Council for Interreligious Dialogue, the Nigerian Cardinal Francis Arinze. "Let us pray for all those who have suffered offences against their human dignity and whose rights have been trampled; let us pray for women, who are all too often humiliated and emarginated, and let us acknowledge the forms of acquiescence in those sins of which

Christians too have been guilty." The prayer with which Pope John Paul II followed up that introduction further specified the sins for which pardon was sought: "The equality of your sons and daughters has not been acknowledged, and Christians have been guilty of attitudes of rejection and exclusion, consenting to acts of discrimination on the basis of racial and ethnic differences." This prayer was most notable for the gender sensitivity of its language and its specification of the church's very mixed record on male-female relations.

• The seventh prayer, led by the Vietnamese Cardinal François-Xavier Nguyen Van Thuan, a political prisoner for thirteen years in his home country, further specified repentance not only by the church but also by the world at large for "sins in relation to fundamental rights of the person." The cardinal specifically prayed for "all the men and women of the world, especially for minors who are victims of abuse, for the poor, the alienated, the disadvantaged." In that company he also included "the most defenseless, the unborn killed in their mother's womb or even exploited for experimental purposes by those who abuse the promise of biotechnology and distort the aim of science." The connection made between ethnic cleansing in countries like the former Yugoslavia, Vietnam, Cambodia, Rwanda, Sudan, and Tibet and the continuing elimination of human life before birth demonstrates vividly the church's broad range of concerns for human rights, including the most basic of all human rights, the right to be born.[1]

What Pope John Paul II did on that Sunday in Rome in 2000 was unprecedented; even if he was once reluctant to engage in such public repentance, Pope John Paul's successor in the chair of Peter, Benedict XVI, had to repeat that gesture many times, especially the seventh prayer of petition, in the aftermath of proliferating charges of sexual abuse by Catholic church personnel. Pope Francis, the successor of Benedict since 2013, has repeated such prayers as well, and, like Benedict, has met more than once with victims of abuse by Catholic clergy. The secular press seems to think such repentance unusual. But is not repentance central not only to the Christian tradition of faith but also

1. "Universal Prayer-Day of Pardon," available at www.vatican.va.

to the tradition of Israel from which Christianity took its origins? Such repentance has often led to fruitful revision of the Jewish and Christian traditions. In the course of this chapter I will suggest that the faith tradition of Islam also knows the reality of such repentance and the revision of its past practices and past formulations of faith.

How can a faith tradition or those who bear that tradition repent? Is it possible for the bearers of a faith tradition to revise their understanding of themselves and of their faith? Are there both faithful and faithless revisions of faith traditions? I would suggest that it is precisely the prophetic charism—the free gift of God's intervention in the lives of certain faithful human beings—that ignites the possibility both of individual repentance and of corporate repentance. In corporate repentance over several generations a faith tradition begins to change because the bearers of that faith tradition change. The call to such repentance and revision has more than once been voiced by prophetic figures outside the power structure of all three faith traditions. These prophetic figures are generally recognized only after they die for the heroism they embodied. Prophets as outsiders speak on God's behalf to you and to me, calling for inner and outer repentance. Such repentance makes revision possible in the root sense of that word: seeing anew the claims of truth. We Jews, Christians, and Muslims have much to learn from each other in this matter, much need to share how our faith traditions have undergone genuine self-criticism. We need to acknowledge how our traditional ways of acting and thinking have endured prophetic rebuke from human beings speaking on behalf of God. As a result of such prophetic rebuke we—as individuals and as a company of the faithful—have been enabled to undergo fruitful change. This assertion flies in the face of the opinions of some interpreters within each of these three traditions of faith who propagate an ahistorical vision of the past, as if nothing important has ever changed or ever can change.

Prophetic Faith, Repentance, and the Development of the Jewish Tradition

In the Torah, the first five books of the Hebrew Bible, it is stated in more than one version of the commandments that the Lord is "a jealous God, punishing children for the iniquity of parents, to the third and the fourth generation of those who reject me" (Ex 20:5).[2] Fortunately, the same passage counterbalances and in some sense revises this word with a promise that the same jealous God shows "steadfast love to the thousandth generation of those who love me and keep my commandments" (Ex 20:6). The context of this baleful threat and glorious promise is the sin of idolatry: "You shall not make for yourself an idol, whether in the form of anything that is in heaven above, or that is on the earth beneath, or that is in the water under the earth. You shall not bow down to them or worship them" (Ex 20:4–5). Unjust as this notion of inherited guilt for sin seems to us today, the fact that we think it unjust derives from the experiences we have undergone of later prophetic revisions and reinterpretations.

Despite this commandment, during the relatively brief experience ancient Israel had with kingship, a period of five centuries, several kings of the Northern and Southern Kingdoms fell into idolatry. Few kings of Judah come in for more obloquy on this account than Manasseh, who ruled in Jerusalem from 687 to 642 BCE. The son of the reformist Hezekiah, Manasseh came to the throne at the age of twelve. Over the next forty-five years he reversed the policies of his devout father and his father's counselor, the prophet Isaiah. The sin of idolatry, and especially the cultus of Baal and Asherah, the fertility gods of the pagan populations among whom the Israelites had settled, was introduced into the Jerusalem Temple under Manasseh. The author of the Deuteronomic history blames Manasseh for the hardships Judah would suffer in the Babylonian Exile half a century later (2 Kgs 21:10–12):

The LORD said by his servants the prophets, "Because King Manasseh of Judah has committed these abominations, has done things more wicked than all that

2. For thematically similar citations see Ex 34:7, Dt 5:9, Lv 26:39–40.

the Amorites did, who were before him, and has caused Judah also to sin with his idols; therefore thus says the LORD, the God of Israel, I am bringing upon Jerusalem and Judah such evil that the ears of everyone who hears of it will tingle."[3]

Despite the reforms introduced into the cultus at Jerusalem under Manasseh's second successor on the throne of Judah, Josiah (r. 640– 609 BCE), nothing could save the Southern Kingdom from the punishment enunciated by prophets in the era of Manasseh. It was probably only in the reign of Josiah that the Book of Deuteronomy, a quintessentially revisionist work developed out of traditions postdating the covenant laws of the Book of Exodus, first questioned the justice of punishment visited on anyone other than the perpetrator of sin: "Parents shall not be put to death for their children, nor shall children be put to death for their parents; only for their own crimes may persons be put to death" (Dt 24:16). When the Babylonian Exile eventuated, the prophet Ezekiel, another revisionist, rejected the notion that descendants to the third and fourth generation could be punished for the idolatry of their forebears (Ezek 18:1–4):

The word of the LORD came to me: What do you mean by repeating this proverb concerning the land of Israel, "The parents have eaten sour grapes, and the children's teeth are set on edge"? As I live, says the Lord GOD, this proverb shall no more be used by you in Israel. Know that all lives are mine; the life of the parent as well as the life of the child is mine: it is only the person who sins that shall die.

A late voice in the tradition of Jeremiah concurs with this notion of individualized moral responsibility and the need for individual repentance: "All shall die for their own sins; the teeth of everyone who eats sour grapes shall be set on edge" (Jer 31:30).[4]

---

3. It is interesting to note, however, that the Deuteronomic historian's utterly negative judgment on Manasseh was not entirely shared by the Chronicler, who maintains that late in his career Manasseh repented of his idolatry: "While [Manasseh] was in distress, he entreated the favor of the LORD his God and humbled himself greatly before the God of his ancestors. He prayed to him, and God received his entreaty, heard his plea, and restored him again to Jerusalem and to his kingdom. Then Manasseh knew that the LORD indeed was God" (2 Chr 33:12–13).

4. Scripture scholars generally ascribe to the influence of Ezekiel during the Babylonian Exile this passage in Jeremiah's Book of Consolation that rejects inherited or multigenerational guilt.

Ezekiel dwells on this revisionist theme at some length. He specifies, in particular, the happy fate that awaits the person who observes
the Law and avoids idolatrous practice, various forms of sexual misbe-
havior and economic crimes such as the abuse of debtors and robbery.
More positively Ezekiel praises the same person who cares for the poor
and practices true justice: "Such a one is righteous; he shall surely
live, says the LORD God" (Ezek 18:9). But the virtue of a parent does not
transfer automatically to a child (Ezek 18:10–13):

If he has a son who is violent, a shedder of blood, who does any of these things
(though his father does none of them), who eats upon the mountains, defiles
his neighbor's wife, oppresses the poor and needy, commits robbery, does not
restore the pledge, lifts up his eyes to the idols, commits abomination, takes
advance or accrued interest; shall he then live? He shall not. He has done all
these abominable things; he shall surely die; his blood shall be upon himself.

Ezekiel even brings up the possibility that sinners can repent; perhaps he knew the Chronicler's tradition that the wicked Manasseh had
repented towards the end of his life. "But if the wicked turn away from
all their sins that they have committed and keep all my statutes and do
what is lawful and right, they shall surely live; they shall not die" (Ezek
18:21). But Ezekiel also mentions the opposite possibility, that the just
can go astray (Ezek 18:24). Easy repentance can as easily evaporate.
How could one forget Solomon, the son of David? "For when Solomon
was old, his wives turned away his heart after other gods; and his heart
was not true to the LORD his God, as was the heart of his father David"
(1 Kgs 11:4).

Obvious as Ezekiel's prophecy on this subject may seem to us in
modern times, it was not entirely obvious to his listeners and readers,
people raised in the ancient understanding of human persons as inextricably identified with family, clan, tribe, or nation, a notion typical of the
era before what the German philosopher Karl Jaspers called the Axial
Period. "This axis of history," Jaspers wrote, "is to be found in the period around 500 B.C., in the spiritual process that occurred between 800
and 200 B.C." Jaspers, more of a philosopher than a historian, maintains
that it is in this era "that we meet with the most deepcut dividing line in

history. Man, as we know him today, came into being."[5] Jaspers and his sources recognize both Jeremiah and Ezekiel as actors on this age.[6]

But even long after the Axial Period, hearers of the parable of Jesus about the unforgiving debtor would not have been surprised that this major economic criminal deserved punishment along with his immediate family: "For this reason the kingdom of heaven may be compared to a king who wished to settle accounts with his slaves. When he began the reckoning, one who owed him ten thousand talents was brought to him; and, as he could not pay, his lord ordered him to be sold, together with his wife and children and all his possessions, and payment to be made" (Mt 18:23–25). The sum of ten thousand talents was an unimaginably large amount squandered by the king's slave; the presumption was that the slave's family had collaborated in his economic crime. Even today, in post-Axial Age New York City, some would like to jail the family members of major economic malefactors of recent times, taking it for granted that they must have colluded with the guilty perpetrator of economic fraud.[7]

The revolutionary nature of Ezekiel's prophetic critique and revision of Torah moral teaching about guilt is recognized by the prophet himself, who responds to the objection of those of his fellow exiles who say that "the way of the LORD is unfair" (Ezek 18:25, 29). Here Ezekiel is referring to God's new way of punishing only the sinner rather than the sinner and his or her whole family. On God's behalf the prophet completes this revolutionary new teaching with a general rule from God: "I have no pleasure in the death of anyone, says the LORD God. Turn, then, and live" (Ezek 18:32). The turning involved is the most basic physical image for repentance: *teshuva* in Hebrew.

5. Karl Jaspers, *The Origin and Goal of History*, trans. Michael Bullock (New Haven, Conn.: Yale University Press, 1953), 1.

6. In his first enumeration of prophetic voices of this Axial Period Jaspers mentions prophets in Israel "from Elijah, by way of Isaiah and Jeremiah to Deutero-Isaiah" (ibid., 2). Later he quotes approvingly the nineteenth-century German Sinologist Viktor von Strauss und Torney, who maintained that "during the centuries when Lao-tse and Confucius were living in China, a strange movement of the spirit passed through all civilised peoples. In Israel Jeremiah, Habakkuk, Daniel and Ezekiel were prophesying" (ibid., 8). Both Jaspers and his nineteenth-century source seem to have been unaware of the second-century BCE provenance of the Book of Daniel.

7. See Diana Henriques, *The Wizard of Lies: Bernie Madoff and the Death of Trust* (New York: Times Books/Henry Holt, 2011), esp. 274–75 and 321–24.

In the Babylonian Talmud, the great collection of the Oral Law composed between the first and sixth centuries CE, it is suggested in the tractate *Berakot*, in mitigation of the threat of multi-generational punishment of idolaters and other major sinners, that children will be punished for the sins of their parents only if they themselves continue in the same sinful behavior.[8] Much more radically, the tractate *Makkot* in the Babylonian Talmud quotes Rabbi Jose ben Hanina, a sage of the third and fourth centuries CE, who states quite boldly that the Law of Moses was revised by prophets. After revisions of the Torah attributed to Amos and Jeremiah, and before one attributed to Isaiah, Rabbi Jose cites the example of Ezekiel: "Moses had said, *The Lord ... is visiting the iniquity of the fathers upon the children and upon the children's children, unto the third and unto the fourth generation*; Ezekiel came and declared, *the soul that sinneth, it shall die*."[9] Indeed, the Talmud as a whole is replete with such examples of what the late Rabbi Ben-Zion Bokser (1907–84) called "daring illustrations of the independence with which the rabbis reacted to biblical texts."[10]

But after the death of the last prophets (for Jews Haggai, Zechariah, and Malachi, who probably lived in the late sixth and early fifth centuries BCE), was there a possibility within the Jewish tradition for prophetic critique and revision of that tradition? The example of the Babylonian Talmud suggests that there was, but did that possibility persist in the era after the Talmud was substantially complete? The great scholar of the Jewish Theological Seminary in New York City, the late Abraham Joshua Heschel (1907–72), once suggested that the prophetic charism continued in the Jewish tradition later than the Talmud. Appearances of Elijah the prophet and voices from heaven (examples of what has been called a *bat qol* in Hebrew) emboldened not a few medieval rabbis to speak on God's behalf with the boldness of the biblical prophets. "The master-rabbi of all generations"—as Hes-

8. *Berakot* 7a in *The Babylonian Talmud (Seder Zera'im)*, ed. and trans. Maurice Simon (London: Soncino Press, 1958), 33.

9. *Makkot* 24a in *The Babylonian Talmud (Seder Nezikin)*, ed. and trans. H. M. Lazarus (London: Soncino Press, 1935), 173.

10. In his introduction to selections from this Tractate in *The Talmud: Selected Writings*, trans. Ben Zion Bokser (New York: Paulist Press, 1989), 213.

chel calls Rashi (Rabbi Shlomo Itzhaki, 1040–1105)—"hinted that he had been granted divine illumination."[11] Even though Rashi usually cited earlier authorities as sources for his judgments on a scriptural or Talmudic passage, he could set out independently in new directions. Rashi even went so far as to say at one point in his commentary on the prophecy of Ezekiel, "As for me, neither teacher nor helper aided me in explaining this entire matter. So it has been shown to me from heaven." On another occasion Rashi asserted, "I have never heard nor found the correct interpretation of this verse … but I say …"[12] So bold were Rashi's assertions of his own inspired interpretations that some modern editors of Rashi have eliminated completely from the text of his commentaries such claims to divine inspiration and independence from human authorities.[13]

Rabbi Heschel concludes his essay on continuing prophecy in the Jewish tradition and its critique of the status quo: "One cannot grasp the innermost thought of the holy men of Israel without remembering that in their eyes, prophetic inspiration hovered over human reason, and, at times, heaven and earth would meet and kiss. They believed that the divine voice which issued from Horeb was not stilled thereafter."[14] That voice from Horeb still strikes our ears and moves our hearts to repentance and deeper faith. The word of God enunciated by prophets corrects our waywardness even today.

Heschel himself was thought by many to take on the prophetic mantle in the United States in the 1960s when he called for repentance from the citizens of his adopted country. It was not the first time he spoke with a prophetic voice. Three decades earlier he had addressed some of his fellow Jews in Germany in a 1936 essay on repentance published in Berlin on the eve of Yom Kippur:

Before the judgment and memory of God we stand. How can we prove ourselves? How can we persist? How can we be steadfast? Through repentance.

11. *Prophetic Inspiration after the Prophets: Maimonides and Other Medieval Authorities*, ed. Morris M. Faierstein (Hoboken, N.J.: Ktav Publishing House, 1996), 38.
12. Ibid.
13. Ibid., 68n3.
14. Ibid., 67.

The most unnoticed of all miracles is the miracle of repentance.... In the dimension of time there is no going back. But the power of repentance causes time to be created backward and allows re-creation of the past to take place. Through the forgiving hand of God, harm and blemish which we have committed against the world and against ourselves will be extinguished, transformed into salvation. God brings about this creation for the sake of humanity when a human being repents for the sake of God.[15]

The timing of this exhortation, three years into the chancellorship of Adolf Hitler, is ominous. Heschel knew that many of his fellow Jews in Germany were completely secularized. They had proven no more than lukewarm in their embrace of the faith tradition of their forbears. He compares them ironically with Marranos, Jews who attempted to pass as Christians in post-*Reconquista* Spain, perhaps because some of these German Jews in 1936 were just beginning to take their Jewishness more seriously, just beginning to identify themselves as Jews in the hostile environment created by rising Nazism: "Marranos of a new metamorphosis: Jewish on the outside. Marranos of different degrees multiply within our ranks. Such victims of insincerity—as historical experience—can become tragic.... When one wants to become a Jew because of the 'situation,' not out of honesty, the result is conflict and misery. Jewishness cannot be feigned! There is no return to Judaism without repentance before God."[16]

In his last years Heschel spoke with a prophetic voice not only to American Jews but also to American Christians on two principal subjects: the civil rights movement and American military engagement in Vietnam. After he participated in the 1965 march on Selma under the leadership of Rev. Dr. Martin Luther King Jr., Heschel reflected that all too many American Jews active in the civil rights movement were motivated principally by secular political commitments. Heschel felt that the "Jewish religious institutions have again missed a great opportunity, namely, to interpret the civil-rights movement in terms of Judaism. The vast number of Jews participating actively in it are totally

---

15. "The Meaning of Repentance," in Abraham Joshua Heschel, *Moral Grandeur and Spiritual Audacity: Essays*, ed. Susannah Heschel (New York: Farrar, Straus and Giroux, 1996), 69.
16. Ibid., 70.

unaware of what the movement means in terms of the prophetic traditions."[17] On Vietnam and on modern warfare in general, he spoke not only to Jews and Christians but to all human beings in his lecture, "No Religion is an Island," delivered at his inauguration in 1966 as Harry Emerson Fosdick Visiting Professor at New York's Union Theological Seminary.

What is needed at this very moment is to mobilize all human beings for one great task, to achieve world peace.... Let us assume that the religions represent moral powers in the world. They could do something, but they are scarcely on speaking terms. The ecumenical movement has made some progress in human relations, but on the top level I don't see much progress. It is conceivable for states to get together and have a United Nations, but it is still inconceivable to have a United Religions. The question is, Why do we not see the writing on the wall? ... What we must do is to alarm the world.[18]

Prophets like Heschel, willing to "alarm the world," continue to call us to the critique of what is past, repentance for our sins and *tikkun olam*, the repair of the broken world in which we live.

Prophetic Faith, Repentance, and the Development of the Christian Tradition

The New Testament offers many examples of prophetic voices that criticize, revise, or call to repentance what has gone before in the tradition of Israel or even in the traditions of the first Jewish Christians. The very name by which we know the uniquely Christian scriptures, the New Testament, derives from a Christian reinterpretation of the prophet Jeremiah's hope for a new covenant to be struck between the LORD and Israel in the aftermath of the Babylonian Exile (Jer 31:31–34). Jesus and the New Testament writers, referring to this passage in Jeremiah, seem to have had something radically different in mind, and in this they departed from Jewish exegesis of the same text. In the Christian understanding of Jeremiah's new covenant, the New Testament writers

---

17. As quoted in Susannah Heschel, "Introduction," from ibid., xxiii–xxiv.
18. Ibid., 255–56.

imitate the style of Jesus as a prophet, or even as a rabbinical commentator on the Torah, revising the Law and sometimes even contradicting it. Ezekiel, Rabbi Jose ben Hanina, and Rashi, to cite only a few names in the Jewish tradition, have also made such prophetic critiques and revisions, as noted earlier. That this should happen in the New Testament is not surprising in historical terms, given the rabbinical formation of Paul and the nearly contemporary careers of the Gospel writers and the principal contributors to the Mishnah, most notably Yohanan ben Zakkai (d. 90 CE).

For Christians, Jesus is understood fully as much more than a prophet, but he *is* understood as a prophet and all four Gospels make this clear. Luke's Gospel symbolically associates with Jesus many of the wonders attributed to Elijah and Elisha in the First and Second Books of Kings.[19] John's Gospel narrates how Jesus encounters a Samaritan woman, who first thought of him as nothing but a thirsty Jew in search of water. She eventually recognizes to her chagrin something much more important about him when he discloses his knowledge of her complicated marital history: "'Sir, I see you are a prophet'" (Jn 4:19). Matthew's Gospel, in particular, preserves in its five great discourses of Jesus many traits of prophetic and rabbinic critique and revision of the Torah. Six times in the first chapter of the Sermon on the Mount Jesus contrasts his teaching on the Ten Commandments with what has gone before; like Ezekiel and Rashi, Jesus speaks on his own authority, an authority derived from God. "You have heard that it was said to those of ancient times.... But I say to you ..." (Mt 5:21–22).

Paul of Tarsus, not an immediate disciple of Jesus and even an enemy of the first Christians, whom he considered deviant Jews, narrates most succinctly in his letter to the Galatian Christian community, dated no later than 55 CE, how he went from a persecutor of those who followed Jesus to the most ardent witness to Jesus. Paul's account of how he changed is best understood as a prophetic call narrative, not unlike that of Jeremiah (Gal 1:13–18):

---

19. On the parallels between the stories of Elijah and Elisha and the story of Jesus in Luke's Gospel, see Fitzmyer, *The Gospel According to Luke (I–IX)*, 213–15.

You have heard, no doubt, of my earlier life in Judaism. I was violently persecuting the church of God and was trying to destroy it. I advanced in Judaism
beyond many among my people of the same age, for I was far more zealous for
the traditions of my ancestors. But when God, who had set me apart before I
was born and called me through his grace, was pleased to reveal his Son to [or
"in"] me, so that I might proclaim him among the Gentiles, I did not confer with
any human being, nor did I go up to Jerusalem to those who were already apostles before me, but I went away at once into Arabia, and afterwards I returned
to Damascus. Then after three years I did go up to Jerusalem to visit Cephas and
stay with him fifteen days.[20]

Note the insistence of Paul writing to the Galatians on the independence of his call from that of Cephas (Peter) and the other disciples
who had known Jesus in his lifetime. Like Ezekiel and Rashi, Paul took
an independent line, although he did admit, when later challenged
as to the authenticity of his proclamation to Gentiles of salvation by
faith apart from works of the Law, that he returned to Jerusalem for "a
private meeting with the acknowledged leaders" (Gal 2:2b). Paul the
prophet did this not because of some summons from headquarters but
"in response to a revelation" (Gal 2:2a) from God.

The prophet Paul felt emboldened by God to contradict the leaders of the Jerusalem community when they divided on the question of
whether Gentiles had first to convert to Judaism before they could become Christians. Emissaries from the Jerusalem church had evidently
disturbed the consciences of the Gentile Christian community in Galatia, urging them to be circumcised and adhere to Jewish dietary practice, implying in the process that Paul had not proclaimed the whole
Gospel to them. Paul, nothing if not irascible, struck back: "If anyone
proclaims a gospel contrary to what you have received, let that one be
accursed" (Gal 1:9). Paul even tells us how he took on Cephas (Peter),
who had earlier eaten with Gentiles but later, influenced by James, the
relative of Jesus and head of the Jerusalem church, had withdrawn
from such table-fellowship: "When Cephas came to Antioch, I opposed
him to his face, because he stood self-condemned" (Gal 2:11).

In the same letter Paul elaborates an extraordinary rereading of the

---

20. Note earlier translation in chapter 2, p. 63. For Jeremiah's prophetic call, see Jer 1:4–19.

story in Genesis about the two wives of Abraham, Sarah and Hagar, and their sons, Isaac and Ishmael. In the process of this rereading, Paul identifies those freed by Christ from observance of the Law with Sarah and her freeborn son, Isaac; those still bound to observe the Law he assimilates to the slave spouse of Abraham, Hagar, and her son, Ishmael (Gal 4:21–5:1). As the Hebrew Bible identifies Sarah and her son as the progenitors of the people of Israel and Hagar and her son as the progenitors of non-chosen peoples, most notably the Arabs of the Sinai peninsula (Gn 25:12–18), Paul's *midrash* or scholarly meditation on this narrative in Genesis runs directly against normative Jewish understanding of the story (Gn 21:8–21). Note that Paul is here rebuking and criticizing the teaching not of Jews but of his fellow Jewish Christians, most notably James, Peter, and John, an apostolic trio Paul calls, possibly with some irony, "pillars" of the Jerusalem church (Gal 2:9). Paul sums up the radical nature of his prophetic teaching by denying the relevance of any traditional barrier to first-class status in the church: "There is no longer Jew or Greek, there is no longer slave or free, there is no longer male and female; for all of you are one in Christ Jesus" (Gal 3:28). It has taken the Christian churches throughout the world a long time to receive fully this teaching of St. Paul's letter to the Galatians.

Although Ethiopia preserves a version of Judeo-Christianity[21] and certain nineteenth-century American-originated Christian groups have taken up some Jewish dietary restrictions,[22] most Christians today reject such practices. As to Paul's declaring the cessation of the distinction between slave and free, it must be admitted that slavery was taken for granted as a fact of economic and political life in the Roman era, as several other passages in the New Testament make clear, although Paul's letter to Philemon begins to offer seeds for a justification of abolition.[23] Abolitionism in some sense began in sixteenth-century

21. For an introduction to Judeo-Christianity in Ethiopia, see Adrian Hastings, *The Church in Africa 1450–1950* (Oxford: Clarendon Press, 1994), 11–17.

22. Seventh-day Adventists are connected with the promotion of vegetarianism, and they popularized breakfast cereals first in the nineteenth century. See *Seventh-day Adventist Church Manual*, 173, available at www.sda.org.

23. The Epistles to the Ephesians (6:5–9) and Colossians (3:22–4:1) take for granted the continuance of slavery in the Christian community. But the Epistle to Philemon (15–16) hints at something approaching emancipation.

Spanish America with the change in the thought of Bartolomé de las Casas, who had once encouraged African slave labor in preference to the enslavement of Native Americans. He finally opposed all forms of slavery.[24] Total opposition to slavery in any form arose in European Pietist and Quaker circles in the late eighteenth century, but it only burst into flame in the Americas in the nineteenth century.[25] The redoubtable Sojourner Truth (ca. 1797–1883), once a slave herself, took up the prophetic mantle not only for an end to slavery but also for the rights of women.[26]

If the reception of Paul's teaching on the abolition of the distinction between slave and free took a long time to be accepted among Christians, his assertion that in Christ Jesus "there is no longer male and female" has, like Thursday's child in the nursery rhyme, "far to go." Although most churches in the Reformation traditions do ordain women to all ranks of the ministry, Catholicism in all its branches and most of the Christian churches of the East do not. Will these latter churches ever change their discipline? Only time will tell.

But this much must be noted. The Christian tradition in all its forms celebrates a vast company of saintly women who have exercised the prophetic charism in ways that are quite extraordinary. This Christian tradition, at least partly derived from the Hebrew Bible's accounts of prophets like Miriam (Ex 15:20), Deborah (Jgs 4:4), and Huldah (2 Kgs 22:14, 2 Chr 34:22), starts with the prophetic words of Elizabeth and Mary and the unspecified prophecy of the widow Anna in the infancy narrative of Luke (Lk 1:41–55, 2:36). In the history of Christianity, and especially in the Catholic tradition, women saints have often spoken out prophetically. They have criticized and advised popes and have stood up, when necessary, to many other male ecclesiastics. Hildegard of Bingen in the twelfth century, Catherine of Siena in the fourteenth century,

24. See Juan Comas, "Historical Reality and the Detractors of Father Las Casas," in *Bartolomé de las Casas in History: Towards an Understanding of the Man and His Work*, ed. Juan Friede and Benjamin Keen (DeKalb: Northern Illinois University Press, 1971), 487–539.

25. See Hastings, *The Church in Africa*, esp. 182–88. See also Lamin Sanneh, *Abolitionists Abroad: American Blacks and the Making of Modern West Africa* (Cambridge, Mass: Harvard University Press, 1999), esp. 22–65.

26. See Margaret Washington, *Sojourner Truth's America* (Urbana: University of Illinois Press, 2009).

and Teresa of Avila in the sixteenth century all exercised considerable influence on the church and on churchmen in their respective times and places. Along with the late nineteenth-century Carmelite mystic, Thérèse of Lisieux, a less public figure in her lifetime, they have been officially recognized as doctors of the church in recent years.[27] They continue to exercise great influence in modern times as well, when the social subordination of women is gradually being reversed.

On October 17, 2010, Pope Benedict XVI canonized Mary MacKillop (d. 1909), the Australian co-founder of a congregation of religious sisters. Her determination from her earliest years to educate poor children in the isolated outback of Australia, an area hitherto educationally disadvantaged, led her to found the Sisters of Saint Joseph of the Sacred Heart, a congregation of religious women dedicated to that project. The Irish Franciscan Bishop of Adelaide, Laurence Bonaventure Sheil, a notoriously bad administrator frequently absent from his diocese, tried to wrest the Sisters' schools away from their control and in the process excommunicated Mary MacKillop for a period of five months because she had resisted his encroachment on her schools. That excommunication was only rescinded on Sheil's deathbed in 1872.[28] The excommunication was also partly motivated as revenge for the fact that some of Mary MacKillop's Sisters, as well as the co-founder of her congregation, the Australian priest Julian Tenison Woods, had exposed an Irish priest in Australia who was a sexual predator. The exposure of the Irish priest who was involved in the crime caused Irish priests in Australia who were the criminal's friends to slander Mary MacKillop, falsely accusing her of having a drinking problem, insinuating as well that she was mismanaging the affairs of her congregation.[29] Extraor-

27. On Hildegard of Bingen's prophetic life, see her *Scivias*, trans. Mother Columba Hart and Jane Bishop (New York: Paulist Press, 1990); on Catherine of Siena's outspoken career, see Mary Catherine Hilkert, *Speaking with Authority: Catherine of Siena and the Voices of Women Today* (New York: Paulist Press, 2001); on Teresa of Avila, see her autobiography, *The Life of Teresa of Jesus: the Autobiography of Teresa of Avila*, ed. and trans. E. Allison Peers (New York: Image Books, 1991).

28. See Kathleen Jones, *Women Saints: Lives of Faith and Courage* (Maryknoll, N.Y.: Orbis, 1999), 250–55.

29. For a clarification on the involvement of some of St. Mary MacKillop's fellow Josephites, along with her co-founder, Fr. Julian Tenison Woods, in the exposure of this priest, and the only indirect connection of this matter with the excommunication of MacKillop, see the October 15, 2010, interview on Vatican Radio with the Australian Josephite sister who was the promoter of MacKil-

dinary women like MacKillop and many others exemplify what Peter, quoting the prophet Joel, proclaimed in his sermon on the day of Pentecost: "In the last days it will be, God declares, that I will pour out my Spirit upon all flesh, and your sons and your daughters will prophesy" (Acts 2:17a).

In the United States in the twentieth century, one of the greatest prophets in the Christian tradition was Dorothy Day (1897–1980). Growing up in a Protestant family of modest means, she experienced strong religious attraction, even as a teenager, to things Catholic. During her two years as an undergraduate at the University of Illinois, however, she began to identify herself more dramatically with radical politics. She left college and embarked on a somewhat unconventional, even bohemian young adulthood, finding employment as a journalist popularizing the plight of the urban poor, socialists, anarchists, and opponents of American entry into World War I. Just after her twentieth birthday in 1917 she was arrested for participating in a demonstration outside the White House for women's suffrage. This led to the first of several short periods of her life spent in jail, times that shaped her identification with outcasts. She became pregnant by a fellow journalist with whom she had a brief affair in 1918 but aborted the fetus. She married another man in 1920 and traveled with him in Europe but that relationship also proved to be short-lived, ending in divorce.

Day published an autobiographical novel in 1924 and with the proceeds bought a small cottage on Staten Island in New York Harbor where she lived from 1925 on with a fellow anarchist whose theoretical commitments precluded anything so bourgeois as marriage. Attracted to Catholicism for some time already, in March 1927 Day gave birth to a daughter whom she named Tamar Teresa; Day had Tamar baptized four months after her birth and she herself was also baptized a Catholic shortly afterwards, an event that ended her relationship with her common-law husband. Day found this separation very painful. The

lop's cause, Maria Casey, RSJ. See "'Whistleblower' label for St. Mary MacKillop called inaccurate and wrong," October 18, 2010, available at www.catholicnewsagency.com. The fact remains, however, that the excommunication of MacKillop resulted from the animus of those Irish priests against her co-founder and sisters under her administrative direction.

stabilization of her faith life in Catholicism, however, did not entail any compromise of her radical political views. Day's radical political and social views seemed strange to many American Catholics during her lifetime; her ardent Catholicism seemed equally strange to Day's fellow American radicals.

In 1932 Day first met an itinerant French Catholic utopian named Peter Maurin, a man twenty years her senior. Day maintained that the most important phase of her life and the development of her ideas dated from that encounter. On May Day 1933, Day and Maurin sold the first edition of their monthly newsletter, *The Catholic Worker,* "one cent a copy"—its price even to the present day. Shortly afterwards they began the first Catholic Worker house of hospitality for the homeless and hungry, and she lived the rest of her life in such settings.

Day's radical commitments to social justice, especially as it was outlined in papal social teaching after 1891, the year of Pope Leo XIII's encyclical letter *Rerum Novarum,* finally led to conflict in 1949 between Day and the archbishop of New York at that time, Cardinal Francis Spellman. When the cemetery workers of the archdiocese went on strike for better hours and compensation, Spellman "volunteered" his major seminarians to dig graves in their stead, thus breaking the strike. Day and other members of the Catholic Worker community picketed the cemeteries and even the cardinal's residence while Spellman raged about communists having infiltrated the gravediggers' union.[30] Two years later, Spellman, still fuming, delegated his vicar general, Monsignor Edward Gaffney, to inform Day and the Catholic Worker community that they could not use the word "Catholic" in their title. They asked if the Catholic War Veterans would also have to give up that adjective; the archdiocese did not pursue the issue any further.[31] By a curious irony, Spellman's second successor as archbishop of New York, Cardinal John O'Connor, a former navy chaplain and auxiliary bishop for the Military Vicariate in the United States, introduced in Rome the cause for the canonization of Dorothy Day, in the year 2000, shortly be-

30. For a detailed analysis of this series of events, see David L. Gregory, "Dorothy Day, Workers' Rights and Catholic Authenticity," *Fordham Urban Law Journal* 26 (1999): 1371–92.

31. See William D. Miller, *Dorothy Day: A Biography* (New York: Harper, 1982), 427–28.

fore O'Connor's own death. Even O'Connor had to admit, however, that Day had reservations about such honors: "Don't trivialize me by trying to make me a saint."[32]

Three years after the death of Peter Maurin, Day published in 1952 an autobiography that expressed repentance for her past but also explained the prophetic style of life she had come to embrace over the years, especially as she and Maurin founded their monthly newsletter and the first of their houses of hospitality. Somewhat in the style of Maurin's "easy essays," prose-poems outlining his Catholic social ideals, Day ended her autobiography with what she called a "Postscript," not only an ending for her autobiography but also a summation of her prophetic life, and the lives as well of the band of prophets who gathered around her and Peter Maurin:

We were just sitting there talking when Peter Maurin came in.

We were just sitting there talking when lines of people began to form, saying, "We need bread." We could not say, "Go, be thou filled." If there were six small loaves and a few fishes, we had to divide them. There was always bread.

We were just sitting there talking and people moved in on us. Let those who can take it, take it. Some moved out and that made room for more. And somehow the walls expanded.

We were just sitting there talking and someone said, "Let's all go live on a farm."

It was as casual as all that, I often think. It just came about. It just happened.

I found myself, a barren woman, the joyful mother of children. It is not easy always to be joyful, to keep in mind the duty of delight.

The most significant thing about *The Catholic Worker* is poverty, some say.

The most significant thing is community, others say. We are not alone any more.

But the final word is love. At times it has been, in the words of Father Zossima, a harsh and dreadful thing, and our very faith in love has been tried through fire.

32. See Cardinal John O'Connor, "Dorothy Day's Sainthood Cause Begins," *Catholic New York*, March 16, 2000, available at www.catholicworker.org/dorothyday/canonizationtext.cfm?Number=82. Cardinal O'Connor in his column seemed more interested in the canonization of Dorothy Day because of her repentance for the abortion she had once procured: "To be sure," he wrote, "her life is a model for all in the third millennium, but especially for women who have had or are considering abortions."

We cannot love God unless we love each other, and to love we must know each other. We know Him in the breaking of bread, and we know each other in the breaking of bread, and we are not alone any more. Heaven is a banquet and life is a banquet, too, even with a crust, where there is companionship.

We have all known the long loneliness and we have learned that the only solution is love and that loves comes with community.

It all happened while we sat there talking, and it is still going on.[33]

In the context of prophetic women like Mary MacKillop and Dorothy Day, I am reminded of the Chinese proverb variously ascribed both to Confucius and Mao Zedong: "Women hold up half the sky." They certainly hold up half, and perhaps a great deal more than half the Catholic sky. Both MacKillop and Day, women outside the male clerical hierarchy of Catholicism, called for repentance, a change of heart, from that religious establishment. Change of heart is a gradual matter, and the innovations in church attitudes urged by MacKillop and Day have, in some instances, come to pass. Bishops the world over have become extremely cautious about the whole problematic of sexual abuse of minors by church personnel. The American hierarchy is much less prone today than it was several decades ago to give unthinking support to American military engagements. "It is by little and by little that we are saved," Dorothy Day often said, words she sometimes attributed to St. Paul, but no one has been able to trace their source.[34] The prophets who have lived in our midst have alerted all of us to the imperative demand for change and development in our lives of faith.

Prophetic Faith, Repentance, and the Development of the Muslim Tradition

The Qur'an itself and the whole prophetic career of Muhammad (610–32) can be construed as a critique of and a repentance for much of what had gone before in the traditions of the Arabs, and also, but to a lesser extent,

---

33. Dorothy Day, *The Long Loneliness* (New York: Harper, 1952), 285–86.
34. On this usage by Dorothy Day, see the preface by Robert Ellsberg to *By Little and By Little: The Selected Writings of Dorothy Day*, ed. Robert Ellsberg (New York: Alfred A. Knopf, 1983) reprinted as *Dorothy Day: Selected Writings*, ed. Robert Ellsberg (Maryknoll, N.Y.: Orbis Books, 1992), xiii.

what had gone before in the traditions of Judaism and Christianity as these faith traditions were known among the Arabs of the seventh century. *Tawba*, repentance, is a central element in the faith of Muslims. Can it also be said to characterize the person of Muhammad? The later development in the Muslim tradition of the doctrine of Muhammad's impeccability or immunity from sin (*'isma'*)[35] has tended to obscure the reality of the repentance and repeated revision that characterized his prophetic life, repentance, and revision very vividly chronicled in the first histories of that era. The attribution of impeccability to Muhammad—and to the Twelve Imams in the Shi'ite tradition, as well—may owe some of its origin to a similar theme enunciated about Jesus in the New Testament, where he is described as "a high priest ....who in every respect has been tested as we are, yet without sin" (Heb 4:15). The apparent similarities between Jesus and Muhammad, however, are outweighed by the major dissimilarities. According to Wilfred Cantwell Smith, "Muhammad plays in the Islamic scheme the role played in the Christian system by St. Paul or St. Peter; namely, that of an apostle who proclaims among men God's gift to them, which in the Islamic case is the scripture."[36]

Growing up in the mercantile environment of the Meccan *entrepôt* that connected the Persian, Byzantine, and Ethiopian worlds, Muhammad had identified himself, even before he received revelation, with a small moral elite, the Confederacy of the Virtuous. These confederates were Meccan merchants who stood up for the rights of non-Meccan merchants who had previously suffered at the hands of some of the less scrupulous Meccan entrepreneurs. "They bound themselves by a solemn agreement," the early chronicler Ibn Ishaq (d. ca. 767) writes of this confederacy. "If they found anyone, either a native of Mecca or an outsider, had been wronged they would take his part against the aggressor and see that the stolen property was restored to him."[37] Even before Muhammad received revelation, the confederates were a community of repentance for past economic crimes, a community bent on holding the Meccan trading community to higher standards of mercan-

---

35. See W. Madelung and E. Tyan, "'Isma,'" *EI2*, 4:182b–184a.
36. Wilfred Cantwell Smith, *The Faith of Other Men* (New York: New American Library, 1965), 61.
37. Ibn Ishaq, *The Life of Muhammad*, 57.

tile decency than what had previously prevailed in pagan Arab trading communities.[38]

At least one early Meccan passage in the Qur'an refers to an event in Muhammad's own life in which he seems to have experienced a divine call to repentance: *Surat 'abasa* ("He frowned," Qur'an 80). The title ascribed to the sura derives from the first word in the opening passage, which begins with a brief narrative of and commentary on an event in the Prophet's career as a preacher in Mecca. A man blind from birth, usually identified as 'Abd Allah ibn Umm Maktum, had approached Muhammad in Mecca just when the Prophet was engaged in earnest conversation with an influential Meccan pagan with whom Muhammad was trying to share his prophetic message (Qur'an 80:1–10):

> He [the Prophet] frowned and turned away
> because the blind man approached him.
> But what would convince you [Prophet] that he [the blind man] might
>   grow in purity
> or even heed the Reminder [the Qur'an] to his benefit!
> As for the type who is self-sufficient—
>   to someone like that you [the Prophet] pay attention!
>   It is no concern of yours that he [the self-sufficient one] does not
>   grow in purity.
>   But for the [blind] man who came to you making an effort
>   and filled with reverential fear,
>   you [the Prophet] prove oblivious of him.

In a fourteenth-century commentary the Syrian Qur'an exegete, Ibn Kathir, expands the last verse in that passage in such a way as to underline the egalitarianism of the Quranic message and its implicit rebuke of the Prophet: "Here God commands his Messenger not to single out anyone with the warning. Rather he should equally warn the noble and the weak, the poor and the rich, the master and the slave, the men and the women, the young and the old. Then God will guide whomever he chooses to a path that is straight."[39]

---

38. W. Montgomery Watt, *Muhammad at Mecca* (Oxford: Clarendon, 1953), 6–7 and 13–16.
39. See *Tafsir Ibn Kathir* to Qur'an 80:10 available online at www.qtafsir.com. I have slightly revised the English translation available on the website.

Muhammad was attracted to the faith traditions of Jews and Christians, but these traditions were only partially represented or understood in Mecca and Medina of the early seventh century. Muhammad identified himself more clearly with *hunafa'* (singular, *hanif*), a term that means something like "monotheistic Arabs."[40] This term designates non-Jewish and non-Christian monotheists, upholders of higher moral principles in Mecca antecedent to the prophetic call of Muhammad. It would seem that even before he experienced the first revelation Muhammad had rejected the polytheistic worship of Mecca centered on the Ka'ba. This great cubic shrine is said in the Qur'an to have originated many centuries earlier as a place of worship dedicated by Ibrahim (Abraham) and his son Isma'il (Ishmael) to the worship of one God alone (Qur'an 2:125–29). Over the centuries between Ibrahim and Muhammad, however, the Ka'ba had gradually accommodated every cult in Arabia, possibly as a way of welcoming trade from any quarter of the peninsula. A central goal of Muhammad's prophetic career, achieved two years before his death, was the purification of the idolatrous Ka'ba and its rededication to the worship of God alone. A return to monotheism for the Ka'ba would also ideally entail a return to upright behavior by those who worshiped there, Meccan and non-Meccan alike.

When Muhammad began to share the revelations he was receiving with the Meccan public after the year 613, some of his fellow citizens immediately perceived the monotheistic drift of his preaching as a challenge to the Ka'ba and its plural divinities. As the years of his Meccan preaching continued Muhammad experienced a great deal of resistance by the devotees of various divinities worshiped not only in Mecca but also in some other nearby cultic centers. Three goddesses, al-Lat and al-'Uzza who were venerated in al-Ta'if and Nakhla near Mecca, as well as Manat, another goddess venerated along the route between Mecca and Medina, exercised a particularly strong attraction for many of Muhammad's Arab contemporaries.[41] Referred to as the "daughters of God" or as "the high-flying cranes," these goddesses proved a major distraction from genuine monotheism for the Meccans and their

40. See Andrae, *Mohammed*, 108–11. See also Excursus C in Watt, *Muhammad at Mecca*, 162–64.
41. See *Muhammad at Mecca*, 103–4.

neighbors. It would seem, from the earliest histories of Muhammad's life, that Muhammad himself fell into that distraction or temptation, at least briefly, possibly because of pressure exerted on him by prominent members of his own tribe, the Quraysh. These proponents of compromise may have urged Muhammad not to embrace total polytheism but rather a more diffuse monotheism, with the possibility of subordinate devotion to these three popular goddesses within the parameters of a more general monotheism. Such compromise might assure the safety and even survival of Muhammad's persecuted religious community in Mecca. The inclusion of these three goddesses as legitimate but secondary celestial powers might make life easier for Muhammad and his followers.

Most Muslim commentary on the Qur'an written in the last two centuries, composed under the influence of the aforementioned doctrine of the Prophet's impeccability, has tended to deny that this lapse or any other ever occurred in the Prophet's lifetime.[42] But the earliest historical narratives of the Prophet's lifetime prove more frank. Ibn Ishaq provides us with an important early narrative, dating from the eighth century, noting that this incident took place shortly after the Prophet had sent some of his disciples to Ethiopia to protect them from the hostility of their polytheistic fellow Meccans. Ibn Ishaq hints at a very natural desire on Muhammad's part to seek compromise with the Meccan guardians of official polytheism. The repetitiousness of Ibn Ishaq's style suggests the author's desire to explain away an embarrassing, albeit temporary lapse:

Now the apostle [Muhammad] was anxious for the welfare of his people, wishing to attract them as far as he could. It has been mentioned that he longed for a way to attract them.... When the apostle saw that his people [the pagan Quraysh] turned their backs on him and he was pained by their estrangement from what he brought them from God he longed that there should come to him from God a message that would reconcile his people to him. Because of his love for his people and his anxiety over them it would delight him if the obstacle that made his path so difficult could be removed; so that he meditated on the project and longed for it and it was dear to him. Then God sent down [the Qura-

42. See Shahab Ahmed, "Satanic Verses," EQ.

nic verses] "By the star when it sets, your comrade errs not and is not deceived, he speaks not from his own desire [Qur'an 53:1–3]," and when he reached [God's] words "Have you thought of al-Lat and al-'Uzza and Manat the third, the other [Qur'an 53:19–20]," Satan, when he [Muhammad] was meditating upon it, and desiring to bring it (sc. reconciliation) to his people, put upon his [Muhammad's] tongue "these are the Gharaniq [cranes] whose intercession is approved." When Quraysh heard that, they were delighted and greatly pleased at the way in which he spoke of their gods and they listened to him; while the believers were holding that what their prophet brought them from their Lord was true, not suspecting a mistake or a vain desire or a slip, and when he [Muhammad] reached the prostration [mentioned in Qur'an 53:62] and the end of the Sura in which he prostrated himself the Muslims prostrated themselves when their prophet prostrated confirming what he brought and obeying his command, and the polytheists of Quraysh and others who were in the mosque believer and unbeliever prostrated.... Then the people dispersed and Quraysh went out, delighted at what had been said about their gods, saying, "Muhammad has spoken of our gods in splendid fashion. He alleged in what he read that they are exalted Gharaniq whose intercession is approved."[43]

The embarrassment felt by many modern Muslims about this incident in the Prophet's life need not be felt if the words of Abu Bakr, the first caliph of Muhammad, uttered on the day of Muhammad's death, were taken seriously: "O men, if anyone worships Muhammad, Muhammad is dead; if anyone worships God, God is alive, immortal."[44] Immediately thereafter, in the text of Ibn Ishaq, Abu Bakr quotes the words of a late-revealed Quranic passage: "Muhammad is only a messenger; messengers have died before him" (Qur'an 3:144). Prophets had died as well, and while they lived they often had to repent and revise.

The brief verses about the "daughters of God" that Muhammad received and construed at first to be genuine divine revelation suggested a slight modification of absolute monotheism. Whatever hope for allegiance Muhammad had been tempted to expect from the Quraysh devotees of these "daughters of God" were soon disappointed and Muhammad recognized the serious mistake into which he had fallen. These three verses about the exalted cranes and their intercession emanat-

43. Ibn Ishaq, *Life*, 165–66.
44. Ibid., 683.

ed from Satan and these verses were abrogated by God, with genuine revelation substituted for them: "They are only names which you have called them, you and your ancestors: God has not sent down anything authorizing this" (Qur'an 53:23a).

The abrogation (*naskh*) of these verses in the Qur'an and the substitution of other verses for that which was abrogated may be taken as an example, within the revelation Muhammad experienced over a period of twenty-two years, of divine critique and revision, and therefore prophetic repentance, critique, and revision of what has gone before.[45] Not unlike figures in the prophetic history of Israel like Isaiah and Jeremiah who needed purification by God (Is 6:5–7, Jer 1:6–7) or the often faithless disciples of Jesus who became his apostles, Muhammad was led by God to a clearer and purer understanding of the implications of his core experience of the oneness of God. The Qur'an provides many examples of Muhammad's receiving revisions of revelations previously communicated, each revision serving to deepen Muhammad's understanding of God's self-disclosure. In the tradition of Quranic scholarship the understanding of these revisions has been called "the science of the abrogating and the abrogated" (*'ilm al-nasikh wa'l-mansukh*).[46] The subject of this science bears a family relationship, however distant, to the radical revisions both Ezekiel and Jesus made to the Ten Commandments.

In the later history of Islam, some of the great mystics took on themselves the unenviable task of revising accepted interpretations of the Qur'an. Al-Husayn ibn Mansur al-Hallaj, the great Muslim mystic of tenth-century Baghdad, courted danger with the guardians of orthopraxy in his time and place when he reinterpreted the story of Iblis, the angel who in Quranic tradition refused to bow down at God's command before Adam. The Qur'an summarizes the rebellion of Iblis with the angel's defiant words about the inferiority of Adam to an angel: "I am bet-

---

45. In referring to a certain parallelism between divine critique and revision and prophetic critique and revision I am influenced by the thought of the late Prof. Fazlur Rahman (1919–88) who noted that most medieval Muslim thinkers "lacked the intellectual capacity to say both that the Qur'an is entirely the Word of God and, in an ordinary sense, also entirely the word of Muhammad." See his seminal work, *Islam*, 2nd ed. (Chicago: University of Chicago Press, 1979), 31.

46. See John Burton, "Naskh," in *EI2*, 7:1009b–1012a.

ter than he: You created me from fire and him from clay" (Qur'an 7:12). Most Qur'an interpreters consider Iblis the quintessential fallen angel. Al-Hallaj and some other Muslim mystics quixotically looked on Iblis as the greatest monotheist of them all, one who endures God's wrath rather than bow down before anything less than God. Al-Hallaj imagines a dialogue between the disobedient angel and God: "[Iblis] was told: 'Bow down!' [Iblis] said '[to] no other!' [Iblis] was asked, 'Even if you receive my curse?' He said, 'It does not matter. I have no way to an other-than-you. I am an abject lover.'"[47] It was not for nothing that al-Hallaj, the author of these daring words, was executed—some say crucified—in Baghdad in the year 922.[48]

Some latter-day revisers of the Qur'an have also suffered a martyr's fate not unlike that of al-Hallaj. The Sudanese thinker Mahmud Muhammad TaHa (1909–85) distinguished between a Meccan and a Medinan message of Islam. The Meccan message of Islam Muhammad received from God between 610 and 622 when he had no political role. The Medinan message of Islam Muhammad received during the last decade of his life when he found himself exiled from Mecca and catapulted into power over a fractious community faced with military, political, and economic challenges. TaHa maintained that many of the Medinan passages in the Qur'an, and especially the regulations they enshrine for male-female relations, criminal law, and other civil matters, need to be understood in their historical setting and do not represent the most basic message of Islam first received in Mecca.

Only the Meccan message continues to be of enduring religious importance, according to TaHa. Somewhat counter-intuitively TaHa refers to Medinan Islam as the first message of Islam and Meccan Islam as the second message of Islam, the one that needs emphasis today:

The Meccan and Medinese texts differ, not because of the time and place of their revelation, but essentially because of the audience to whom they are ad-

---

47. This dialogue between God and Iblis composed by al-Hallaj is ably translated by Michael Sells of the University of Chicago as part of "The TaSin of Before-Time and Ambiguity in the Understanding of Understanding Concerning the Validity of Proclamations with Inversion of Meanings," in *Early Islamic Mysticism* (ed. Sells), 274.

48. The master work on al-Hallaj is Louis Massignon, *The Passion of al-Hallaj: Mystic and Martyr of Islam*, trans. Herbert Mason (Princeton, N.J.: Princeton University Press, 1982).

dressed. The phrase "O believers" addresses a particular nation, while "O mankind" speaks to all people. The verses "You have received a messenger from amongst yourselves who is deeply distressed by your suffering, cares for you, and he is tender and merciful to the believers" ([Qur'an] 9:128) in contrast to the verse "God is truly tender and merciful upon mankind" ([Qur'an] 2:143) demonstrates the different audiences to which the Qur'an speaks.... The hypocrites were mentioned for the first time in Medina, during the ten years of revelation, but never during the Meccan thirteen years of revelation, because there were no hypocrites in Mecca. People were either believers or unbelievers in Mecca, since there was no compulsion, the verses of persuasion prevailed.... After the migration to Medina, and the abrogation of the verses of peaceful persuasion, the verses of compulsion by the sword prevailed.... Under this threat of violence some people had to seek refuge by concealing one view and declaring another, thereby introducing hypocrisy into the Islamic community.[49]

TaHa denied that *jihad*, slavery, capitalism, male-female inequality, polygamy, divorce, female veiling, and male-female segregation were integral elements of "original precept[s] in Islam."[50] Alas, TaHa was put to death in 1985 for his opposition to the rigorist enforcement of Islamic law in the late part of the Numayri (Nimeiri) dictatorial regime in Sudan.

The tragic ending of TaHa's life has not discouraged his disciples—most notably 'Abdullahi Ahmed An-Na'im of Emory University—and many other prominent reformist and modernizing scholars in the contemporary Muslim world, about whose prophetic inner critique of Islam we hear too little in the United States. These reformist scholars, like TaHa, have remained within the faith tradition of Islam but have ventured to raise critical voices, voices that I would characterize as prophetic. Like the prophet Muhammad, too many of these modern Muslim scholars have been driven into *hijra*, exile from their homelands. I hope, however, that they or their disciples will return someday to their homelands on *yawm al-fath*, the day of victory.

49. *The Second Message of Islam*, ed. and trans. Abdullahi Ahmed an-Na'im (Syracuse, N.Y.: Syracuse University Press, 1987), 125–26.
    50. Ibid., 132–45.

Repentance, Self-Criticism, and Developing Faith

What Pope John Paul II and the seven prelates of the Roman Curia did in the liturgy for the First Sunday of Lent in the year 2000 was a frank admission that sinful human action has all too often distorted the faith of the church, its fidelity to God and to Christ. Their action might be construed as a response to a prophetic critique of the church; their response became itself prophetic, human words delivered on God's behalf to all of us who are Christians, indeed, to all of us who try to live faithful lives in any monotheistic tradition. Sometimes we sinfully betray our faith, we betray our God, and we need to repent.

How far can a faith tradition go in its repentance, its willingness to engage in self-criticism? Is there a limit beyond which a people of faith cannot go without renouncing one form of faith and embracing another—or embracing no form of faith whatsoever? One of the most radical self-criticisms of Judaism developed into Christianity. So radical was the criticism as to give birth to a separate community and the development of something utterly new, although the parting of the Jewish and Jewish-Christian communities was probably not complete until the end of the fourth century CE.[51] Rabbinic Judaism also criticized the tradition enshrined in the Hebrew Bible, especially the priestly elements in the Torah, but continued within the tradition of Israel right down to the present day.[52]

Precisely by their rejection of the Oral Law and their total commitment in faith to Jesus as much more than a teacher, Christians eventually departed from the ranks of Judaism. Centered not on the Law of Moses but on an inner Law enfleshed in the person of Jesus, Christians rely in faith on the saving fidelity of Jesus to effect their reconciliation

51. On this subject, see several of the essays in *The Ways That Never Parted: Jews and Christians in Late Antiquity and the Early Middle Ages*, ed. Adam H. Becker and Annette Yoshiko Reed (Minneapolis, Minn.: Fortress Press, 2007).

52. The late Jewish scholar Alan Segal (d. 2011) described rabbinic Judaism "as an unacknowledged new religion, a later offshoot of Israelite religion that formulated its principles after Christianity had already gone its own way. And rabbinic Judaism defined itself in conscious opposition to the sectarian battles and dogmatism that had characterized the time of that separation." See "The Jewish Tradition," in *World Religions: Western Traditions*, ed. Willard G. Oxtoby (Oxford: Oxford University Press, 1996), 59.

with God. That fidelity of Jesus is made accessible to Christians by faith and baptism into the dying and rising of Jesus and the gift of God's Spirit that creates the church. Any offshoot of Christianity that compromises this graced identification of the Christian with Jesus, for instance, by rejecting the concreteness of the historical Jesus, as did Marcion and the Gnostics of the second century CE, ceases to be Christian.

Islam began principally as a critique of Arab paganism, theological and moral. Rejecting plurality in God, Muhammad and the first Muslims also rejected divisive plurality in the human race, calling all people to acknowledge their unity and the moral obligations this unity entails as the less than perfect reflection of God's absolute unicity. Muhammad's exemplarity—the path (*sunna*) he trod in his prophetic life—offers men and women of faith a way to come close to the one and only God of creation. Those who have departed from the unique Word of God that is the Qur'an and have wandered from the path of practice taken by Muhammad cease to be counted as Muslims by themselves or by anyone else, as is obvious in the case of such distant offshoots of the Shi'i tradition in nineteenth-century Iran as the Babis and the Baha'is.[53]

There are limits to the critique of faith traditions. Beyond a certain frontier the critic is entering into a new homeland of faith, perhaps, or is wandering into a limbo of unfaith. St. Vincent of Lérins in the fifth century first sketched the outlines of what can be seen as legitimate development of a faith tradition—development that does not distort the core of the tradition but that may involve what I have called prophetic critique of the tradition. Needless to say, he was writing about the Christian tradition of faith, but I think his words can shed light on the faith traditions of Jews and Muslims as well.

The religion of souls should follow the law of the development of bodies. Though bodies develop and unfold their component parts with the passing of the years, they always remain what they were. There is a great difference between the flower of childhood and the maturity of age, but those who become

---

53. On the Babis, see Alessandro Bausanit, "Bab" and "Babis" in *EI2*, I:833a–835b and 846b–847b. On the Baha'is, see Alessandro Bausani, "Baha' Allah and "Baha'is" also in *EI2*, I:911a–912a and 915b–918b.

old are the very same people who were once young. Though the condition and appearance of one and the same individual may change, it is one and the same nature, one and the same person.[54]

A great English writer and theologian of the nineteenth century, John Henry Newman, saw in the development of doctrine, not only in a religious or theological setting, the possibility, at least, of a healthily organic growth of great ideas. Vincent of Lérins envisioned the development of doctrine through the model of the development of a human body between childhood and maturity. Newman's imagery of the development of ideas also compared that process to the way a tiny stream develops into a mighty river:

It is indeed sometimes said that the stream is clearest near the spring. Whatever use may fairly be made of this image, it does not apply to the history of a philosophy or belief, which on the contrary is more equable, and purer, and stronger, when its bed has become deep, and broad, and full. It necessarily rises out of an existing state of things, and for a time savours of the soil. Its vital element needs disengaging from what is foreign and temporary, and is employed in efforts after freedom which become more vigorous and hopeful as its years increase. Its beginnings are no measure of its capabilities, nor of its scope. At first no one knows what it is, or what it is worth. It remains perhaps for a time quiescent; it tries, as it were, its limbs, and proves the ground under it, and feels its way. From time to time it makes essays which fail, and are in consequence abandoned. It seems in suspense which way to go; it wavers, and at length strikes out in one definite direction. In time it enters upon strange territory; points of controversy alter their bearing; parties rise and fall around it; dangers and hopes appear in new relations; and old principles reappear under new forms. It changes with them in order to remain the same.[55]

The development of an idea is a gradual, historical process, and Newman recognized that with this earthbound, riverine imagery. Looking at how the faith traditions of Judaism and Christianity have developed over many centuries, Newman cited within the Jewish and Christian scriptures the contributions made by the cumulative writings of pro-

54. *Commonitorium*, available at www.documentacatholicaomnia.eu.
55. John Henry Cardinal Newman, *An Essay on the Development of Christian Doctrine* (London: Longmans, Green, 1909), 40.

phetic and wisdom figures, constantly reinterpreted by later figures in those same traditions:

> The prophetic revelation is ... a process of development: the earlier prophecies are pregnant texts out of which the succeeding announcements grow; they are types. It is not that first one truth is told, then another; but the whole truth or large portions of it are told at once, yet only in their rudiments, or in miniature, and they are expanded and finished in their parts, as the course of revelation proceeds.... The books of Wisdom and Ecclesiasticus are developments of the writings of the Prophets, expressed or elicited by means of current ideas in the Greek philosophy, and ultimately adopted and ratified by the Apostle in his Epistle to the Hebrews.[56]

Jews may experience more than a little difficulty in accepting that the charism of prophecy continues in the writing of the New Testament. Jews and Christians both will experience difficulty in the Muslim claim that the prophetic charism continued as well into the era of Quranic revelation. Jews, Christians, and Muslims have all found it difficult to see the prophetic charism continuing down to the present day, well beyond the time of scriptural canonization. Recognizing the continuation of prophecy right up the present, however, may be at least one key to understanding of what is most important—what is purest in its development—in the Jewish, Christian, and Muslim traditions of faith.

There are vast possibilities within each of these monotheistic traditions for faithful and legitimate critique, faithful and legitimate development and change. The history of these traditions gives us ample evidence that such change has happened; it also gives us hope that such change can happen again. Repentance—*teshuva* in the Jewish tradition, *metanoia* in the Christian tradition, *tawba* in the Muslim tradition—has occurred over and over again. Prophetic voices outside and after the definition of respective scriptural canons have alerted the faithful to changing circumstances, new perspectives, and further challenges. The living nature of the faith traditions of Jews, Christians, and Muslims demands such changes. Newman summed up the possi-

---

56. Ibid., 64–65. Many scholars in the nineteenth century still continued to refer to the Epistle to the Hebrews as a work authored by St. Paul "the Apostle."

bility of such development pithily and realistically: "In a higher world it is otherwise, but here below to live is to change, and to be perfect is to have changed often."[57]

But in the arid lands of the Middle East, the birth place of each of these faith traditions, it is not hard to go astray in a sand storm. There are few landmarks in a desert to guide the voyager. Only by looking up at the stars—celestial navigation—can travelers find their way to their destination, their ultimate home. Each of us—Jew, Christian, and Muslim—must look upwards for guidance in the sand storms of life, the desert through which we travel. Our only God, we pray, will help us to hear the prophetic voices that can guide us home along the ways of truth, the paths of peace.

57. Ibid., 40.

CHAPTER 5

Faith Facing Death:
Hopes and Fears

I know, D., that you have also lived in Ghana. When you were there, did you ever go to a funeral? Permit me to take you with me on an Ashanti journey through death, life after death and the mystery of faith.

Three decades after I taught at the University of Ghana (1974–83), I noticed on a visit to the campus that many streets had recently been given names. The sign on one of those streets—Agyei Barimah Crescent—brought back memories I had not expected to confront again. Agyei Barimah was a first-year student in May 1979, a time when Ghana was living through the last months of a despotic military dictatorship that had begun in 1972. Participating with some of his boisterous fellow students from the University of Ghana's Commonwealth Hall in a street cleanup exercise in central Accra one Saturday morning, Agyei Barimah met a dreadful end. The nervous police—always worried about the political volatility of students in a crowded urban center—shot randomly at the students and killed him.

The young man shot dead by the police was a Catholic and also an Asante ("Ashanti"), a member of a matrilineal society that dominates the middle of Ghana. Furious with the military government, his fellow students had demonstrated after his death not only in Accra but all along the 200 miles of road to his village by the river Tano where he was to be buried a week later. The corpse, which had been frozen in the University Teaching Hospital mortuary, was now incongruously dressed in a mortar board and the academic gown of his residential hall. When I arrived at Agyei's village early on the morning of the funeral, the body lay within an elaborately canopied bier in an open field near the local Catholic church. I had arrived shortly after dawn. A young Ghanaian Presbyterian minister, one of my students at the time, beckoned for me to approach the bier and conduct the transfer of the body to the coffin in what he called "the Catholic way." I had no idea what "the Catholic way" might entail, but I didn't let on. I started to pray aloud; nearby students, drunk and rowdy until then, fell silent. Agyei Barimah's relatives, tired from a sleepless night of wake-keeping, approached the bier. His mother's brothers, draped in the fulsome clay-red cloth that is the mark of matrilineal relatives in mourning, gathered around me. Patrilineal relatives, draped in black, removed their toga-like outer garments and surrounded me, the matrilineal uncles and the corpse with a wall of cloth. Gently we lifted the corpse, now wet from defrosting, and laid it in the coffin.

For one who had died so young, childless and the victim of sudden violence, Asante funeral rites are traditionally curtailed, or even suppressed. Such a "bad death," as it is called, prevents the deceased from providing for his matrilineal ancestors a channel of rebirth, precisely because the youth died childless. Furthermore, the violent nature of a murder is said to "offend" the Earth, which must be pacified for every burial, but especially when the one to be interred has met a violent end. Such a death may in some sense be thought culpable, the result of a willful bad choice made at the moment before birth when God gives, or the human being chooses, a destiny (nkrabea). The victim may have died like this because of some offense that brought on the ire of witches or other invisible forces. Such a youthful victim of sudden death was traditionally buried hastily and at noonday, an unpropitious hour. But traditions are changing, especially under the influence of Christianity. The relatives of Agyei Barimah insisted that his burial be delayed until the later afternoon, to avoid the stigma of "bad death." Having arrived just after dawn, I suddenly realized that I had a long day ahead of me.

Within the wall of cloth surrounding the corpse, one of his matrilineal uncles reached into his pocket and produced two coins which he wished to place in the coffin with the corpse. Another uncle, looking remorsefully at me, remonstrated with him: "No! This is a Christian funeral." I looked up from the corpse, tears in my eyes. "Let it be." I said, "Let him give the coins." The uncle was offering his nephew the coins of passage across the river of death, a motif known both in the ancient Greek and Roman worlds as well as in Asante. But in the old

Asante tradition, the possibility of such blessed survival, such a crossing of the river of death, was denied to one who had died a "bad death." The gift of the uncle's coins transcended Asante cultural expectations and bespoke a faith in Christ who gives hope for life after death, who makes life after death possible. "Let it be," I repeated, and Agyei Barimah, just before his Catholic funeral, a Liturgy of the Resurrection, was given the fare to cross the river to the land of his ancestors (*asamando*).[1]

There are many hopes and fears we may all share about life after death and many different ways in which we Jews, Christians, and Muslims have imagined life after death over the centuries. My interest in life after death in this chapter centers on faith in God as the source of survival that includes rising from the dead, understood quite concretely not as the resuscitation of a corpse but as resurrection of the body. I thought of that in 1979 as I helped to lift the cold and wet corpse of Agyei Barimah into his coffin. Greek aspirations for survival of the soul, but not the body, may have satisfied philosophers in ancient Athens, but the peasants in the Greek countryside may have wanted something a bit more concrete. Even the hero Achilles in the underworld tells the visiting Odysseus that he would much rather be a living slave than a ruler among the shades of the dead. "No winning words about death to *me*, shining Odysseus! By god, I'd rather slave on earth for another man—some dirt-poor tenant farmer who scrapes to keep alive—than rule down here among all the breathless dead."[2] So would many of us. Let me take you now on a rapid tour of Jewish, Christian, and Muslim hopes and fears about death and the gradual development of faith in God as the source of afterlife, quite concretely imaged as bodily resurrection.

    1. On Asante funeral customs, see R. S. Rattray, *Religion and Art in Ashanti* (Oxford: Clarendon, 1927), and many modern studies, especially Judith A. Vollbrecht, *Structure and Communitas in an Ashanti Village: The Role of Funerals* (Ann Arbor, Mich.: University Microfilms, 1979).
    2. See *Odyssey* 11:488–91. For this translation see Homer, *The Odyssey*, trans. Robert Fagles (New York: Viking Penguin, 1996), 265.

Life after Death in the Jewish Tradition

There is some evidence in ancient Israel, at least in the Iron Age (after 1200 BCE), for something normally connected, and on a much grander scale, with the neighbors of Israel in Egypt: the depositing of grave goods in tombs.[3] Presumably such grave goods signified popular belief in ancient Israel that the deceased could use these things after death, unless the Israelites had a sense of humor in the face of death, like some modern Americans—friends of mine—who slip into the coffins of favorite relatives such treasured objects as good cigars, Oreo cookies, and mini-bottles of single-malt whiskey.

Hope for a particular form of life after death, resurrection of the body, not mere survival of the soul (not in its origins a particularly Jewish notion), developed late in the tradition of Israel, probably most clearly in the final two centuries BCE. Earlier Israelites were more interested in the survival of Israel through progeny. There were, however, some yearnings and even positive hope expressed for rescue from the grave, which was envisaged as the entry into the pit of the underworld (*Sheol*). "God will ransom my soul from the power of Sheol," one voice cries out in the Psalms, "for he will receive me" (Ps 49:15). The nature of that divine rescue from the pit of death, or of the reception that God might provide for one so rescued, was left fairly vague. There is, however, at least one substantial portion of the prophetic work ascribed to Isaiah of Jerusalem, possibly interpolated into his corpus by later thinkers in that prophetic school, that has been characterized as the Isaiah apocalypse (Is 24:1–27:13). The prophetic speaker in this context sees different fates awaiting the wicked and the just. The former have no hope for survival: "The dead do not live; shades do not rise—because you have punished and destroyed them, and wiped out all memory of them" (Is 26:14). But the same fate will not be visited on the just: "Your dead shall live, their corpses shall rise" (Is 26:19). A more cor-

---

3. See Claudia Setzer, *Resurrection of the Body in Early Judaism and Early Christianity: Doctrine, Community and Self-Definition* (Leiden: Brill, 2004), 6–7. I am much indebted to this excellent work of Professor Setzer for my understanding of hopes for life after dead in the early Jewish and early Christian traditions.

porate rather than individual version of such hope can be found in a passage from Ezekiel who was writing sometime after the end of the Babylonian Exile in the late sixth century BCE. Ezekiel envisions the return of the Jews from Babylon to their homeland as the revival and enfleshment of a valley of dry bones for whom God promises resurrection of the body: "You shall know that I am the LORD, when I open your graves, and bring you up from your graves, O my people" (Ezek 37:13). But was such a resurrection motif only literary imagery in the Isaiah apocalypse and the work of Ezekiel?

Why did genuine hope for the resurrection of the body eventually arise among some Jews in the early second century BCE? The Seleucid or Syrian Greek rulers, who had inherited from Alexander the Great in the late fourth century BCE the political domination of much of the territory that is the modern Middle East, tended to take a dim view of the Jews within their realm, especially by the early second century BCE. The feeling of antipathy was mutual. The last of the major Syrian Greek rulers, Antiochus IV Epiphanes (r. 175–164 BCE), slaughtered many faithful Jews who resisted his wholesale campaign to promote *hityavnut*, Hellenization of every aspect of Jewish life, including the Temple worship in Jerusalem. The priest Mattathias and his sons, the Maccabee brothers, spearheaded an eventually successful revolt against the tyranny of Antiochus IV, but before it succeeded not a few Jews lost their lives in battle or as individual martyrs for the faith. It may have been such deaths of young people that motivated Jews to hope for a completed, resurrected bodily life in "the world to come" (*ha-olam ha-ba*: the phrase can also be translated "the age to come").

The Books of Maccabees, of which only a Greek version survives, were probably composed soon after the events they describe in the second century BCE. In several vivid passages these works reflect a strong hope for life after death, precisely in the form of resurrection of the body, nowhere more dramatically presented than in the account of the martyrdom of seven Jewish brothers and their mother who refuse to eat pork at the command of Antiochus. The second son defies Antiochus before he dies: "'You accursed wretch, you dismiss us from this present life, but the King of the universe will raise us up to an everlasting renewal of life, because we have died for his laws'" (2 Mc 7:9). When only one son is left, his valiant mother urges him to maintain the same faith in God who can raise the dead. Note the parallelism in her words between the wonder of procreation and the wonder of resurrection (2 Mc 7:27–29):

My son, have pity on me. I carried you for nine months in my womb, and nursed you for three years, and have reared you and brought you up to this point in your life, and have taken care of you. I beg you, my child, to look at the heaven and the earth and see everything that is in them, and recognize that God did not make them out of things that existed. And in the same way the human race came into being. Do not fear this butcher, but prove worthy of your brothers. Accept death, so that in God's mercy I may get you back again along with your brothers.

The Book of Daniel, purportedly narrating events taking place during the Babylonian Exile of the sixth century BCE, actually reflects the same Syrian Greek persecution of the Jews in the early second century BCE. The last chapter of Daniel looks forward to a deliverance from persecution that is much less this-worldly than the exodus from Egypt or the return of the Jewish exiles from Babylon, the prime examples of the deliverance of Israel in earlier portions of the Hebrew Bible. The future hope of the author of Daniel centers on deliverance from the ultimate captivity, the ultimate exile: death. Like the Isaiah apocalypse, the Book of Daniel sees different fates awaiting the faithful and the faithless. "Many of those who sleep in the dust of the earth shall awake, some to everlasting life, and some to shame and everlasting contempt. Those who are wise shall shine like the brightness of the sky and those who lead many to righteousness, like the stars forever and ever" (Dn 12:2–3).

By the time of Jesus, the Jewish community living in the Roman-ruled Middle East, and especially in Judea and Galilee, was of two minds about the resurrection of the dead, and I will treat the New Testament account of these quandaries below. But the lay movement known to us as the Pharisees (Perushim) continued the hopes of the Maccabees for resurrection of the body, while the Sadducees, an older aristocracy surrounding the Temple and its officiants, rejected the notion of resurrection. With the Roman destruction of the refurbished Second Temple in 70 CE, the influence of the Sadducees declined dramatically, and the rabbis in the Pharisee tradition who preserved Judaism in the early centuries CE considered bodily resurrection of the dead a central component of Jewish faith. The Babylonian Talmud, in the *Tractate Sanhedrin*, cites several texts from the Torah that imply the resurrection of the dead: "It is written 'and you shall contribute from it the Lord's offering to Aaron the priest' (Num 18:28). Would Aaron live forever? ... This indicates that [Aaron] was to be resurrected and the children of Israel would give him offerings."[4]

There were dissenters on this theme over the centuries before modern times, but Orthodox Jews to the present day, as well as many Conservative Jews, still place their hope in the God who raises the dead to life. Maimonides in the twelfth century expressed a consensus on the resurrection of the dead that prevailed in most Jewish circles until the nineteenth century. "The great reward is the life of the world to come and the punishment is the cutting off of the soul [in the world to come]" (Principle XI). But Maimonides also specifies the possibility of some sinners, weak but basically faithful, making it into the world to come. Such a sinner "will be punished for his sins, but he still has a share in the world to come and is among the sinners of Israel" (Principle XIII).[5] Maimonides was also affected by the Aristotelian philosophical tradition and did not confuse resurrection of the dead and the reality of the world to come with the restoration of normal physical life. For Maimonides, "the human soul returns to the body. This is the intended meaning of *Resurrection of the Dead*,"[6] but such return of the soul to the body does not mean that eating, drinking, and sexual activity will characterize the life of the resurrected.[7] In the *Mishneh Torah*, Maimon-

---

4. Tractate Sanhedrin 90b, in *The Talmud: Selected Writings*, 211.

5. For this translation of the Thirteen Principles of Maimonides, see Marc Mermelstein, "The 13 Foundations of Judaism," available at www.mesora.org/13principles.

6. Moses Maimonides, "Treatise on the Resurrection," trans. Hillel G. Fradkin, in Ralph Lerner, *Maimonides' Empire of Light: Popular Enlightenment in an Age of Belief* (Chicago: University of Chicago Press, 2000), 165–66.

7. Ibid., 157.

ides insists that those "who have no share in the world to come, who are cut off and destroyed and are judged on account of great wickedness and sins forever and ever" include "heretics, atheists and those who reject the Torah and deny the resurrection and the coming of the Messiah" as well as "the apostate."[8]

Many modern Jews in Europe and America, and especially those who adhere to the Reform tradition, do not share Maimonides's convictions about the world to come. They evade any clear reference to a hope for resurrection of the dead and the world to come when they pray to God "who has implanted within us eternal life."[9] The perspectives of such Reform Jews underline the moral importance of what happens or does not happen in a particular person's life, and as such this serves to motivate a life of disinterested morality. The 1885 Declaration of Principles ("the Pittsburgh Platform") of Reform Jews in the United States affirms "the doctrine of Judaism that the soul is immortal" but "rejects as ideas not rooted in Judaism, the beliefs both in bodily resurrection and in Gehenna and Eden (Hell and Paradise) as abodes for everlasting punishment and reward."[10] (Ironically, the immortality of the soul was originally a Greek notion that only gradually became "the doctrine of Judaism," while "bodily resurrection" took root as an idea in Judaism in the Hellenistic era.) By the time of the 1999 Pittsburgh Convention of the Central Conference of American Rabbis, this 1885 Reform doctrine had been considerably modified, perhaps even mollified, especially in view of the overwhelming Jewish experience of the Shoah: "We continue to have faith that, in spite of the unspeakable evils committed against our people and the sufferings endured by others, the partnership of God and humanity will ultimately prevail." The vagueness of that formula is immediately followed by a more positive affirmation of the soul's survival: "We trust in our tradition's promise that, although God created us as finite beings, the spirit within us is

---

8. *The Book of Knowledge from the Mishneh Torah of Maimonides*, trans. H. M. Russell and Rabbi J. Weinberg (New York: Ktav, 1983), 116.

9. "Morning Service for Week-Days," in *The Union Prayer Book for Jewish Worship*, rev. ed. (New York: The Central Conference of American Rabbis, 1940), 321.

10. "The Pittsburgh Platform" of 1885, available at ccarnet.org/rabbis-speak/platforms/declaration-principles/.

eternal."[11] Reform Jews to the present day ask many questions about the status of the dead, sensing their continued survival of death in some way or another.

Life after Death in the Christian Tradition

Jesus and his disciples had much in common on the subject of the resurrection with the Pharisees in the first century. In the Gospels of Mark, Matthew, and Luke, Jesus takes on the Sadducees on this topic with some vigor. The Sadducees posed a conundrum to Jesus. They told him the hypothetical tale of seven brothers, married according to levirate law, one by one, to the same childless bride.[12] Such an unlucky widow poses a difficulty for the doctrine of the resurrection. "'In the resurrection, whose wife will she be? For the seven had married her'" (Mk 12:23). The reply of Jesus to the Sadducees' conundrum argues that even in the Torah, the first five books of the Bible (the only ones Sadducees regarded as authoritative), the resurrection of the dead is implicit in God's words spoken to Moses in the burning bush: "I am the God of Abraham, the God of Isaac, the God of Jacob" (Mk 12:26, quoting Ex 3:6). Following principles not untypical of Jewish exegetes in the early centuries of the Common Era, as we can see in the passage from the *Tractate Sanhedrin* cited above,[13] Jesus interpreted the divine proclamation to Moses of God's present relationship ("I AM") to the dead patriarchs as an assertion of continuing relationship, even beyond the physical death of the patriarchs. "'He is God not of the dead, but of the living'" (Mk 12:27). In the world to come the unlucky widow is granted a *get*, a rabbinical divorce (Dt 24:1); she becomes a free agent. "When they rise from the dead, they neither marry nor are given in marriage, but are like angels in heaven" (Mk 12:25). What did Jesus mean by quoting

11. "A Statement of Principles for Reform Judaism" of 1999, available at ccarnet.org/rabbis -speak/platforms/declaration-principles/.

12. On the levirate law, see Deuteronomy: "When brothers reside together, and one of them dies and has no son, the wife of the deceased shall not be married outside the family to a stranger. Her husband's brother shall go in to her, taking her in marriage, and performing the duty of a husband's brother to her, and the firstborn whom she bears shall succeed to the name of the deceased brother, so that his name may not be blotted out of Israel" (Dt 25:5–6).

13. See Daniel J. Harrington, SJ, "The Gospel of Mark," in *NJBC*, 622b.

this text? He meant to say that the present and future meaning of the divine name—"I AM WHO I AM" or "I WILL BE WHAT I WILL BE"—must be taken seriously with regard to Abraham, Isaac, and Jacob as well as with regard to the father of Moses. The LORD who spoke to Moses in the burning bush was assuring Moses that his father and the ancestors of Israel—Abraham, Isaac, and Jacob—were still living in God's presence: "I AM" their God even now, and "I WILL BE" their God forever.

When Paul, according to the Acts of the Apostles, was brought to trial before a Sanhedrin made up of both Pharisees and Sadducees, Luke maintains that he divided them among themselves: "Brothers, I am a Pharisee, a son of Pharisees. I am on trial concerning the hope of resurrection of the dead" (Acts 23:6). The earliest written documents of the New Testament come from the pen of Paul, composed over a period of a decade starting about 51 CE. Paul's experience of Jesus, very different from that of the disciples who had accompanied Jesus during his public career, began in the early 30s of the first century. The Gospel writers, especially Luke, record visions of the risen Jesus by his disciples over a period of forty days (Acts 1:3). But after their experience of the ascension of Jesus and the descent of the Holy Spirit, the apostles claimed no further visions of the resurrected Jesus. Paul, however, insists that he personally experienced, some five to eight years after the death and resurrection of Jesus, a genuine vision of the risen Jesus. After listing the male eyewitnesses of the resurrection of Jesus, Paul boldly asserts that "last of all, as to one untimely born, he appeared also to me" (1 Cor 15:8). By this vision Paul apparently means his call experience: "God, who had set me apart before I was born and called me through his grace, was pleased to reveal his Son to me, so that I might proclaim him among the Gentiles" (Gal 1:15–16).[14] The Acts of the Apostles three times fleshes out these two testimonies by Paul with accounts of his experience on the road to Damascus.[15] Was the vision Paul had of the risen Jesus on the road to Damascus mainly an interi-

14. The Greek of this passage can be read literally as follows: "when he [God] who had set me apart before I was born and called me through his grace, was pleased to reveal his Son *in* me." The most important aspect of this passage is the way it denotes the revolution worked within Paul by what he experienced that day.

15. On Paul's call experience as narrated three times by Luke, see Acts 9:1–31, 22:1–21, 26:2–23.

or event? If it was, such a vision, especially given Paul's insistence on its significance for Gentiles, could not but be controversial in the early Jewish-Christian church, especially because of Paul's recent career as a persecutor of Jewish Christians.

The traditions that Paul received about the resurrection of Jesus concentrate only on the eyewitness testimony of men, the sort of testimony that might be accepted in a rabbinical setting; they run counter to the four evangelists' insistence that the first witnesses of the risen Jesus were women. But the importance of the resurrection for Paul's preached theology appears most clearly in a passage from the First Letter to the Corinthians (1 Cor 15:20–24):

Christ has been raised from the dead, the first fruits of those who have died. For since death came through a human being, the resurrection of the dead has also come through a human being; for as all die in Adam, so all will be made alive in Christ. But each in his own order: Christ the first fruits, then at his coming those who belong to Christ. Then comes the end, when he hands over the kingdom to God the Father, after he has destroyed every ruler and every authority and power.

The image of the risen Christ as "the first fruits of those who have died" returns in a different form a few verses later, and should keep us from confusing the resurrection of Jesus or the resurrection of anyone else with what may be called the resuscitation of the dead, as in the raising of Lazarus. Lazarus, called forth from his tomb, has to be untied from his grave wrappings (Jn 11:44); the risen Jesus, by contrast, leaves the grave wrappings behind (Jn 20:5–7). Michelangelo's famous statue of the risen Jesus in the Roman Church of Santa Maria sopra Minerva shows Christ notably unclothed, apart from a swirl of bronze added over the sculptor's objections by ecclesiastical censors.

Paul answers a hypothetical question: "How are the dead raised? With what kind of body do they come?" (1 Cor 15:35). Paul compares the corpse that is buried to a seed planted in the hopes of fruition: "You do not sow the body that is to be, but a bare seed, perhaps of wheat or some other grain" (1 Cor 15:37). In the Gospel of John, Jesus uses a similar image to describe what will happen to him after his glorification (Jn 12:24). Paul goes even further and refers to the risen body as something radically transformed: "It is sown a physical body, it is raised a spiritual body" (1 Cor 15:44). Does this image compromise the reality of the resurrection? I think not: instead, it helps us to comprehend the four Gospels' accounts of the risen Jesus, able to come and go mysteriously, even though the doors are locked (Jn 20:19), not always recognized at first (Lk 24:16, Jn 21:4), and demanding what seems to be more than normal cognition. Matthew tells us quite frankly that when the eleven disciples went to the mountain in Galilee where they were told to meet the risen Jesus, "when they saw him, they worshiped him; but some doubted" (Mt 28:17). One such doubter in another Gospel narrative, Thomas, even insisted that he would not accept the reality of the resurrection unless he could put his finger into "the mark of the nails in his hands" and put his hand into the wounded side of Jesus (Jn 20:25). Thomas got what he wanted—or perhaps stopped short of such probing when confronted a week later by the risen Jesus. Thomas and all of us are bidden, along with Mary Magdalene, not to cling physically to the risen Jesus but to recognize that he has entered into a new dimension of his relationship with his Father: "'I am ascending to my Father and your Father, to my God and your God'" (Jn 20:17). The risen body bears a direct relationship to the body of the person who has died, but it is the relationship of full flowering or fruition to what was only a seed, the mortal body. There is not much more we can say sensibly about this mystery, as we have no personal experience of it. The Lutheran theologian Wolfhart Pannenberg suggests that "the fate of Jesus Christ" is "the anticipation of the end"[16] and will only become

16. Wolfhart Pannenberg, "Dogmatic Theses on the Doctrine of Revelation," in *Revelation as History*, ed. Wolfhart Pannenberg, trans. David Granskou (London: Macmillan, 1968), 143. For Pannenberg the whole purport of the teaching of Jesus was the announcement of the imminent eschatological reign of God. Jesus proclaimed the relativization of the Law and the resurrection of the dead as elements of this coming age. The fact that Jesus and his contemporaries may have expected the verification of these claims in imminent events of cosmic dimension does not mean that Jesus has been proven false or deceived, as Albert Schweitzer might maintain. Rather, Jesus has been proven paradoxically right by his own resurrection as the first fruits of the harvest of the dead; the resurrection of Jesus, then, can be understood as the proleptic dawning of the endtime. Pannenberg's theology gives a new seriousness to the earliest stratum of Paul's writing: "The dead in Christ will rise first. Then we who are alive, who are left, will be caught up in the clouds together with them to meet the Lord in the air; and so we shall be with the Lord forever" (1 Thes 4:16–17). Unfortunately, this passage from Paul has been trivialized by fundamentalists hopeful of being caught up in "the rapture," in the process abandoning their cars in heavy traffic.

intelligible when understood in its setting, the general resurrection of the dead.[17]

In the early church there were differences on how the resurrection of the dead was to be interpreted. The great theologian of the early third century, Origen (d. ca. 254), affirms the resurrection of the dead but insists that the gross materiality of human bodies will play no part in the resurrected life. In this Origen does not differ very much from Paul.

So must we suppose that our bodies, like a grain of corn, fall into the earth, but that implanted in them is the life-principle which contains the essence of the body; and although the bodies die and are corrupted and scattered, nevertheless by the word of God that same life principle which has all along been preserved in the essence of the body raises them up from the earth and restores and refashions them. Just as the power that exists in a grain of wheat refashions and restores the grain, after its corruption and death, into a body with stalk and ear.[18]

Later thinkers identified as "Origenists" in the sixth century, especially monks of the Monastery of Mar Saba outside Bethlehem, seem to have gone well beyond Origen and suggested that risen bodies would be quite different from mortal bodies and would even be spherical in shape.[19]

Did the Syriac homilist of the late fifth and early sixth century, Mar Jacob of Serugh, write his poetic account of the Sleepers of Ephesus as an apologetic against such "Origenists"?[20] His Sleepers are, however,

17. See Wolfhart Pannenberg, "The Revelation of God in Jesus of Nazareth," in *Theology as History*, ed. James M. Robinson and John B. Cobb, Jr., New Frontiers in Theology: Discussions among Continental and American Theologians 3 (New York: Harper and Row, 1967), 101–33, and Pannenberg's response to the other authors in the volume, 221–76.

18. *Origen on First Principles*, trans. G. W. Butterworth (New York: Harper and Row, 1966), 141. Origen's analogy of the resurrection as a transformation like that of a grain into a full ear of wheat derives in part from Paul (1 Cor 15:37–41) and John (Jn 12:24).

19. The "theologian emperor" Justinian (r. 527–65) pushed in 543 for a condemnation at a Synod in Constantinople of nine theses attributed to Origen, who had been dead for nearly three centuries. The fifth of those condemned theses, nowhere to be found in the texts of Origen that deal with resurrection, entails the notion that "in the resurrection the bodies of human beings will be raised spherical in shape" (Greek: *sphairoedei*; Latin: *orbiculata*). See DS, §207/407. For a judicious account of Origen and the difference between Origen and later "Origenists," see H. Crouzel, "Origen and Origenism," in *The New Catholic Encyclopedia*, ed. Thomas Carson, 2nd ed. (Detroit: Thomson, Gale, 2002) (hereafter, *NCE2*), 10:653a–61.

20. On the possibility of the story as anti-"Origenist," see Sidney Griffith, "Christian Lore and

decidedly non-spherical boys. Mar Jacob's poem opens with an apostrophe to the Son of God, asking him to help the poet-homilist to tell the story of "the children of light" who are also described as "lambs from the midst of [God's] flock" and "wheat [selected] from the tares." All of these images derive from the Gospels and their perspective on life after death. Then the poem goes on to narrate how the Roman emperor Decius, whose short reign (249–51) was marked by vigorous persecution of Christians, tried during a visit to Ephesus to impose the duty of sacrificing to the gods on Christian Ephesians, including eight boys who hid in a cave outside the city to avoid apostasy. There they slept, they thought, for a night. Mar Jacob of Serugh says that "the Lord saw the faith of the dear lambs and ... took their spirits and raised them up above, to heaven, and left a watcher to be guarding their limbs." Decius, outraged by their refusal to sacrifice to the gods, has the entrance to the cave blocked with cut stones. Two wise men, however, evidently Christians, mark the location of the tomb with an inscription "on tablets of lead" that preserves the names of the boys, leading to their veneration as martyrs for the faith.

About two centuries later, well into the history of the Eastern Roman Christian Empire, a wealthy Ephesian wants to build a sheepfold near that cave and in the process removes some of the stones from its entrance. Thus "light entered in and awoke the children of light." Thinking they had only slept one night, the boys send one of their number secretly into Ephesus to buy food with coins they had brought with them two hundred years earlier. Entering the city, the boy sees crosses everywhere, to his amazement. The coins he brings, two centuries old, arouse a commotion among Ephesians who think they must come from a hidden treasure. Eventually, the boy bearing the ancient coins is dragged before the local bishop, who rescues him from the crowd. The boy finally leads the Christians of Ephesus to the mountain retreat where he and his companions have slept since the persecution of Decius. Later, the Byzantine emperor, Theodosius II, is brought into the

the Arabic Qur'an: The 'Companions of the Cave' in *Surat al-Kahf* and in Syriac Christian Tradition," in *The Qur'an in its Historical Context*, ed. Gabriel Said Reynolds (London: Routledge, 2008), 120.

picture; he tries to persuade the boys to relocate to downtown Ephesus, but the boys prefer their mountain retreat, declaring that "the shepherd who chose us is the one who bade us be here." They envision their role to be witnesses to the reality of the resurrection: "For your sake has Christ the Lord awoken us so that you might see and hold firm that the resurrection truly exists." Covered with the emperor's mantle they return to sleep until the general resurrection.[21]

These youthful witnesses to the resurrection, eight in number according to Jacob of Serugh (seven of them fairly taciturn, plus one spokesperson), exhibit a distinctive family resemblance to the seven martyred brothers and their valiant mother in the Second Book of Maccabees. We shall meet them once again, much transformed, in the Qur'an.

Life after Death in the Muslim Tradition

Few themes play a more central role in the earliest passages of the Qur'an, those first experienced by Muhammad as revelation while he was still in Mecca (610–22), than "the day of the resurrection" (*yawm al-qiyama*), a phrase that occurs seventy times in the Qur'an. The seventy-fifth chapter of the Qur'an actually bears the title, Sura of the Resurrection, and it begins with a startling, almost macabre vision of the resurrection of all the dead, good and evil, and the accompanying realization by the evil of their condemnation (Qur'an 75:1–15):

No, I swear by the day of resurrection—No, I swear by the reproach-laden soul! Do human beings think that We [God] will not collect their bones? Yes indeed! We can even piece together their fingers! But they want to continue living in sin. They ask: "When will this day of resurrection occur?" When sight is dazzled, when the moon is eclipsed, when sun and moon clash: on that day they will say: "Where can we escape?" But there will be no hiding place! With your Lord, though, on that day there will be a place of rest. On that day human beings will be told what they put first and what they put last. Yes indeed! Human

---

21. For the full text of this work by Jacob of Serugh, see Sebastian Brock, "Jacob of Serugh's Poem on the Sleepers of Ephesus," in *I Sowed Fruits into Hearts (Odes Sol. 17:13): Festschrift for Professor Michael Lattke*, ed. P. Allen, M. Franzmann, and R. Strelan, Early Christian Studies 12 (Strathfield: St. Paul's Publications, 2007), 13–30.

beings will act as clear witnesses against themselves, despite all the excuses they proffer for themselves.

Muhammad's preaching about the day of resurrection, as well as the day of judgment that inevitably follows, struck his uncaring Meccan contemporaries as nonsense. The Qur'an reports their skepticism: "'Beyond our one death there is nothing; we will not be raised up. Bring back our ancestors if what you say is true!'" (Qur'an 44:35–36). Unlike the New Testament, which can point to the resurrection of Jesus as a foretaste of what lies in store for all who keep faith, the Qur'an proffers no clear example of a past resurrection.[22] But the Qur'an does adduce arguments in favor of the hope for resurrection, noting the parallelism between God's creating everything in the beginning and God's revivifying the dead at the end (Qur'an 17:49–52):

They also say, "When we are reduced to bones and dust, will we really be raised up as a new creation?" Say: "Even if you are stone or iron or some created thing even greater in your minds." Then they will say, "Who will bring us back?" Say: "The One who made you the first time." Then they will shake their heads at you and say: "When will that be?" Say: "Perhaps it will be soon, someday when

---

22. Two passages from the second chapter of the Qur'an are sometimes said to refer to previous resurrections. The first passage consists of two verses, Qur'an 2:72–73, addressed to Jews: "Behold, you killed someone and began to blame each other on this matter. But God was the One who brought to light what you were trying to hide. Then We [God] said: 'Strike [the corpse] with a piece of it [a heifer mentioned in v. 71]. Then God brings the dead person back to life and makes you see some of God's signs so that you will be able to understand." The modern Qur'an translator and interpreter A. Yusuf 'Ali has suggested that this passage develops further Dt 21:1–9, a passage from the Hebrew Bible that describes a ceremony for cleansing neighbors from blood-guilt for a person found murdered in the countryside without any evidence for who committed the crime. See *The Holy Qur'an*, trans. A. Yusuf Ali, 2nd ed. (n.p.: American Trust Publications, 1977), 36n81. The Quranic verses do not so much describe a resurrection as a resuscitation of the dead for the purpose of establishing guilt or innocence of the potentially guilty. The second passage from the same sura (Qur'an 2:259) is quite different: "[Take the example] of the person who passed by a town in ruins. He said 'How will God bring it back to life after its death?' God made him die for a hundred years and then [God] revived him and asked him: 'How long did you stay [there]?' and he said, 'I stayed a day or part of a day.' But [God] said: 'No, you stayed there a hundred years. Look at your food and drink: they have not gone stale. Look at your donkey. Thus do We [God] make you a sign for people. Look at the bones and how We will assemble them and even clothe them with flesh.' Thus, when it became clear to him, the person said: 'Now I know that God is powerful in every matter.'" Like the Seven Sleepers of Qur'an 18, the anonymous witness to what God can do for a town in ruins has no idea how much time has passed since he died. His own revival by God may not so much be resurrection as resuscitation of the dead, to prove to this anonymous person that God can do as much to revive the ruined city he had seen and thought beyond hope. Many Qur'an commentators see this passage as having some relationship to Ezekiel's vision of the valley of dry bones (Ezek 37:1–14). See A. Yusuf 'Ali, *Qur'an*, 105n304.

[God] will call you and you will respond with praise of Him, and you will presume that you have delayed only a little bit."

Note that in this passage from the Qur'an the resurrection of the body is
imaginatively linked with the original creation of the body, a frequent
Quranic motif. The Qur'an also offers analogies to the resurrection of
the dead in natural phenomena, awe-inspiring for Arabs in a desert
environment, such as the growth of vegetation (Qur'an 41:39) and the
transformation of dry soil by rain (Qur'an 53:11).

There is one story told in the Qur'an, not entirely unlike the Christian story of the Sleepers of Ephesus, a story that may serve as a promise of future resurrection of the dead as the ultimate awakening of
those who have kept faith with God. In the Sura of the Cave (Qur'an
18:9–26) we are told about seven young men whose fidelity to the oneness of God motivated them to take refuge from persecution in a cave
where they fell asleep—they thought for only one night, but actually
for three centuries or more. When they awoke they served as witnesses to the intimate connection between fidelity to that one God and the
hope for the resurrection of the dead that is so central to the Quranic
message. The Quranic story of the Seven Sleepers lacks most of the
specifically Christian details in the version preserved by Mar Jacob of
Serugh or later Christian writers. As with so many stories in the Qur'an,
however, it presumes familiarity with the narrative already, not because Muhammad had read it (Muslims generally deny his literacy)
but probably because the story of the Seven Sleepers had entered into
the oral tradition of Arabia through Christians living there. Muhammad may have known this story already, but it was re-experienced by
him as revelation only when his Meccan compatriots challenged his
teaching about the hour of judgment and the resurrection of the dead.
God speaks once again in the plural of majesty: "Thus did We bring
them [the Companions of the Cave] to their attention so that they might
know God's promise is true and that there is no doubt about the hour
[of judgment], even though they hold various opinions about this matter" (Qur'an 18:21).

Originally Greek intellectual pursuits—loosely grouped together as *falsafa* (a word quite obviously borrowed from the Greek word *philoso-phia*)—began to find enthusiastic practitioners among a minority of Muslims by the ninth century. Many of these Muslim philosophers fell into a skeptical attitude about both protology and eschatology: the central doctrines of the Qur'an about creation of the universe in time and the consummation of that universe at some future point in time. *Falsafa* never had a large numerical following, but it did have an elite clientele among some Arab and even more Iranian and Turkish Muslims for whom it provided an alternative worldview to that of normative Islam. Looking at the universe, the *faylasuf* tried to discover more about *what it was* rather than about *Who made it*. For the Muslim philosopher the cosmos was less the result of God's creative activity than the result of interacting causes, first the four qualities (moist, dry, hot, cold) and then the derivative four elements (air, fire, water, earth). Change could be explained as the mixture of qualities and elements rather than as the result of divine initiative.

For the *faylasuf*, the world, constructed of constitutive principles, could not have derived directly from God without sullying the abso-luteness and changelessness of God, conceived in Aristotelian terms as the Uncaused Cause and First Principle of Movement, eternally at rest. To avoid the notion that God went from not-creating to creating—and therefore underwent change—the Muslim practitioners of *falsafa* speculated that the visible universe was eternally created: absolutely dependent or contingent on God but co-eternal with God. In such an eternally contingent world, there was no place for an end of the world and no place for the day of resurrection.[23] *Falsafa* so conceived and practiced was heading down a collision course with Islam, although leading Muslim philosophers tried various ways to reconcile their ideas about God and creation with revelation.

The great Muslim thinker al-Ghazali was at one time more involved in the practice of *falsafa* than he later thought was spiritually healthy. As noted earlier, al-Ghazali developed many arguments to refute the principal teachings of the philosophers about God and the universe in

23. See Hodgson, *The Venture of Islam*, 1:428.

his polemical work *Tahafut al-falasifa* ("The Incoherence of the Philosophers"). This work of al-Ghazali's later provoked Averroes to write his line-by-line refutation, *Tahafut al-tahafut* ("The Incoherence of the Incoherence"). Al-Ghazali in an autobiographical work takes on the philosophers in a briefer scope, singling out three principal teachings of the philosophers (especially al-Farabi and Avicenna) for which they must be accounted faithless (*kuffar*). The first and most egregiously faithless teaching of the philosophers, according to al-Ghazali, was their affirmation "that men's bodies will not be assembled on the Last Day, but only disembodied spirits will be rewarded and punished, and the rewards and punishments will be spiritual, not corporal."[24] The other two teachings of the philosophers that amounted to total infidelity, according to al-Ghazali, include their assertion that "God Most High knows universals, but not particulars" and "their maintaining the eternity of the world, past and future."[25]

The last two errors of the philosophers provide the intellectual underpinning for the first, the denial of the resurrection of the body. The word "particulars," in Aristotelian terms, at least as interpreted by Thomas Aquinas, points to the unique individual (the *individuum* in classical terms, that which is undivided in itself) that is "signed" by matter, which differentiates one individual from another within a species, the universal or form that is generic. Thus, if I may play with these terms, Jesuit might be construed as a generic species or universal form, while Pat Ryan is an individual within that species, a particular differentiated by his unique matter from any other Jesuit. If God only knows Jesuits in general and not Pat Ryan in particular, my hope for life after death sinks into the grave. Even worse, the eternity of the world, past and future, reduces Pat Ryan to undifferentiated prime matter.[26]

In the last book of his forty-volume work *The Revival of the Disciplines of Piety*, suitably entitled *The Remembrance of Death and the Afterlife*, al-Ghazali dwells at great length on every aspect of death and

24. Al-Ghazali, *Deliverance from Error*, 66.

25. Ibid.

26. I am grateful to Christopher Cullen, SJ, of Fordham University's Department of Philosophy for his help in formulating these sentences.

life after death and ends with an exhortation for all of us who must, willy-nilly, face the inevitability of death: "These Traditions, gathered together with those we have related in the *Book of Hope*, give us the glad news of the wide compass of God's Mercy (Exalted is He!). It is our hope that He will not deal with us as we deserve, but will rather grant us that which is appropriate to Him, in His generosity, abundant indulgence, and mercy."[27] I think of these words every time I hear the news of the death of any of my former students and colleagues in Ghana and Nigeria, and especially my Muslim friends in both countries.

Conclusion: Funerals Remembered

I began with a memory of death and the hope for life after death at a funeral in Africa. Let me conclude with some memories that will mark me out as what I am: an Irish New Yorker. I spent a significant part of my childhood attending wakes. For many Americans, that experience is much more occasional—if it ever happens at all. Some Americans consider it downright dreadful. They prefer the later memorial service, far removed from the corpse in place and time. But the Irish sources of my culture have developed a whole ethic of wake and funeral behavior. "I'm sorry for your trouble" is often said as an opener to the nearest family members standing by the coffin of the deceased. Prayer is uttered while kneeling beside the open coffin. Rising from that prayer one says that the dead person "looks so natural," even if he or she doesn't. A Mass card is left near the coffin and a memorial card is picked up. Then the lively talk and bursts of humor begin, sometimes even including the principal mourners, depending on how expected or unexpected the death of their relative was. I have found, at least in New York, that Italian wakes are much more somber than Irish wakes; Jewish wakes, usually without the body displayed, in my experience, at least, are both solemn and serious. Muslims bury their deceased as quickly as Jews, with only the immediate family involved in washing and clothing the corpse.

27. Al-Ghazali, *The Remembrance of Death and the Afterlife* [*Kitab dhikr al-mawt wa-ma ba'dahu*], Book XL of *The Revival of the Religious Sciences* [*Ihya' 'ulum al-din*], ed. and trans. T. J. Winter (Cambridge: Islamic Texts Society, 1989), 261.

Irish wakes are great places to meet old friends and exchange the latest news, the most hilarious jokes, happy reminiscences of times past. They provide a joyful setting for looking forward to life after death. James Joyce took the title of his last work of fiction, *Finnegans Wake*, from a Dublin music hall song that told the story of Tim Finnegan, a hod-carrier at whose disorderly wake whiskey (*uisce beatha* in Irish, "the water of life") was accidentally spilled on the corpse, causing Finnegan to rise from the dead.

There is something much more satisfying, intellectually and spiritually, about life after death conceived as the resurrection of the body than of life after death as the pale survival of a soul in the manner of the shades in the Greek underworld. Jews, Christians, and Muslims have all looked forward to resurrection as a bodily event, albeit a transformed bodily event, the fruition or flowering of the spiritual-corporeal whole that is you or me. None of us is hoping for the resuscitation of our aging carcasses, so that we can grow older and older, more and more feeble, in some preternatural Florida. Resurrection of the body promises much more and much better than bodily prolongation. In that resurrected future I hope to meet not only the risen Jesus, but my family and friends as well, including my student whom I buried more than three decades ago, Agyei Barimah.

In an early short story entitled "Pigeon Feathers," John Updike (1932–2009), a man who lived and died with this same hope for the resurrection of the dead, has his fourteen-year-old protagonist, David, find in the remains of pigeons he has shot down as nuisances in the family's barn a promise of very concrete life after death. David is dumbfounded to discover the beauty and variety of the dead pigeons' feathers, and what he sees confirms him in his faith that God is able to conquer death. "He was robed in this certainty," Updike writes, at the conclusion of the story, "that the God who had lavished such craft upon these worthless birds would not destroy His whole Creation by refusing to let David live forever."[28] I try to live robed with the same certainty, although nothing is pellucidly clear on this side of the grave.

---

28. John Updike, *Pigeon Feathers and Other Stories* (New York: Knopf, 1962), 150.

D., I have outlived just about all the men among my paternal and maternal ancestors. My father died at forty-five, his only brother at forty-three; their father
died at sixty. My mother's father died at fifty-six, her brother at seventy-six.
There was a paternal great-great-grandfather of mine who lived much longer,
to judge from the family headstone in Ireland. John Ryan, the founder of the
Ryan Lacken family of Knockfune, near Newport, County Tipperary, died in 1879
at the age of ninety-six, which means he was born in 1783. He moved in the
1840s, the time of the famine, from lowland Tipperary, good farmland, to moun-
tainous north Tipperary, bad farmland. He did this, as far as we can determine,
as a consequence of an unspecified encounter with local agents of Queen Vic-
toria. Needless to say I am not descended from a long line of Irish Anglophiles.

My father's death in his forties was more than partially caused by his life
"on the run" during the Irish war of independence (1919–22) and the subsequent civil war (1922–23). Two cases of rheumatic fever (before the invention of
penicillin and other antibiotics) made major contributions to weakening my father's heart. I would have liked to know my father better, as did my older sister,
but I was only four when he died in January 1944.

This mention of my father's relative youth at death brings me to the subject of contemplating my end and the challenge it poses to faith in the God
who raises the dead. I have a very vivid memory of being beaten up by the bul-
ly who lived next door in Woodside, a neighborhood in Queens. The boy who
beat me up was a young contemporary of mine named Jimmy. There were three
tribes who lived on our block in Woodside back in the 1940s: Irish, Italians, and
Jews. We Irish got along with our fellow Irish and with the Jews, especially the
Weinbergs, a widow with two daughters—one a beauty queen and the other a
charming tomboy. It was only when I joined the Boy Scouts at the age of eleven
that I met my first Protestant, and I'm not sure if he really counted: he was a
Quaker.

To get back to my unfortunate encounter with Jimmy: it must be noted that
he belonged to the Italian tribe on 65th Street. One late summer afternoon Jimmy beat me up, an act of miscreancy on his part that resulted in my mother
going next door to remonstrate with his mother. While my mother was out of
sight, engaging in dialogue with Jimmy's mother, my father returned—I'm not
sure from where. He stood by me and held my hand, smiling gently and a little ironically as my mother continued her conversation with Jimmy's mother.
I asked my mother about that event many years later and she said I never had

any trouble with Jimmy until we were both in grade school, which would have been nearly two years after my father's death. Did I only dream his presence with me that afternoon?

My father and my mother are still with me, seventy-four years after his death and twenty-seven years after hers. The older I become, the more I realize that I am accompanied in my living by those who have died, and especially by my dead relatives in Ireland and America as well as my dead friends in Nigeria and Ghana, where I have lived and loved for a long time.

I think of life and death as a turbulent sea in which we survive for a while but finally drown. There is hope, however, beyond the drowning and through the drowning. T. S. Eliot phrased it well in one of his Four Quartets, a short passage in the full quartet he entitled "The Dry Salvages." In this passage he reflects not only on a bell heard across the waves from a Catholic church near Cape Ann in Massachusetts—the Angelus bell commemorating three times a day the Virgin Mary's conception of Jesus—but also the sound of a bell heard ringing from a buoy warning sailors of treacherous rocks just beneath the surface of the turbulent sea, the Dry Salvages of the poem's title. The Virgin Mother of Jesus reigns not only as queen of heaven in this situation but also as guardian of all those on earth and on the seas whose faith is shaken by the surging waters and treacherous rocks of death.

> Lady, whose shrine stands on the promontory,
> Pray for all those who are in ships, those
> Whose business has to do with fish, and
> Those concerned with every lawful traffic
> And those who conduct them.
>
> Repeat a prayer also on behalf of
> Women who have seen their sons or husbands
> Setting forth, and not returning:
> Figlia del tuo figlio,
> Queen of Heaven.
>
> Also pray for those who were in ships, and
> Ended their voyage on the sand, in the sea's lips
> Or in the dark throat which will not reject them
> Or wherever cannot reach them the sound of the sea bell's
> Perpetual angelus.[29]

29. T. S. Eliot, *Collected Poems 1909–1962* (New York: Harcourt, Brace and World, 1963), 197–98.

CHAPTER 6

Circling around God: The Faith of Pilgrims

Have you ever gone on a pilgrimage, D.? My first pilgrimage took place in the fall of my freshman year in high school. With my fellow pilgrims I traveled by train from New York City to Auriesville, New York, a village in the Mohawk River Valley. Six decades ago, all the Jesuit institutions in and around New York City hired a full train so that students, staff, and other friends of the Jesuits could travel together on pilgrimage to the Shrine of the North American Martyrs near the village of Auriesville about thirty-five miles west of Albany. Auriesville today is probably the location of what was once the Mohawk settlement called Ossernenon. Three saints died as martyrs there: the French Jesuits René Goupil (d. 1642), Isaac Jogues (d. 1646), and Jean LaLande (d. 1646). The recently canonized Mohawk woman, Catherine Tekakwitha, was born at Ossernenon in 1656 but died in what is now Canada. Needless to say, the martyrdom of those French Jesuits not only testified to their faith but also, quite realistically, to the forebodings the Mohawks harbored about encroaching French presence in the middle of the seventeenth century.

Our pilgrimage to Auriesville in 1953 was not all prayer and solemnity, although there were both at the Mass in the Martyrs' Shrine that Sunday, and along the paths that took us past trees marked with simple crosses and the name of Jesus in imitation of a practice once followed by the seventeenth-century missionaries. But the train ride on either end of the visit to Auriesville was more fun, as I recall. In 1953 we were not that different from Chaucer's fourteenth-century pilgrims to Canterbury, or the young people who journey on foot today along the Camino de Santiago to Compostela in Spain.

Let me take you, D., on pilgrimage, in fact three pilgrimages—Jewish, Christian, and Muslim—each one featuring a unique pilgrim, each of these pilgrims very different from each other and yet each of them very like you and me. PRAYER CHANGES THINGS, I once read many years ago on a sign outside a Holiness Church in Washington, D.C., and I have come to understand what that means over the years. Prayer, although addressed to God, mainly changes you or me. Pilgrimage is a type of prayer in motion, a geographical prayer, not a variety of tourism or any other secular journey. Pilgrimage as prayer changes things in the pilgrim. The roads we follow as pilgrims take us to sacred places that have been waiting for our arrival all our lives. Those destinations welcome us—they welcome us, but they also transform us.

That late September visit to Auriesville remains very vivid in my mind, as have subsequent visits to Aurieville in the depths of winter when I was a Jesuit novice and a mid-summer spent there in the last phase of Jesuit formation, when I made the full thirty days of the Spiritual Exercises of St. Ignatius Loyola for the second time in my life, immediately after finishing graduate studies. The outer pilgrimage was then replaced by inner pilgrimage. I think not only of the French Jesuit martyrs and the young Mohawk woman who once lived there but also of the many other Native Americans, both those who accepted the Gospel and those who did not, those much displaced and abused people whose faith is known to God alone. The Mohawks found in those woods and valleys and the flowing river that passes them insight into the mighty power of God.

At the state funeral in April 2013 of Baroness Thatcher, for eleven years prime minister of the United Kingdom (1979–90), the congregation sang a hymn that caught my fancy. The hymn said much about the Methodist origins of Margaret Thatcher, even though she died a member of the established Church of England. Written by the famous prose writer John Bunyan, it occurs toward the conclusion of his book *The Pilgrim's Progress*. Modern English hymn books usually present a bowdlerized version of Bunyan's original, as in the version sung at

Thatcher's funeral; I much prefer the Puritan vigor and wild imagery of Bunyan's original:

> Who would true Valour see
> Let him come hither;
> One here will Constant be,
> Come Wind, come Weather.
> There's no Discouragement,
> Shall make him once Relent
> His first avow'd Intent
> To be a Pilgrim.

> Who so beset him round
> With dismal Storys,
> Do but themselves Confound;
> His Strength the more is.
> No Lyon can him fright,
> He'l with a Gyant Fight,
> But he will have a Right,
> To be a Pilgrim.

> Hobgoblin, nor foul Fiend,
> Can daunt his Spirit:
> He knows, he at the end,
> Shall Life Inherit.
> Then Fancies fly away,
> He'l fear not what men say,
> He'l labour Night and Day,
> To be a Pilgrim.

An African Muslim friend of mine over the past five decades stayed with me a few years ago at Fordham University. One morning, as he was preparing his breakfast, I suddenly realized that he was whistling that hymn. "Where did you learn that?," I inquired. "We used to sing it in primary school back in the colonial days," he admitted, and we laughed. "It's a pity," he went on, "but nowadays the children don't learn any hymns in school." I am sure that is true in the public schools of his home country, a nation more than 90 percent Muslim.

As I thought over my friend's fond recollection of learning Bunyan's hymn as a child, it also struck me that the hymn is surprisingly interreligious, if you wish, although Bunyan might have been horrified to discover this. At the heart of the Jewish, Christian, and Muslim traditions of faith, pilgrimage plays an enormous role. Each tradition has a sense that at its core lies a journey that all must undertake if they are to reach the destination of life. Pilgrimage is not the same in each tradition, but in many ways all three faith traditions map their visions of the world in a geography of faith, largely as a result of their pilgrimage traditions, traditions of worldly travel that are really various ways in which we human being circle around God.

Aliya: Pilgrim Ascent to Mount Zion

The desire of Jews to go on pilgrimage (*aliya*) to the Holy Land, and especially to Jerusalem—to ascend to Zion, to translate the Hebrew expression literally—derives from legislation in the Torah. In the Book of Exodus, the people of Israel are commanded to worship God at regular intervals: "Three times in the year you shall hold a festival for me" (Ex 23:14). The word for "festival" in this context is *hag*, the cognate in Hebrew of the Arabic word *hajj*, and it suggests a pilgrimage as well as going around in a circle.[1] Psalm 48 seems to refer to such ritual circumambulation: "Walk about Zion, go all around it, count its towers" (Ps 48:13). All of the psalms between Psalm 120 and 134 are prefaced with the note that each is "A Song of Ascents." Psalm 122 begins with words placed in the mouth of a pilgrim to Jerusalem and its Temple: "I was glad when they said to me, 'Let us go to the house of the LORD'" (Ps 122:1).

The times of those three festivals mandated in the Book of Exodus were connected with stages of the agricultural cycle: the Feast of Passover (*Pesach*) or Unleavened Bread, at the time of planting; the Feast of Weeks or First-Fruits (*Shavuot*), occurring when the first grains can be harvested; and the Feast of Tabernacles (*Sukkot*), associated with the

---

1. See Richard C. Martin, "Pilgrimage: Muslim Pilgrimage," *Encyclopedia of Religion*, ed. Lindsay Jones, 2nd ed. (Detroit: Macmillan Reference USA, 2005), 7154–61, esp. 7155.

completion of the harvest. The Book of Exodus does not specify where these feasts are to be held, saying only that "Three times in the year all your males shall appear before the Lord GOD" (Ex 23:17). The Book of Deuteronomy, however, a document of the seventh century BCE—several centuries after King David's centering of the united Israelite kingdom and its worship on Jerusalem—insists on the unity of Israelite cultus, implicitly at Jerusalem, referred to anonymously as "the place where the LORD your God will choose out of all your tribes as his habitation to put his name there" (Dt 12:5). When Solomon consecrated the Temple in Jerusalem in the tenth century BCE, he insisted that everyone, even Gentiles attracted to the faith of Israel, should ever afterward utter their prayers while facing in the direction of the Jerusalem Temple (1 Kgs 8:41–43):

When a foreigner, who is not of your people Israel, comes from a distant land because of your name—for they shall hear of your great name, your mighty hand, and your outstretched arm—when a foreigner comes and prays towards this house, then hear in heaven your dwelling-place, and do according to all that the foreigner calls to you, so that all the peoples of the earth may know your name and fear you, as do your people Israel, and so that they may know that your name has been invoked on this house that I have built.

The Jerusalem-centeredness of faith in the Israelite and, eventually, the Jewish tradition, raises some questions about people who trace their origins as a people to the call of Abraham (Abram) and his immediate descendants, Isaac and Jacob, ancestors in faith much anterior to the era of David and Solomon. Each of the earliest patriarchs is identified with particular sacred places where they worshiped God, many of them quite far from Jerusalem. Abraham, for instance, built an altar to worship God at Shechem (Gn 12:6), where he originally entered the Land of Promise. Abraham built altars at several other locales as well: between Bethel and Ai (Gn 12:8), at Hebron (Gn 13:8), at Beer-sheba (Gn 21:33), and finally at Moriah (Gn 22:14). Isaac also worshiped God at Beer-sheba (Gn 26:23–25), and Jacob, more famously, at Bethel (Gn 28:18–19, 35:1–3).

Later Israelite tradition identified Moriah, where Abraham had been willing to sacrifice his son Isaac, with the site of the Temple in Jerusalem (2 Chr 3:1), although this geographical reference is not entirely explicit in scripture. The Book of Genesis also manages symbolically to identify Abraham's worship of God with Jerusalem by arranging an encounter between the patriarch and the mysterious priest-king of Salem, Melchizedek, who blesses Abram in the name of "God Most High" (Gn 14:19). One possible translation of Psalm 110 considers the incumbent Davidic-descended ruler in Jerusalem as the heir of Melchizedek (Ps 110:4). Abram pays to Melchizedek (Gn 14:20) the tithe later identified in Israelite tradition as the tax for the support of Jerusalem Temple officiants (Nm 18:31). The unity of Israelite faith assured by the centering of the cultus on Jerusalem in the era of David and Solomon broke down with the collapse of the united monarchy after Solomon's death. Almost immediately, Jeroboam, the first ruler of the Northern Kingdom, realized that the continuation of worship of the LORD at Jerusalem would undermine his throne. Thus he instituted or reinstituted worship of the LORD at Dan and Bethel, at the northern and southern ends of his kingdom. The Jerusalem-centered account of this Northern Kingdom worship refuses to recognize the worship at these shrines as anything but idolatry of the worst sort, adoration of a golden calf (1 Kgs 12:25–33). We have no alternate theological or historical narrative from a Northern Kingdom perspective that might contradict this accusation. In the eighth century BCE the Southern Kingdom prophet Amos made his way north and excoriated the worship at Bethel and other shrines outside Jerusalem's control (Am 5:5). Amaziah, the priest at Bethel and a loyalist of the Northern Kingdom's ruler, Jeroboam II, reacted vehemently to the preaching of Amos. "'O seer, go, flee away to the land of Judah, earn your bread there, and prophesy there; but never again prophesy at Bethel, for it is the king's sanctuary, and it is a temple of the kingdom'" (Am 7:12–13).

The experience of exile entered into the lives of the people of the Northern Kingdom in the late eighth century BCE, and into the lives of the people in the Southern Kingdom in the early sixth century. Neither Northern Kingdom shrines nor the Southern Kingdom Temple at Jerusalem survived as centers of worship. The Book of Daniel nevertheless portrays its eponymous hero as one who refused, even in Persia, to submit to the public cultus of the divinized king in that place of exile. Instead, in the privacy of his room Daniel prayed to the God of Israel alone, and he prayed in a room with a precise geographical orientation, "windows in its upper room open towards Jerusalem" (Dn 6:10). After the Babylonian Exile, the Jews built the Second Temple in Jerusalem at the urging of prophets like Haggai (Hg 1:1–11). In the final century BCE the Judean-Idumaean king, Herod the Great, undertook a massive rebuilding of that Second Temple to please his Jewish subjects, but the project was more or less completed only a few short years before the Zealot uprising which resulted in the Roman destruction of the Second Temple in the year 70 CE. Jews resumed the Babylonian Exile tradition of prayer facing Jerusalem and its one God, especially after the Romans forbade access to Jerusalem for Jews in the aftermath of the Bar Kokh-ba Revolt (132–35). Even if Jews have been acculturated in many differ-ent social and educational backgrounds over the centuries, especially after the Diaspora effected by the Romans, they have continued to turn to God in the direction of the hill in Jerusalem where the Temple once stood.

No Jew of later centuries exemplified this prayerful geographical orientation better than the scholar and poet of eleventh- and twelfth-century Spain, Judah Halevi. His social and educational background had profoundly immersed Halevi in the Muslim culture of Spain, but his inner life as a Jew—and especially as a Levite (*ha-Levi*)—oriented him to the Land of Israel and Jerusalem, referred to as Zion. Halevi's most famous prose work in Arabic, *The Kuzari* (*Kitab al-Khazari*, "The Book of the Khazar") purports to be the record of an extensive conver-sation between a Jewish scholar and the king of the Khazars, an ethnic group of southwestern Asia who had tented in what is now the Cau-casus. Some of the Khazar nobility converted to Judaism in the eighth century, but Halevi's king is a creation of the writer's imagination in twelfth-century Spain. According to Halevi, the superiority of revealed knowledge of God over philosophical knowledge of God corresponded

also with the superiority of the Jewish religious tradition over other traditions. That superiority also attached to the Jewish homeland, which
Halevi always referred to as *al-Sham*, the normal Arabic word for the
whole area of today's Syria, Lebanon, Jordan, Israel, and the Palestinian territories.[2] In this geographical and theological centeredness (not
to say ethnocentrism), Halevi continues the tradition of many other
ancient and medieval writers, Hellenistic, Christian, and Muslim, who
constructed geographies of various climes proving that one or another
homeland provided the world with its true center.[3]

At the end of his life Halevi left Spain for the Land of Promise, dying
shortly after his arrival there. Halevi's most famous poem, his "Ode to
Zion," is used in the annual Jewish commemoration of the Ninth of Av,
the day in the Jewish calendar that commemorates the destruction of
both the First and the Second Temples. It looks forward to what would
be Halevi's pilgrimage at the end of his life. "Jerusalem! Have you no
greeting for your captive hearts, your last remaining flocks, who send
you messages of love? Here are greetings for you from west and east,
from north and south, from near and far, from every side—greetings
also from a certain man, a captive of your love."[4] Although the poem
addresses itself to Zion, the poet cites various places of encounter between God and the patriarch Jacob that are unconnected with Jerusalem: "My heart is aching for Beth-el, Peniel, Mahanayim, every place
where saints met messengers from God."[5] Halevi's Zion is much larger
than Jerusalem and the Temple Mount; it encompasses every place in
the Land of Promise where Israelites of old encountered the reality of
the LORD God dwelling in their midst, what has been called the *Shekhina*. Halevi describes in an almost folksy manner the goal of his pilgrimage as to arrive at the place "where the *Shekhina* is your neighbor."[6] It

---

2. See C. E. Bosworth, "al-Sham," *EI2*, 9:261.

3. See S. Maqbul Ahmad, "Djughrafiya," *EI2*, 2:575–87, esp. 575.

4. For this translation, see Scheindlin, *The Song of the Distant Dove*, 172–77. For the very first
word of this ode in translation (173), I prefer the more literal rendering of the Hebrew in English by
the translators of Franz Rosenzweig, *Ninety-Two Poems and Hymns of Yehuda Halevi*, ed. Richard
Cohen, trans. Thomas Kovach, Eva Jospe, and Gilya Gerda Schmidt (Albany: State University of New
York Press, 2000), 272: "Zion! You do not inquire about those who carry Your yoke."

5. Scheindlin, *Song*, 173.

6. Ibid.

is God dwelling among his people, the *Shekhina*, that consecrates not only Mount Zion but all of Israel.

We know very little about how Judah Halevi ended his days, except that his death apparently occurred shortly after his arrival in the Holy Land in 1141. What we do know is that Halevi, the descendant of Levites who had once served in the Temple, was finally able to follow in their footsteps. At the end of his life he found it possible to pray not only in the direction of Jerusalem, but right there. "God chose to dwell in you [Zion]," Halevi wrote, "and happy is the man He chooses to bring near / to make his home within your courts."[7] That centeredness on Mount Zion, Jerusalem, and the Land of Promise continues in the faith tradition of Jews to the present day. Zionism bears a family resemblance to many other nationalistic traditions of the late nineteenth century, especially in central and eastern Europe, but the Jewish theological orientation to Jerusalem and to the hill of Zion—and especially, the Jewish tradition of the pilgrim ascent to Zion (*aliya*)—makes it unique, although not every Israeli or every Jew recognizes this.

Decentered, but Christocentric Pilgrimage

Jesus as Lord and Messiah stands at the center of the Christian faith tradition, and therefore at the center of Christian pilgrimage. This holds true even for those Christian pilgrimages that seek out shrines commemorating localized visions of the Virgin Mary, such as Lourdes, Fatima, Częstochowa, and Knock, or the tombs of martyred saints like Peter and Paul in Rome, James the Greater at Compostela, and Thomas Becket at Canterbury. When Jesus Christ is not at the center of any Christian pilgrimage, it too easily degenerates into a cult surrounding dubious visionaries or fictionalized saints. The altar where the Eucharist is celebrated at a pilgrimage shrine often stands over or near the tomb where the martyred saint is buried, or very close to the locale where the visionary experienced the presence of the Virgin Mary.

Although there are many Christian pilgrimage sites in Jerusalem

7. Ibid., 177.

and the Holy Land more generally, for more than a millennium and a half the road of Christian pilgrims coming from outside the Holy Land led not to Mount Zion, the goal of Jewish pilgrimage, but slightly off center, as it were, to the nearby Church of the Holy Sepulcher in Jerusalem, which commemorates both the death and the resurrection of Jesus. Christian pilgrims to the Holy Land have also sought out the holy places commemorating the birth of Jesus in Bethlehem and his ascension from the Mount of Olives. Only the soldiers of the First Crusade, after enacting a brutal pogrom against the Jews of the Rhineland in 1096, directed their marauding and murderous path toward the Temple Mount.[8] Upon their arrival in Jerusalem in 1099 they slaughtered many, possibly most, of the Muslims and Jews living there,[9] profaning with their blood the Muslim site called the Noble Sanctuary (*Haram al-Sharif*), the place where the Jerusalem Temple had once stood.[10]

For Jesus himself, however, *aliya* or ascent to Mount Zion in Jerusalem played an important role during his lifetime. But after the destruction of the Temple in Jerusalem by the Romans, Christians of Jewish origin no longer focused their lives of prayer on the Temple Mount in the same way that Jesus had, or that Jews in the Diaspora from the late first century CE continued to do. This historical fact may be taken as one aspect of the melancholy but gradual history of separation of Christianity from its Jewish roots; it also points to the great difference that Jesus introduces into the monotheism inherited from Israel.

Luke's Gospel depicts Jesus as a man on a journey, in some sense a pilgrimage, to Jerusalem.[11] "When the days drew near for him to be taken up," Luke writes, "he set his face to go to Jerusalem" (Lk 9:51). At the conclusion of Luke's Gospel, Jesus leaves Jerusalem by ascending

---

8. See P. M. Holt, *The Age of the Crusades: The Near East from the Eleventh Century to 1517* (London: Longman, 1986), 22.

9. See Simon R. Schwarzfuchs, "Crusades," *EJ2*, 5:311.

10. See the anonymous contemporary chronicle of these events entitled *Gesta Francorum et aliorum Hierosolymytanorum* as translated by A. C. Krey in *The First Crusade: The Accounts of Eyewitnesses and Participants* (Princeton, N.J.: Princeton University Press, 1921), available at www.fordham.edu/halsall/source/gesta-cde.asp.

11. According to Fitzmyer (a specialist on the Lucan writings) in *The Gospel According to Luke (I–IX)*, "the overarching geographical perspective in Luke-Acts can be seen as the author's preoccupation with Jerusalem as the city of destiny for Jesus and the pivot for the salvation of mankind" (164).

into heaven from Bethany on the Mount of Olives (Lk 24:50–51). The infancy narrative of Luke, a highly symbolic presentation of the significance of the life, death, and resurrection of Jesus worked out in the account of his earliest years, brings Jesus to Jerusalem twice: the first time to be presented as an offering to God in the Temple and redeemed by his parents (Lk 2:22–39), and the second time as a pre-adolescent pilgrim who ascends to Jerusalem with his parents for Passover. Luke narrates in this context how Jesus was separated from his parents in Jerusalem for a period of three days and then reunited with them in the Temple, symbolically presaging his death in Jerusalem and his resurrection after three days (Lk 2:41–52).

John's Gospel more realistically portrays Jesus as making at least three canonical pilgrimages to Jerusalem.[12] The first and the last of these canonical ascents to Jerusalem took place at Passover at the beginning of the public career of Jesus and at its conclusion. In his account of the first Passover pilgrimage of Jesus, John describes the uproar Jesus caused when he drove the sellers of animals for sacrifices and the changers of profane coinage into Temple shekels out of the Court of the Gentiles (Jn 2:13–22). The other three evangelists (Mk 11:15–18, Mt 21:12–13, Lk 19:45–46)[13] narrate this event as something of a prelude to the final conflict between Jesus and the Temple authorities: "Is it not written, 'My house shall be called a house of prayer for all the nations? But you have made it a den of robbers'" (Mk 11:17).

John's Gospel places the cleansing of the Temple at the beginning of his narrative, depicting it as an event of even greater symbolic and theological importance: "'Destroy this temple,'" Jesus says in John's Gospel, "'and in three days I will raise it up'" (Jn 2:19). John assures us that Jesus was not speaking literally about the Second Temple, but figuratively about "the temple of his body," maintaining that "after [Je-

12. Jesus also visits Jerusalem for the non-canonical feast of Hanukkah (Jn 10:22), a feast which commemorates the Maccabees' renewal of the Temple after its profanation by Antiochus IV Epiphanes in the second century BCE.

13. In these Synoptic narratives Jesus identifies his symbolic action with three motifs in the Hebrew Bible: Third Isaiah's vision of a Temple open even to Gentiles (Is 56:6–7), Jeremiah's hostility to the Temple as a source of false hope for the citizens of Jerusalem just before the Babylonian Exile (Jer 7:11), and Zechariah's visionary critique of the presence of traders (or Canaanites) in the Temple (Zec 14:21).

sus] was raised from the dead, his disciples remembered that he had said this; and they believed the scripture and the word that Jesus had spoken" (Jn 2:21–22).

On his final Passover pilgrimage to Jerusalem, Jesus, according to John's Gospel, is put on trial before priestly and Roman authorities. John's Pharisees and priests fear that the work of Jesus might provoke the Romans to "destroy both our holy place and our nation" (Jn 11:47–48). The Gospels of Mark and Matthew recall among the accusations leveled against Jesus a very literal interpretation of his words that he would "destroy this temple that is made with hands, and ... build another, not made with hands" (Mk 14:58; see also Mt 26:61). The Gospels of Mark, Matthew, and Luke all agree that a certain symbolic destruction of the Temple occurred at the time of the death of Jesus, the tearing of the veil that separated the Holy of Holies from the rest of the Temple (Mk 15:38, Mt 27:51, Lk 23:45). The Gospel writers, composing their written accounts of Jesus after 70 CE, saw in that tearing of the veil a hint of the disaster that would eventually befall the Temple.

In between the two Passover pilgrimages to Jerusalem in John's Gospel, Jesus visits the Temple for the Feast of Tabernacles (*Sukkot*). He figuratively presents himself on the last day of that festival as the fulfillment of, or even replacement for, some of the central symbolic elements of *Sukkot*. When water from the fountain of Gihon is poured out in the Temple by the High Priest "on the last day of the festival, the great day," Jesus symbolically associates that water with himself: "Let anyone who is thirsty come to me, and let the one who believes in me drink" (Jn 7:37–38).[14] Likewise, when four enormous golden candlesticks are lit in the Court of the Women on the first night of *Sukkot*, illuminating much of Jerusalem, Jesus claims the image for himself: "I am the light of the world. Whoever follows me will never walk in darkness but will have the light of life" (Jn 8:12). A similar claim to replacement or even abolition of aspects of the Temple worship at Jerusalem comes up in the account in John's Gospel of the meeting between Jesus and a

---

14. On the symbolic significance of this statement of Jesus in John's Gospel, see Raymond E. Brown, SS, *The Gospel According to John (I–XII)*, The Anchor Bible 29 (Garden City, N.Y.: Doubleday, 1966), 327.

Samaritan woman at Jacob's well, near Mount Gerizim, where the Samaritans centered their ritual lives. Jesus relativizes all sacred geography in that dialogue, telling his Samaritan interlocutor that "the hour is coming when you will worship the Father neither on this mountain nor in Jerusalem" (Jn 4:21). It is no wonder, then, that some Judeans accused Jesus of being a Samaritan and possessed by the devil (Jn 8:48).

For all the hints at the future destruction of the Second Temple in the four Gospels, the Acts of the Apostles depicts the first Jerusalem Christians as people who still feel at home in the Temple (Acts 2:46). Preaching the message of Jesus and performing a miraculous healing in that sacred setting bring the disciples into conflict with the Temple authorities (Acts 3:1–4:31), but the disciples still continue "every day in the temple and at home ... to teach and proclaim Jesus as the Messiah" (Acts 5:42). A break with the Temple cultus, however, begins among some of the Greek-speaking members of the Jerusalem Christian community. Stephen, one of the seven Hellenist Jews who served his fellow Greek-speaking Jewish Christians in Jerusalem, is accused by his critics of "saying things against this holy place and the law" (Acts 6:13). In the tradition of Jeremiah, Stephen also relativizes the importance of the Temple: "The Most High does not dwell in houses made by human hands" (Acts 7:48). The Book of Revelation, in its depiction of the future, heavenly Jerusalem, envisions no Temple in that eschatological scenario: "For its temple is the Lord God the Almighty and the Lamb" (Rv 21:22).

Even before the Western Roman emperor Constantine the Great issued the Edict of Milan in 313 CE, making Christianity licit throughout his domain, Christians had begun to undertake pilgrimage or at least visits to the places where Jesus had lived and died and risen.[15] Eusebius of Caesarea makes much of the pilgrimage undertaken in the fourth century by his imperial patron, Constantine, and his redoubtable

---

15. Eusebius records a visit, apparently to the Holy Land, by Bishop Melito of Sardis (in what is now western Turkey) during the reign of Marcus Aurelius (161–80 CE), not for pilgrimage but for research into the scriptures that made up the Hebrew Bible: "I came to the east and reached the place where these things were preached and practiced, and learnt accurately the books of the Old Testament." See *The Ecclesiastical History,* Loeb Classical Library 153 (Cambridge, Mass.: Harvard University Press, 1926), IV.xxvi (393).

mother, Helena. To Constantine we owe the location of the place in Jerusalem where Jesus had died, was buried, and rose again, now the
Church of the Holy Sepulcher.[16] Helena is said to have built the original
Basilica of the Nativity in Bethlehem and an oratory on the Mount of
Olives, marking the locale where the disciples witnessed the ascension
of Jesus.[17] Those three locations may be taken as symbolic of the difference between Jewish *aliyah* leading to the Jerusalem Temple or its
ruins and Christ-centered pilgrimage focused on the whole mystery of
the incarnation. That seemingly small but deeply significant decentering of pilgrimage, away from the Temple Mount and toward Golgotha,
Bethlehem, and the Mount of Olives, reorganized the geography of
faith for Christians.

In the same century Cyril, bishop of Jerusalem, describes how the
baptism of neophytes in the Church of the Holy Sepulcher oriented
them quite literally, directing them toward the east. In the outer cham-
ber of the church the neophytes first faced west—the direction of Egypt,
the land of darkness and of bondage—to renounce their sins. Then
they faced toward the rising sun. Entering the church they stripped
off their clothes and were led by the hand toward "the sacred pool of
divine Baptism, as Christ passed from the cross to the Sepulcher you
see before you."[18] The geographical directedness of those neophytes in
the Church of the Holy Sepulcher in fourth-century Jerusalem may be
taken as an early example in Christian liturgy undertaken *ad orientem*,
facing the east.

Such eastward directedness has proven theologically and liturgi-
cally controversial in the last two centuries, especially in Anglican and
Catholic circles, where the orientation of church buildings, altars, cele-
brants, and congregations has been debated. The pope emeritus, Benedict XVI, published a book on liturgy while he was still Joseph Cardinal
Ratzinger, in which he argued that for early Christians "the east super-

16. See Eusebius of Caesarea, *Vie de Constantin*, Sources chrétiennes 559 (Paris: Les Éditions
du Cerf, 2013), III.25–40 (384–401).

17. Ibid., III.41–43 (401–7).

18. "Mystagogical Lecture II," in *The Works of Saint Cyril of Jerusalem*, trans. Leo P. McCauley,
SJ, and Anthony A. Stephenson, The Fathers of the Church (hereafter, FOTC) 64 (Washington, D.C.:
The Catholic University of America Press, 1970), 2:163–64.

sedes the Jerusalem temple as a symbol." He goes on to note that "we cannot date exactly when this turn to the east, the diverting of the gaze from the Temple, took place, but it is certain that it goes back to the earliest times and was always regarded as an essential characteristic of Christian liturgy (and indeed of private prayer)."[19] It should be noted, in passing, that most churches in Manhattan and the Bronx, at least, follow the city's grid and are placed geographically on a north-south axis, facing either north or south. Saint Patrick's Cathedral and the Cathedral of Saint John the Divine, however, face eastward. The Major Basilica of Saint Peter in Vatican City has always faced west, even in its original construction under Constantine.

The seventh-century conquest of Jerusalem by the armies of 'Umar, the second caliph in succession to Muhammad, started devotional pilgrimage by Muslims to the long abandoned site of Mount Zion, believed in Islamic tradition to be the location of "the furthest place of worship" (*al-Masjid al-Aqsa'*) to which Muhammad had traveled by night (Qur'an 17:1). Although Romans—pagan and later Byzantine Christian—had barred Jews from access to Jerusalem and the Temple Mount, the Umayyad Muslim rulers of Syria originally welcomed both Jews and Christians to visit their own holy places under Muslim sway.[20] Orthodox Jews, however, prefer to pray at the Western Wall of the Temple today rather than on the platform that was once the site of the actual Temple, and especially the Holy of Holies.[21]

When, four centuries after the Muslim conquest of Jerusalem, Christian access to their own holy places in Jerusalem became difficult under later and more antagonistic Muslim regimes, this difficulty—as well as the perilous decline of the Eastern Christian Roman Empire—provided motives for starting what have come to be called the Crusades.[22] But

19. Joseph Cardinal Ratzinger, *The Spirit of the Liturgy*, trans. John Saward (San Francisco: Ignatius Press, 2000), 68.

20. See Grabar, *The Dome of the Rock*, 42–46.

21. A *minyan*—a group of ten men needed for a valid Orthodox synagogue service—in 2013 attempted, in defiance of Israeli law, to pray publicly on the Temple Mount within the precincts of the Noble Sanctuary. See Jodi Rudoren, "Ten Jewish Men Detained at Temple Mount," *New York Times*, October 14, 2013.

22. There is a vast literature on the origin of the Crusades. See, e.g., Jonathan Riley-Smith, *The First Crusade and the Idea of Crusading*, 2nd ed. (London: Continuum, 1993).

the earliest crusaders defined what they were doing as *peregrinatio*. Usually translated as "pilgrimage," the word *peregrinatio* more literally means "foreignness," and it was thought of as penitential exile for sin,[23] even if the crusader pilgrims too often fell into more grievous sin on their journeys toward the Holy Land, as noted earlier with regard to the First Crusade.

A penitent pilgrim of the sixteenth century, Iñigo López de Loyola—better known today as Ignatius Loyola—found a new orientation for his life in 1523 when he traveled to the east as a pilgrim. On the eve of his scheduled departure, after three weeks spent in Jerusalem, Ignatius gave in to "a great desire to go back and visit the Mount of Olives again before he left."[24] In his brief *Autobiography* he mentions no other holy place in Jerusalem. What was Ignatius looking for on the Mount of Olives at the Muslim shrine that had once been the oratory built by Helena? Markings on a stone in the floor of the shrine were said to be the footprints Jesus left behind. It is more probable that they derive from a too-literal understanding by Christians of a verse from an apocalyptic vision of the LORD in the Book of Zechariah: "On that day, his feet shall stand on the Mount of Olives, which lies before Jerusalem on the east" (Zec 14:4).

In any case, Ignatius slipped away from his fellow pilgrims and their Ottoman guides that final day of his pilgrimage and went off alone to the Mount of Olives. The sentries did not want to let him enter, but Ignatius paid the entry fee, not once but twice. He gave them his pen knife the first time, and his scissors the second time, when he wanted to revisit the spot shortly afterward because "he hadn't taken a proper look at where the right foot was or where the left was."[25] When the Franciscans discovered that their Basque pilgrim had gone missing, they sent one of their servants to retrieve him. That servant marched

---

23. On *peregrinatio* as penitential exile, see John Mahoney, *The Making of Moral Theology: A Study of the Roman Catholic Tradition* (Oxford: Clarendon Press, 1987), 11–13. See also, H. E. J. Cowdrey, "The Genesis of the Crusades," in *The Holy War*, ed. T. P. Murphy (Columbus: Ohio State University Press, 1976), 22–23.

24. "Reminiscences or Autobiography," in *Saint Ignatius Loyola: Personal Writings*, ed. Joseph A. Munitiz and Philip Endean (London: Penguin Books, 1996), 34.

25. Ibid., 35.

Ignatius back under arrest to the Franciscan custody in what would to-day be called a "perp walk." Ignatius endured this humiliation with patience, feeling that "he was seeing Christ always over him."[26] His life's Christocentric pilgrimage was not to end finally in Jerusalem but in Rome. Ignatius remained, to the close of his days, "the pilgrim," the term he used for himself in his *Autobiography*. It would no longer matter to him where the right foot and the left foot of Jesus were planted on the Mount of Olives. Ignatius had placed his own feet firmly on the pilgrim road that leads to the presence of God.

The *Hajj*: In the Footsteps of Abraham

The pilgrimage (*hajj*) to the places in the Arabian Peninsula that Muslims associate with Abraham plays a more central role in the practice of Islam than does pilgrimage in either the post-biblical tradition of Jews or the tradition of Christians at any period. One of the five pillars (*arkan*) of Islam, the *hajj* nevertheless is not quite so rigorously required of all Muslims as are the other four pillars.[27] Problems in financing the *hajj*—or performing it at times of civil unrest on the roads to or within Arabia—could excuse a faithful Muslim from undertaking the fulfillment of this pillar of Islam. Every Muslim I have ever known in Africa, at least, wishes to undertake this sacred journey at least once in his or her lifetime. Some undertake it more often.

Although there are other local or sectarian pilgrimages in Muslim societies, the *hajj* uniquely provides all Muslims, Sunni or Shiʻi, with their own geography of faith. All Muslims face Mecca in worship five times a day; within Mecca they face the *Masjid al-Haram*, the Sacred Mosque; within the Sacred Mosque they surround the empty and windowless cubic building at its heart, the Kaʻba, said in some sense to

---

26. Ibid.

27. The other four pillars include the dual witnessing to the oneness of God and the message Muhammad brought (the *shahadatani*); the canonical worship performed five times daily and on Fridays in community at midday (*salat*); the poor-due that purifies legitimate profits (*zakat*); the annual month-long fast usually undertaken in the month of Ramadan (*sawm*). Some Shiʻi Muslims include a sixth pillar in this company: *jihad*, struggle for the cause of God, not necessarily military. See editors, "Rukn," *EI2*, 8:596.

be "the House of God." The Qur'an is quite specific in reporting God's words of command regarding this sacred place: "We arranged for the House to be a refuge for humankind and a sanctuary: 'Take Abraham's place of worship as yours as well.' We made a covenant with Abraham and Ishmael: 'Purify my House for those who circumambulate it, for those who ponder there, for those who bow down there, for those who prostrate themselves there'" (Qur'an 2:125).

Abraham plays some part in Jewish pilgrimage to Mount Zion, especially when later Jewish tradition conflated Mount Moriah in Jerusalem with "the land of Moriah" (Gn 22:2), where Abraham had been called upon to sacrifice his only son.[28] Abraham plays no role at all in Christian orientation in prayer toward the locales of the birth, death, resurrection, and ascension of Jesus. But the patriarch returns to the center of religious attention as Ibrahim in the Muslim pilgrimage.[29] For Muslims, moreover, the stories of Abraham are not connected with the land of Canaan or with a patrilineal inheritance through Isaac. Along with Hagar (*Hajar* in Arabic), the mother of his first-born son (*Isma'il*)—the quintessential human scapegoats in the Book of Genesis—the Quranic Abraham meets his God in the desert vastness of Arabia, precisely in the place where the Sacred Mosque now stands in Mecca. The place of Abraham (*maqam Ibrahim*) is singled out as a small pavilion near the Ka'ba. The hillocks of Safa and Marwa, revered as the places to which the frantic Hagar ran to find water for her baby in the desert, lie today at either end of a colonnaded portico within the precincts of the Sacred Mosque. Muslim tradition, however, maintains that the Ka'ba built by Abraham and Ishmael eventually descended into polytheism, what is called more vividly in Arabic *shirk*, falsely ascribing to God partners in the divine reality.

God's command to Abraham and Ishmael to "purify my House" points to the fact that pre-Islamic Arab festivals were celebrated at regular intervals at or near the Ka'ba in Mecca, pilgrimages that only ended when Muhammad and his exiled compatriots finally conquered

---

28. Grabar, *The Dome of the Rock*, 50.
29. See A. J. Wensinck, J. Jomier, and B. Lewis, "Hadjdj," *EI2*, 3:31–38.

his native city in 630. The pre-Islamic *hajj* seems to have been characterized by a somewhat orgiastic quality, with at least some of the pilgrims, and perhaps most of them, circumambulating the Ka'ba in a state of complete nakedness.[30] Poetic competitions accompanied by considerable levity and exorbitant spending also characterized this polytheistic *hajj*.[31] The mercantile elite of Mecca welcomed strangers to market festivals in certain fixed months of the year, events that featured veneration of multiple divinities enshrined in the Ka'ba. It may be for this reason that, at least until 624, two years after his migration from hostile Mecca to welcoming Yathrib (later, Medina), Muhammad led his valiant band of Meccan and Medinan monotheists in worshiping God while facing northward toward the unseen Temple Mount in Jerusalem. Absence made the heart grow fonder, however, and after 624 the Muslims in Medina directed their worship toward what is called the second *qibla*, the direction of Mecca and the Ka'ba, places still distinctly pagan but safely out of sight.[32]

Muhammad's earliest preaching of God's oneness and the moral demands that one God made may have been deemed to threaten the polytheistic and mercantile identity of the Ka'ba, and Mecca with it. Two of the briefest and earliest suras that Muhammad received in Mecca, *Surat al-Fil* (Qur'an 105: "The Sura of the Elephant") and *Surat Quraysh* (Qur'an 106: "The Sura of Quraysh") assure Muhammad and his earliest listeners that the Ka'ba and the pilgrimage will survive, albeit in a transformed manner, continuing to play a central role in the life of the Quraysh, the Arab tribe to which Muhammad and most of his Meccan disciples and adversaries belonged. The first of these two brief suras sees God's providence at work in the deliverance of Mecca and the Ka'ba from an Abyssinian army that invaded the Meccan area with an elephant, an event dateable to the time of Muhammad's birth around 570. "Have you not seen what the Lord did with the elephant people?

---

30. See Ibn Ishaq, *Life*, 87–88.

31. See the censorious observations on these practices by the twentieth-century Indo-Pakistani moralist, Sayyid Abu'l A'la Mawdudi (d. 1979) in his *Let Us Be Muslims*, ed. Khurram Murad (Leicester: Islamic Foundation, 1982), 254–55.

32. Some authors suggest that Muhammad's break with the Jewish communities in Medina may have also influenced this change of *qibla*. See A. J. Wensinck, "Kibla," *EI2*, 5:82–83.

Did He not bring their clever ploy to confusion?" (Qur'an 105:2–3). The following sura continues in the same vein, asserting that God assured this pre-Islamic victory with the aim of "making the Quraysh secure—making them secure by having caravans come both in the winter and the summer" (Qur'an 106:1–2). But there would be a difference in the purified Ka'ba, once its many idols were toppled. It would now be a place of the strictest monotheism, where "they will worship the Lord of this House, who feeds them in their hunger and saves them from fear" (Qur'an 106:3–5). Polytheism would have to go, but the Ka'ba and its pilgrimage would remain, continuing to make Mecca prosperous right down to the present day.

What purpose does the *hajj* serve in the lives of Muslims? As in many other pilgrimages, there is in the *hajj* not a little of the penitential, entailing hope for the remission of past sins. From the beginning of their *hajj*, pilgrims are ritually separated from their ordinary, day-to-day life, including any prideful elements in that life. They enter into *ihram* (consecrated status) and after making a total ablution (often coming down to a shower) all male pilgrims dress in two unsewn pieces of white cloth that cover the upper and lower parts of the body. This common dress not only separates the male pilgrim from his previous situation as a Muslim of a particular ethnic and national identity, symbolized by distinctive clothing, but it also bonds him with his fellow pilgrims who wear the same uniform. No specific *ihram* garments are prescribed for women, but a coverall is generally worn that leaves only the hands and face visible.

Once Muslim pilgrims have entered into *ihram*, they must abstain from sexual relations and also avoid all quarreling or other bad behavior (Qur'an 2:197), including such otherwise legitimate actions as killing an animal or uprooting a plant, with exceptions made for killing snakes or dangerous insects. A highpoint of the *hajj*—but not the highest—occurs when the pilgrims, newly arrived in Mecca, undertake seven circumambulations of the Ka'ba and the subsequent sevenfold ritual run between the hillocks of Safa and Marwa in imitation of Hagar. The *hajj*, however, is dramatically differentiated from the *'umra*, the devotional visit to Mecca only held outside the pilgrimage season. On the ninth day of the *hajj* all pilgrims stand together on Mount 'Arafat, the "hill of mercy" twenty miles east of Mecca. From midday until dusk, they listen to sermons and beg for God's mercy. The rite of standing (*wuquf*) on Mount 'Arafat for that afternoon and early evening brings the pilgrimage to its climax. The theocentrism of Islam and the *hajj* emerge most eloquently in the often repeated pilgrimage prayer, the *talbiya*: "Here I am, O God, here I am! You have no associate [in Godhead]! To You are due praise, grace and power! Here I am!"[33]

That evening, after the *wuquf*, the pilgrims move hastily from Mount 'Arafat to Muzdalifa, where they stay overnight. On that night of the ninth of *Dhu'l-hijja*, the pilgrims gather stones to prepare for the ritual stoning of what may have been ancient, pre-Islamic idols still preserved for such symbolic repudiation at Mina, halfway back to Mecca. At Mina the pilgrims also ritually reenact Abraham's sacrifice of a ram to replace his only son. Muslims throughout the world join the pilgrims in commemorating this incredible act of self-surrender—Islam, in its most radical sense—on the tenth day of the month of *Dhu'l-Hijja*, calling the day *'Id al-adha'* (The Feast of the Oblation).

For many Muslims the *hajj* also serves, even more importantly, as an education in Islam—either a deepening of what is already known, or an introduction to those elements of the Islamic tradition that have never been emphasized or understood in the previous life of the pilgrim. Several notable African pilgrims in times past have changed their lives and the lives of their neighbors as a result of what they learned in Mecca and its environs, as well as what they learned along the route to and from Mecca. The eleventh-century Almoravid reform of Islam in northwestern Africa and eventually Spain traced its origins to the experiences on the *hajj* of a chief of the Guddala, a subgroup of the Zenaga Berbers who lived on the borders of present-day Mauritania and Mali. That chief, Yahya ibn Ibrahim, when he made the pilgrimage, realized that he and his fellow Guddala knew virtually nothing of their faith as Muslims. As a result he hired a teacher from northern Morocco,

33. See Toufic Fahd, "Talbiya," *EI2*, 10:160–61.

'Abd Allah ibn Ya'Sin, whom he took "with him to his home, where seventy persons assembled to learn and obey."[34]

The Mauritanian pilgrim of the nineteenth century Ahmad ibn Tuwayr al-Janna ("Ahmad, the son of the little bird of paradise") dilates at great length in his memoir on all that he learned not only at Mecca and Medina but also in places on his journey to and from Mecca and Medina as diverse as Cairo and Gibraltar.[35] In more recent times the charismatic African-American Muslim preacher Malcolm X learned on the only *hajj* he ever made, in spring 1964, the racial diversity of the worldwide Muslim community. When he first saw the Ka'ba within the precincts of the Sacred Mosque of Mecca, he was struck by the fact that the worshipers consisted of "thousands upon thousands of praying pilgrims, both sexes, and every size, shape, color, and race in the world."[36] Travel broadens, they say; pilgrimage—ancient and modern—does much more.

Conclusion

Jews still center their faith on Jerusalem and Israel, and more dramatically so over the past century or more since the modern Zionist movement began. Some Orthodox Jews fondly visit the tomb of Maimonides, at Tiberias in Galilee, or the gravesites of other scholars and saints, but Jerusalem still provides all Jews with a direction for prayer. The decentering of Christian pilgrimage continues to the present day, although many Christians still seek out Jerusalem and the Holy Land more generally, to follow the *Via Crucis* or to kneel where Jesus was born, where he died and rose, where he ascended into glory. The labyrinths in certain Gothic cathedrals built in medieval France seem to have substituted for the rigors of pilgrimage to Jerusalem, as did the medieval Franciscan-

---

34. Abu 'Ubayd Allah al-Bakri, *Kitab al-masalik wa'l-masalik*, as excerpted in *Corpus of Early Sources for West African History*, ed. Nehemia Levtzion and J. F. P. Hopkins, trans. J. F. P. Hopkins (Cambridge: Cambridge University Press, 1981), 71.

35. See *The Pilgrimage of Ahmad Son of the Little Bird of Paradise*, ed. and trans. H. T. Norris (Warminster: Aris and Phillips, 1977), 31–33, 45, 94–99.

36. Malcolm X with the assistance of Alex Haley, *The Autobiography of Malcolm X* (New York: Grove Press, 1965), 367.

inspired Stations of the Cross, an attempt to allow non-pilgrims to follow the steps of Jesus on the way to his death on Golgotha. The rigors of ancient Christian pilgrimage to Jerusalem can be found today more concretely acted out along the Camino de Santiago in Spain, or while fasting and walking in the circular stony penitential "beds" of Saint Patrick's Purgatory on Station Island in Lough Derg, County Donegal.

Muslims continue to make the pilgrimage in enormous numbers to the places where Abraham encountered God in the Arabian Peninsula. Secondarily, they may also visit the Prophet's mosque and his tomb in Medina, as well as the Al-Aqsa Mosque and the Dome of the Rock in Jerusalem, but those visits are not part of the canonical *hajj*. Some Shi'i Muslims also seek out the tombs of Muhammad's son-in-law, 'Ali, at Najaf, and his grandson, Husayn, at Karbala, both of those holy places in Iraq, as well as the tomb at Mashhad in Iran of the eighth Imam in 'Ali's lineage, Ali al-Rida. I have also seen Shi'i women, their black chadors billowing in the wind, climbing the circling staircase that mounts the ziggurat in Harissa, Lebanon, where Maronite Catholics have enthroned an image of Notre Dame du Liban. Like so many Muslim women, they seek the intercession of the mother of the Messiah, especially when problems arise with conception, childbirth, or the health of children. As Shi'is they also associate Mary, the mother of the persecuted prophet Jesus, with Fatima, the daughter of Muhammad and the sorrowful mother of the martyred Imams.

Circumambulation of a holy place after a pilgrim journey and before a return journey focuses the pilgrim on the mystery at the core of each pilgrimage. I gave some thought to the possibility of making the pilgrimage to Saint Patrick's Purgatory recently, during a visit to Ireland, but anticipatory arthritic discomfort at the prospect of barefoot circumambulation of those stony beds dissuaded me. Instead, I visited very privately—and well shod—a tiny shrine near the quay on the bank of the Shannon in the village of Terryglass (*Tir-na-ghlas*) in Country Tipperary. Ireland is dotted with holy wells, but this holy well, called Saint Augh's Well, is much better cared for than many others. Saint Augh's Well specializes in the cure of eye problems; suitably enough, it is eye-shaped. A nearby sign informs the pilgrim that St. Augh was a Christian youth and scholar of the ninth century CE who lost his eyes to the cruelty of a pagan Danish chieftain who lived in nearby Slevoir.

St. Augh was healed at this well, and pilgrims to this site seeking help with ophthalmic problems are urged to do so on four Saturdays in May between sunrise and sunset. There they are to start the single cir-cumambulation of the well, beginning at the flagstone that faces east-ward toward the rising run. At each quarter of the circle the petitioner should recite the Apostles' Creed once, as well as the Our Father and the Hail Mary five times each. After completing this prayerful circum-ambulation the pilgrim petitioner should wash his or her eyes with wa-ter from the well. A small token of one's gratitude to God and St. Augh can be left in the form of flowers strung from a nearby bush.

Imaginary lines of latitude and longitude crisscross our globe, but pilgrim routes map the real world. Many pilgrim routes lead to the crossroads of the world where the three segments of the Afro-Eurasian landmass connect and yet divide: in the neighborhood of Mount Zion, the hill of Golgotha, and Mount 'Arafat. Not infrequently our pilgrim paths have transected each other in that crossroads of the world— sometimes in peace, but too often in war, especially over the past cen-tury. In the long run our pilgrim journeys do not call us to advance like crusaders in battle-array, but to walk in peace round and round again, contemplating the great mysteries that lie at the heart of our faith tra-ditions. On my journey as a Christian—and on a Jew's journey as a Jew or a Muslim's journey as a Muslim—we should all look across at each other and see a fellow pilgrim. Let us pray for each other's peaceful arrival at places where all of us can circle around the mysteries at the heart of all reality.

After my initial pilgrimage to Auriesville at the age of fourteen, D., there were many other pilgrimages in my life: to Lourdes, for instance, with my widowed mother in 1957, just before I entered the Society of Jesus. My mother found peace in Lourdes after some months of fear and loneliness as she contemplat-ed my becoming a Jesuit later that summer, as well as the imminent marriage of my sister, my only other sibling. The Lady of Lourdes assured my mother that she would never be utterly alone in her widowhood, any more than the woman entrusted to the care of the Beloved Disciple was ever really alone after that day on Golgotha. I myself also learned something about prayer those days in Lourdes, catching sight one evening of a French boy scout around my own age kneeling and praying by himself in the sanctuary. Following the custom of the local people of the Pyrénées at that time, he was praying with his arms out-stretched. I sensed that his prayer was an act of total self-surrender to God, and I can still picture him all these years later.

In 1936 the great Anglo-American poet T. S. Eliot visited the ruins of the semi-monastic Anglican community at Little Gidding in Cambridgeshire, the place where the devout Ferrar family and eventually even King Charles I took refuge from the religious hatreds that sundered seventeenth-century England. Eliot in his poem, "Little Gidding," the fourth of his *Four Quartets*, bids us to come to Little Gidding not as tourists but as pilgrims:

> You are not here to verify
> Instruct yourself, or inform curiosity
> Or carry report. You are here to kneel
> Where prayer has been valid.[37]

That, finally, is what all pilgrimage is about, a geographical prayer that is valid. Such prayer changes us, if we allow it. Judah Halevi experienced prayer that is valid, prayer that changed him, when he finally reached the soil of the Land of Promise. Iñigo López de Loyola experienced prayer that is valid in the Holy Land, and then over and over again revisiting the Holy Land in contemplation, and he was changed by such geographical contemplation. Malcolm X followed the steps of Abraham on the hajj and, seeing the diversity of his fellow pilgrims, found genuine Islam there, prayer that is valid in the submission of one's whole self to God and to God alone. That experience changed him during the last year of all too short a life. Without traveling anywhere, each of us is still called to be a pilgrim, a woman or man of prayer that is valid. PRAYER CHANGES THINGS. Let prayer transform you, D. That is the point of every pilgrimage, including the pilgrimage of life.

37. Eliot, *Collected Poems*, 201.

CHAPTER 7

Naming the God with Whom We Keep Faith

D., as someone who has lived in Africa and Asia for many years, I think you will appreciate the importance of local languages, even if your work and mine were mainly conducted in English. In summer 2010, a few years after I returned to United States, I was invited to join a group of scholars and curators who had already been meeting for some months to help plan an exhibition of Jewish, Christian, and Muslim materials from the permanent collection of the New York Public Library. The exhibition took place from fall 2010 into the early months of 2011 and can still be found, at least in part, on the NYPL's website under the title "Three Faiths." It was an interesting experience, especially working with curators. I found myself becoming an advocate for some less than obviously beautiful books, especially a small copy of an 1838 translation of one of the Gospels into the Grebo language spoken by fisherfolk from Liberia.

The name of the exhibit, "Three Faiths," is hard to pronounce in English and bothered me a bit because I am not sure you can count "faiths." It was a better title than one suggested by a younger curator for the exhibit who proposed the more contemporary "OMG!" as a possible title, teenage text-speak for "Oh my God!"

It never ceases to amaze me how people who are not very religiously inclined still fall back on the invocation of God's name in moments of frustration and moments of joy. I have heard attributed to the Italian communist politician of an earlier era, Palmiro Togliatti (1893–1964), and also to Woody Allen, the pithy declaration that "I am an atheist—thank God!" The name of God still passes the lips of the faithful and the faithless alike in such unforeseen circumstances as stubbing one's toe or slipping on a wet bathroom floor. But naming God—pronouncing the name of the One whose reality centers the lives of faithful Jews, Christians, and Muslims—has not been taken for granted in every culture or in every historical period.

Henri IV, the Huguenot king of Navarre, finally succeeded in taking the throne of France in 1590 after he renounced his Calvinist roots. An apt but unlikely legend has it that he said at the time that *Paris vaut bien une messe* ("Paris is well worth a Mass"). Despite his Calvinist upbringing and his subsequent conversion to Catholicism, Henri IV continued in bad habits: he kept mistresses and even made two of his illegitimate sons bishops, one at the age of six and the other at the age of four, and this despite the reforms introduced after the Council of Trent. Although many of the local clergy of Gallican sympathies disliked Henri IV, the French Jesuits did their best to deal with the reality of the only king they had, once he was established in Paris.[1]

The Jesuit Pierre Coton even served as the king's confessor. One of the prevailing vices of Henri IV was a habit of blasphemy. *Je renie Dieu*, he would cry out in a moment of exasperation: "I renounce God." In his typically Béarnais pronunciation of French, that exclamation by Henri IV would sound more like *Jarnidieu*. Hoping to help his penitent to renounce the evil habit of renouncing God on a regular basis, Père Coton suggested to Henri IV that he substitute for that blasphemy *Je renie Coton*, "I renounce Coton." In the Béarnais dialect that came out as *Jarnicoton*, and the non-blasphemous curse word entered into the French language. On the Internet you can find information about a Connemara pony over forty years ago named *Jarnicoton*, as well as advertisements for a pricey non-sulfite blend of Cabernet and Merlot from the south of France called *Jarnicoton*. The Jesuits popularized many

1. See Eric Nelson, *The Jesuits and the Monarchy: Catholic Reform and Political Authority in France (1590–1615)* (Aldershot: Ashgate Publishing Company for the Institutum Historicum Societatis Jesu, 2005).

other non-blasphemous curse words in French of that era. *Sacré Dieu!* ("Holy God!") became *Sacrebleu!* ("Holy Blue!"), a favorite exclamation of Agatha Christie's Hercule Poirot. I suspect this French spoken curiosity is the origin of what we call today blue language.[2]

The name of God, and the very fact that human beings are or are not *allowed* to call God by name, has a long history in the world's traditions of faith. In this chapter I will concentrate on the privilege and the danger that confronts Jews, Christians, and Muslims in naming God.

Naming or Not Naming God in the Jewish Tradition

In the Hebrew Bible two principal names are given to God, one rather generic and the other quite unique. The generic name for God, *Elohim*, is plural in form but singular in meaning when it refers to the God of Israel. But other speakers of Semitic languages in the ancient Near East also used words with the same basic root, *el* or *il*, to denote a force or forces external and superior to human beings, gods, or even something approaching God with a capital *G*. In ancient Ugarit, a cultural area that flourished on the Mediterranean coast of present day Syria in the second millennium BCE, the name El designated the highest god in their pantheon. Like many of the so-called high gods in African traditional forms of faith, the Ugaritic *El* "generally fades into the background and plays a minor role in the preserved myths."[3] The same cannot be said of the homonymous God in the ancient tradition of Israel. In the first chapter of Genesis *Elohim* dominates the action of creation: "In the beginning when God created the heavens and the earth, the earth was a formless void and darkness covered the face of the deep, while a wind from God swept over the face of the waters. Then God said, 'Let there be light'; and there was light" (Gn 1:1–3).

A shorter version of the name *Elohim*, or perhaps a vocative form of that name, *El*, appears in what is called grammatically "construct":

2. I am grateful to a French Jesuit, Nicolas Steeves, who introduced me to this aspect of French and Jesuit history.

3. Louis Hartmann and S. David Sperling, "God, names of," *EJ2*, 7:672b.

God of X, Y, or Z or perhaps "O God of X, Y, or Z." There are several such
numinous names by which God is invoked in the Hebrew Bible, not all
of them entirely obvious in their significance. Many of them seem to be
archaisms, especially those found in the Book of Job and in the Psalms.
Examples of such preserved but not entirely understood ancient titles
of God include *El 'elyon*, often translated as God Most High; *El 'olam*, often translated as God the Everlasting; *El shaddai*, usually but probably
erroneously translated as God the Almighty; *El ro'i*, translated either
as God of Vision or God Who Sees; and finally *El berit*, fairly obviously meaning God of the Covenant. The name *Eloah*, found forty times
in the Book of Job, may well be a more formal singular form of *Elohim*
than *El*.[4] The fact that biblical Hebrew uses a plural-sounding word to
designate the utterly singular God of Israel more than two thousand
times should not surprise us. When *Elohim* is used with a singular verb,
it quite obviously means God with a capital G, and when it is used with
a plural form of the verb, it sometimes means "gods." Psalm 82 plays
on this ambiguity, imagining a divine triumph in judicial imagery pic-
turing a single God demoting and finally condemning lesser gods to
death: "God [*Elohim*] has taken his place in the divine council; in the
midst of the gods [*elohim*] he holds judgment" (Ps 82:1). It should also
be noted that the word *elohim*, apparently plural in form, resembles
the plural form of abstract words like *hayyim*, meaning life, and may
simply represent an abstraction, "the Divinity." In any case, the earliest
Israelite perception of God may be better characterized as henotheistic:
exclusive worship of one God ("our God," "the God of Israel") without
denying the existence, power, and even threat of other gods ("the gods
of the nations").

Such henotheism may have prevailed in Israel at least until the era of
Second Isaiah (the late sixth century BCE), when that prophet, famous
for his worldwide vision, speaks with God's voice to declare that "I am
the LORD, and there is no other; besides me, there is no god" (Is 45:5).[5]
The God of Israel was sometimes addressed with respect as a king might

---

4. Ibid., 672b–674b.
5. See John L. McKenzie, "Aspects of Old Testament Thought," in *NJBC*, 1287a.

be, or the owner of a slave, or the husband of a wife, *adoni* ("my lord"). That term of address was rendered in the plural when it referred to God, a plural that corresponded with the plural form of *Elohim*. Thus God could be addressed as *Adonai* ("my LORD"), even apart from the more usual substitution of this royal divine name in speech for the tetragrammaton (YHWH), to be discussed below.

The text of the Book of Genesis and the rest of the Torah are ascribed by scholars to the human authorship of blended literary sources, referred to as the Yahwist (J), the Elohist (E), the Deuteronomist (D), and the Priestly source (P). All four sources use the more generic name for God, *Elohim*, sometimes in combination with the unique name ascribed to God in the account of the experience Moses had at the burning bush. That unique name of God belongs to no category of common or proper nouns and is said to be the third-person-singular form of the name God gave himself (or did not give himself, some would say) when God was speaking to Moses. It is a combination of two identical first-person-singular verbs linked by a pronoun: *Ehyeh-Asher-Ehyeh*. Most English translations of the Bible opt for translating that Hebrew name as something like "I AM WHO I AM" (Ex 3:14), often in small capital letters. The Jewish Publication Society translation (1999) simply transliterates the Hebrew,[6] possibly as a way to avoid controversy as to how it should (or should not) be translated. The name so expressed can be construed as a revelation of the divine name or as a refusal to disclose the divine name, not unlike the refusal to reveal a name by the One who wrestled with Jacob by night: "Jacob asked, 'Please tell me your name.' But he said, 'Why is it that you ask my name?'" (Gn 32:29).

The Septuagint, the Greek translation of the Hebrew Bible, came into existence at various times between the third century BCE and the early second century CE.[7] In the Septuagint, *Ehyeh-Asher-Ehyeh* is ren-

---

6. The JPS *Tanakh* does this as "Ehyeh-Asher-Ehyeh." Franz Rosenzweig in 1929 wrote a most insightful essay on the problems involved in translating the tetragrammaton and the difference between the translation he was working on with Martin Buber and the much earlier translation of the Torah by Moses Mendelssohn (d. 1786): "'The Eternal': Mendelssohn and the Name of God," reproduced in Martin Buber and Franz Rosenzweig, *Scripture and Translation*, trans. Lawrence Rosenwald with Everett Fox (Bloomington: Indiana University Press, 1994), 99–113.

7. See Patrick W. Skehan, "Septuagint," *NCE Supplement* (2009), 920b.

dered in Greek as *Ego eimi ho-ōn*. Translating this Greek can prove as problematic as translating the Hebrew. Let me start with "I AM THE ONE WHO IS," most neutrally, or "I AM THE EXISTENT ONE."[8] As such this translation of the Hebrew original preserves the personal character of God, a God very different from the Greek philosophical term *to on*, which is neuter: "Being," in a general or overarching and nonpersonal sense.[9] But it must be said immediately that the Greek translation of the Septuagint not only suggests a metaphysical definition of God, but also, in using a masculine present participle made into a substantive, suggests subliminally that "THE ONE WHO IS" or "THE EXISTENT ONE" is to be understood as "HE WHO IS." The choice of a masculine present participle serving as a substantive may be less significant than the fact that this Greek translation chooses a personal pronoun, in this case the "unmarked" or generic personal pronoun in the pairing of masculine and feminine possibilities,[10] and by choosing this personal substantive participle it insists on the personhood of God over a concept of God as a transcendent It.

The Hebrew original of what God said to Moses does not specify or even hint at any gender, as first-person-singular verbs in Hebrew have no gender; the same is true of the first-person-singular verb in the Greek Septuagint and the Latin Vulgate. Furthermore, the Greek is not content with the purely verbal form of the first person singular of the verb "to be" (*eimi*), a grammatically possible parallel to the Hebrew *Ehyeh*. The Greek insists on the emphatic specification of "I" (*ego*) as

8. The early Christian writers who relied on the Septuagint Greek of the Book of Exodus often derived rather metaphysical notions of God from this passage. See examples in *Ancient Christian Commentary on Scripture: Old Testament III: Exodus, Leviticus, Numbers, Deuteronomy*, ed. Joseph T. Lienhard, SJ, in collaboration with Ronnie J. Rombs (Downers Grove, Ill.: InterVarsity Press, 2001), 19–23.

9. It may have been the pre-Socratic philosopher Parmenides who first used the term "being" (*to on*) as an abstraction. See "The Poem of Parmenides," 8.35. For commentary on this passage, see *Plato and Parmenides: Parmenides' Way of Truth and Plato's Parmenides*, ed. and trans. Francis MacDonald Cornford (New York: Bobbs-Merrill, 1957), 43.

10. On these linguistic categories, see "Marked and Unmarked Terms," *Concise Oxford Companion to the English Language,* ed. Tom McArthur (New York: Oxford University Press, 1998), available at www.Encyclopedia.com. The article gives a pithy example: "In the pair *horse/mare*, horse is the more general, unmarked term, while *mare* is marked for femaleness. In the pair *cow/bull*, cow is unmarked, while *bull* is marked for maleness." In the last forty years or more, the unmarked quality of masculine pronouns in the English language has been radically challenged.

the subject of the verb, as does the Latin Vulgate. For any human being to speak about God—even for the scriptures to speak about God—is to stammer. To further complicate this subject, the pronoun between the two verbs of the divine name or the refusal to disclose a divine name need not be translated so personally; it could be rendered "I AM WHAT I AM."

But do the verbs in that name so clearly designate a present-tense God? It is quite possible that *Ehyeh-Asher-Ehyeh* means "I AM WHO I WILL BE," or "I WILL BE WHO I AM," or "I WILL BE WHO I WILL BE." Biblical Hebrew has no future tense,[11] dividing all verbs into the continuous (imperfect) and the completed (perfect) modes. Note that within the context of the same chapter of Exodus, just before the revelation of the divine name, future actions planned by God are mentioned: "'I will send you to Pharaoh to bring my people, the Israelites, out of Egypt ... I will be with you, and this shall be the sign for you that it is I who sent you: when you have brought the people out of Egypt, you shall worship God on this mountain" (Ex 3:10, 12).

Rashi, the great medieval Torah commentator, certainly interprets the divine name disclosed to Moses in the burning bush as future-oriented. According to Rashi, *Ehyeh-Asher-Ehyeh* "means that God "'will be' with them [the Israelites] in this predicament [Egyptian bondage] 'what I will be' with them in their [future] subjugation by other kingdoms."[12] Rashi goes on to say that the next words that follow in Exodus 3:14, "'I AM HAS SENT ME TO YOU,'" indicate that God is only informing the Israelites about divine accompaniment in their present Exodus distress, without telling them that there will be many more such situations of distress in their future from which they will have to seek rescue from God. Those future situations necessitating divine rescue are, according to Rashi, implied in the second and third words of the divine name in Hebrew (*Asher-Ehyeh*: "WHO I WILL BE"). Thus Rashi writes that "[Moses] said before [God]: "O Lord of the universe! Why should I mention to them another trouble? They have enough

---

11. Modern Hebrew does have a future tense, created in imitation of European languages.

12. See *The Complete Jewish Bible With Rashi Commentary* on Ex 3:14, available at www.cha bad.org.

[problems] with this one."[13] Rashi here follows the lead of the tractate
Berakot in the Babylonian Talmud, a work probably completed no later
than the sixth century CE:

The Holy One, blessed be He, said to Moses: Go and say to Israel: I was with you
in this servitude, and I shall be with you in the servitude of the [other] kingdoms. [Moses] said to [God]: Lord of the Universe, sufficient is the evil in the
time thereof! Thereupon the Holy One, blessed be He, said to him: Go and tell
them: I AM has sent me unto you.[14]

Much more could be said about the divine self-naming in the Book
of Exodus, or the understanding of that self-naming in later Jewish
writings.[15] Moses, of course, had to transform the first-person-singular
name of *Ehyeh* into the third person singular ("HE IS/HE WILL BE") to
make clear to the people that he was not speaking in his own voice. The
spelling of that third-person verbal name in Hebrew is called the tetragrammaton, usually symbolized by the four consonants YHWH, or simply by writing twice the consonant *yod*, the first of the four consonants
in the tetragrammaton. Although the people of Israel pronounced the
tetragrammaton before the Babylonian Exile, in the Second Temple
period (approximately 515 BCE to 70 CE) it became customary to substitute for the tetragrammaton another divine name mentioned earlier,
Adonai ("my LORD"), with the pronunciation of the tetragrammaton
reserved to Aaron and his descendants, the high priests, alone com-
missioned to bless the people with the divine name: "The LORD bless
you and keep you; the LORD make his face to shine upon you, and be
gracious to you; the LORD lift up his countenance upon you, and give
you peace" (Nm 6:24–26).

When the Masoretic scribes in the late first millennium CE supplied
vowels above and below the consonants of the Hebrew Bible to aid in
the pronunciation of the consonantal Hebrew text, they put above and
below the consonants of the tetragrammaton the somewhat adapted

13. Ibid.

14. *Berakot* 9b in *The Babylonian Talmud (Seder Zera'im)*, ed. and trans. H. M. Lazarus (London:
Socino Press, 1958), 38.

15. See, for a recent example, Avivah Gottlieb Zornberg, *The Particulars of Rapture: Reflections
on Exodus* (New York: Image, 2000), 74–77.

vowels of the word *Adonai*. Christian translators of the Hebrew Bible into German and some other languages after the Reformation mistakenly read the tetragrammaton with the vowels of *Adonai* in such a way as to create the ersatz word "Jehovah." Jehovah's Witnesses continue this usage down to modern times. Most translations of the Hebrew Bible into English simply print "Lord" (the ordinary substitution for the tetragrammaton) in capital letters every time that unique divine name occurs.[16]

In parts of the Torah where the sources are blended, the name of God is, as it were, hyphenated: the tetragrammaton precedes the name *Elohim*, the combination translated as "the Lord God." Thus, in the second account of creation in Genesis, considered the work of the Yahwist, we are told that "In the day that the Lord God made the earth and the heavens ... the Lord God formed the human being [*ha-adam*] from the dust of the ground [*ha-adamah*]" (Gn 2:4b, 7).[17] *Genesis Rabbah*, a commentary on Genesis written by rabbis between the second and fifth centuries CE, compares the combination of the two divine names, "the Lord" and "God," in the Yahwist's story of creation to the combination of hot water and cold water in one glass by a king; each type of water by itself would break the glass, but combined they temper each other. God the King in this parable explains his creative process: "'If I create the world on the basis of mercy alone, its sins will be great; on the basis of judgment alone, the world cannot exist. Hence I will create it on the basis of judgment and mercy, and may it then stand!' Hence the expression, 'the Lord God.'"[18] The tetragrammaton, then, in this

16. When the translators of *The Jerusalem Bible* in English (1966) followed the example of the original French *Bible de Jerusalem* (1956) and rendered the tetragrammaton as "Yahweh," the bishops of England and Wales asked them to substitute "the Lord" in lectionaries for liturgical usage. The Holy See took up this topic later and in 2008 Cardinal Francis Arinze, prefect of the Sacred Congregation for Divine Worship, forbade the usage of the tetragrammaton in liturgical texts. See the Catholic News Agency report of this on September 3, 2008, which can be found at www.catholic newsagency.com. Bishop Arthur Serratelli (Paterson, N.J.), chairman of the U.S. Bishops' Committee on Divine Worship, is quoted in the same source as saying that it might have "some impact on the use of particular pieces of liturgical music in our country." It would seem that hymns like the very popular "Yahweh, I Know You are Near," composed by Dan Schutte, might be affected. From the blogosphere it looks like the revision of this hymn—if it ever happens—will not be popular.

17. This is my slight variation of the NRSV rendering of the Hebrew, meant to underline the connection between the human being and the dust of the earth.

18. "Genesis," in *Midrash Rabbah*, trans. Rabbi Dr. H. Freedman and Maurice Simon (London: Soncino Press, 1939), 1:99.

tradition of Jewish commentary in the early centuries CE, is the name of God's mercy and *Elohim* is the name of God's judgment. We shall return to this tradition in what follows.

Jesus and the Names of God

Over sixty years ago I first heard someone from upstate New York exclaim, "Judas Priest!" The exclamation patently served as a way to avoid the exclamation, "Jesus Christ!," but I had never heard it before and presumed it must be some curious upstate aberration. Christian avoidance of expressing exasperation with the name of Jesus points to what is new about the Christian tradition of faith that emerged from a Jewish matrix: its centering on Jesus as both Messiah and LORD. The Decalogue forbade the Israelites to "make wrongful use of the name of the LORD your God" (Ex 20:7); Christians to the present day surround the name of Jesus, whose very name in Aramaic means "the LORD saves" (see Mt 1:21, Lk 1:31), with special reverence, such as a slight inclination of the head or even doffing of the biretta at the utterance of that name—for those who still wear birettas!

Until the Gospel was brought to Gentiles, there was no need for the preachers of the earliest Christian communities to insist on the theme of monotheism, something that could be presumed among Jews and Jewish Christians. Thus the first Jewish Christian evangelists, preaching to their fellow Jews, focused their preaching on two themes: the Messiahship and Lordship of Jesus. To proclaim the Messiahship of Jesus could be deemed a political act, encouraging allegiance to Jesus as a new king of Israel, even if Jesus eschewed such political aims, whatever may have been the ambitions of his disciples. To proclaim the Lordship of Jesus—his identity with the One who spoke to Moses in the burning bush—proved to be something utterly new in a Jewish setting: insisting on the meeting of the divine and the human in Jesus of Nazareth in a way that would strike most Jews as blasphemous. This proclamation of Jesus as LORD was something very new for Jews, even scandalous, as the Gospels make evident.

The Gentiles to whom Paul and other evangelists of the late first century brought the good news about Jesus were peoples who revered "many gods and many lords" (1 Cor 8:5) in their traditional religious setting, ranging from Zeus (Jupiter) on the most exalted level to *Divus Augustus*, the divinized Roman emperor, on the lower end of the scale. For such non-Jewish hearers of the Gospel, the first Jewish and Gentile Christian missionaries had to insist not only on the Lordship and Messiahship of Jesus but also on the oneness of God. Christian preaching ever since has had to steer a difficult course, as it were, through choppy theological waters between the rock of God's oneness and the shoals of the identity of Jesus as "true God and true man."[19] What eventually developed as the doctrine of the Trinity in the early church took its origins from the New Testament, the first crystallization of how Jewish Christians understood and proclaimed Jesus in the second half of the first century. The Jews and eventually Gentiles who embraced the way of Jesus had to find new language to express their faith in one God only, as well as their faith in Jesus as Messiah and LORD. How did they manage to do that? In some sense, the naming of God was all-important in this process.

Jews at the time of Jesus, the late Second Temple era, had for some time avoided pronunciation of the tetragrammaton, the unique name of God in the Jewish tradition. Many references to "the name" (*to onoma*) of God in the New Testament would be better understood, in my opinion, if we recognized in those words in Greek a rendering of the Hebrew *ha-Shem* ("your Name"), the surrogate for the tetragrammaton. Thus, for instance, in the prayer of Jesus quoted in the Gospels of Matthew and Luke, the phrase "the Name" occurs at the very beginning: "Our Father in heaven, hallowed be your name" in Matthew 6:9 and "Father, hallowed be your name" in Luke 11:2.[20] What does it mean to "hallow" the divine Name? I would suggest that this first sentence

19. See *Catechism of the Catholic Church*, no. 469.
20. Luke's version may be more original while Matthew's, beginning with "Our," reflects the liturgical use of the Lord's Prayer in the early church. The late first-century *Didache*, a catechetical treatise in Greek contemporaneous with most of the New Testament writings, orders that the Our Father in Matthew's form be said by Christians three times a day (*Didache* 8.2), available at www.annomundi.com/bible/didache.

in the Lord's Prayer, both in Matthew and Luke, is really an interjec-
tion, urging the first Christians, Jewish and especially Gentile, to keep
in mind the contemporary Jewish tradition of the utmost reverential
avoidance of pronouncing God's unique name (*ha-Shem*). Paradoxically that avoidance of pronouncing the divine name is combined with
addressing the One whose name is so reverentially avoided as Father,
in Aramaic, *Abba*.

In his mortal lifetime the Aramaic-speaking Jesus called God *Abba*,
especially in prayer. Mark tells us that Jesus in the Garden of Gethsemane cried out: "'Abba, Father, for you all things are possible; remove
this cup from me; yet, not what I want, but what you want'" (Mk 14:36).
The Aramaic word *Abba* is simply the equivalent of the Hebrew *ha-ab*,
"the Father," understood as vocative in form: "O Father!"[21] In so addressing God as *Abba*, Jesus seems to claim a unique personal relationship to God, a relationship based on themes already adumbrated in the
Hebrew Bible. But the relationship of Jesus to the One he called Father
seems more intimate, more individualized and uniquely personal than
the Father-Son relationship of God to the whole of Israel, expressed so
eloquently in Third Isaiah: "For you are our father, though Abraham
does not know us, and Israel does not acknowledge us; you, O LORD,
are our father" (Is 63:16).[22] The closest parallel in the Hebrew Bible to
the use of *Abba* by Jesus may perhaps be found in the Psalms where
God suggests to David that he should address the LORD with such in-
timacy: "'You are my Father, my God, and the Rock of my salvation!'"
(Ps 89:26). The Second Book of Samuel likewise promises a personal
Father-son relationship between the LORD and King David: "I will be a
father to him, and he shall be a son to me" (2 Sm 7:14). Such family in-
timacy between David and God led to the tradition of the king of Israel
being characterized as an adoptive son of God in a royal psalm, possibly one used at an enthronement: "I will tell of the decree of the LORD:
He said to me, 'You are my son; today I have begotten you'" (Ps 2:7).

21. Note that this interpretation modifies the supposed status of the name "Abba" as a term of
childlike endearment, not unlike "Papa" or "Daddy." See Máire Byrne, *The Names of God in Judaism, Christianity, and Islam: A Basis for Interfaith Dialogue* (London: Continuum, 2011), 56–75.

22. The prophet Jeremiah (3:19 and 31:9) as well as Malachi (1:6 and 2:10) both allude to God as
a Father to Israel in a corporate sense.

The use of the vocative *Abba* by Jesus so struck some of the writers of the New Testament that they simply transcribed the Aramaic word *Abba* in Greek. We have already seen Mark's transcription of that word in the prayer of Jesus in Gethsemane. Paul in the Epistle to the Galatians, written no later than the year 55, tells us that those redeemed by the death and resurrection of Jesus become adopted children of God: "And because you are children, God has sent the Spirit of his Son into our hearts, crying, 'Abba! Father!'" (Gal 4:6). In his Epistle to the Romans, written a few years later, Paul returns to the theme: "You have received a spirit of adoption. When we cry, 'Abba! Father!' it is that very Spirit bearing witness with our spirit that we are children of God, and if children, then heirs, heirs of God and joint heirs with Christ" (Rom 8:15–17). One could perhaps say that Christian trinitarian faith centers on the way Jesus addressed God as *Abba*, and the way God's Spirit enables those redeemed by Jesus to do the same.

Let me return to the importance of *ha-Shem*, the unpronounced name of God in the Jewish tradition, for understanding the New Testament account of Jesus. The Gospel of Matthew ends with the so-called great commission: "Go therefore and make disciples of all nations, baptizing them in the name of the Father and of the Son and of the Holy Spirit" (Mt 28:19). I would suggest that the Greek of this verse in Matthew's Gospel has not been translated adequately in NRSV or in many other translations. So translated, it give the impression that the disciples are deputized to baptize on behalf of the Father, the Son, and the Holy Spirit. But the text more radically declares that the first disciples should make disciples among all the Gentiles, and that they should do so by plunging those disciples *into* the name (*eis to onoma*)—into the ineffable divine reality (*ha-Shem*), the Lordship of the Father, the Son, and the Holy Spirit. Having so plunged these new disciples into the inner life of God, and having taught them to obey "everything that I have commanded you," Jesus promises both the original Jewish followers of Jesus and their later Gentile disciples that the Exodus accompaniment of God's people will continue into their future: "Remember, I am with you always, to the end of the age" (Mt 28:20). There is perhaps a parallel here with the Talmud's tractate Berakot and Rashi in their future-oriented understanding of the tetragrammaton: "I was with you in this servitude, and I shall be with you in the servitude of the [other] kingdoms."

The one who is praying, Jewish or Gentile, must remember the privilege involved in addressing God by name as *ha-Shem*. The secular Greek word *kyrios*, usually rendered in English as "lord" with either a small *l* or a capital *L*, denotes in Greek what the Hebrew word *adon* signifies. In the Septuagint, the related periphrasis for the tetragrammaton, *Adonai* in Hebrew, is also rendered *kyrios*, LORD in small capital letters. Translators of the New Testament are sometimes unsure how to translate *kyrios* in key New Testament passages, and especially how to translate its vocative form, *kyrie*. In secular Greek it could be used for any gentleman, and especially for an exalted ruler. Should *kyrie* be rendered "Sir," or "LORD" in this passage or another? It depends on the context.

Even when the word is addressed to Jesus, it may have begun its history as simply a polite "Sir," or even a somewhat ironic "Sir," as when the woman of Samaria reminds Jesus that he has no means to supply her with fresh water from a well: "Sir [*Kyrie*], you have no bucket, and the well is deep. Where do you get that living water?" (Jn 4:11). But even within that intriguing dialogue, the woman of Samaria comes to use the term with less irony: "Sir [*Kyrie*], I see that you are a prophet" (Jn 4:19). John's Gospel reaches one of its two conclusions with the clearest example of the divine use of the word *Kyrios*. The disciple Thomas, who had doubted the testimony of his fellow disciples about the risen Jesus, was confronted by the risen Jesus in the midst of the disciples a week later: "Thomas answered [Jesus], 'My Lord and my God!'" (Jn 20:28). In those words of Thomas, linking the words Lord and God in reference to Jesus, one senses a certain parallel with the theme enunciated in *Genesis Rabbah* commenting on Genesis 2:4, where we are told that those two divine names, *Elohim* and the tetragrammaton, express God's judgment and God's mercy, cold water and hot water combined so as not to break the glass. In this context the glass involved was the fragile faith of doubting Thomas.

Paul in his epistles uses the word *Kyrios* most obviously in the way that his Jewish contemporaries used *Adonai* or even *ha-Shem*. In a famous hymn he quotes in the Epistle to the Philippians, written in the late fifties of the first century, the divine name of the LORD (*ha-Shem*) is bestowed on Jesus in his resurrection and ascension as a result of his suffering and death: "Therefore God also highly exalted him and gave him the name that is above every name, so that at the name of Jesus every knee should bend, in heaven and on earth and under the earth, and every tongue should confess that Jesus Christ is Lord, to the glory of God the Father" (Phil 2:9–11). That hymn echoes a passage in Second Isaiah in which the LORD exults: "To me every knee shall bow every tongue shall swear" (Is 45:23). Note, however, that those knees in Paul's hymn should bend not exactly for the name Jesus, a not uncommon Jewish man's name, but for the tetragrammaton (YHWH), the unique divine name, "the name that is above every other name," bestowed upon Jesus as LORD.

In John's Gospel, however, even if others address Jesus as Lord (*Kyrie*), Jesus himself seems to use the phrase "I AM" of himself in a way that signifies the same thing as *Ehyeh* in the tetragrammaton, and in speaking of himself this way he astounds and even horrifies his hearers. Many English translations of John do no justice to that phrase, rendering the Greek *ego eimi* as if it simply meant "I am he" or "It is I." But Jesus says "I AM" quite starkly, without a predicate, several times in John's Gospel, three times in chapter 8 alone: "I told you that you would die in your sins, for you will die in your sins unless you believe that I AM" (8:24); "When you have lifted up the Son of Man, then you will realize that I AM, and that I do nothing on my own, but I speak these things as the Father instructed me" (8:28); "Amen, Amen, I tell you, before Abraham was, I AM" (8:59).[23] The third of those usages of *ego eimi* provokes outrage: "So they picked up stones to throw at him, but Jesus hid himself and went out of the temple" (8:59). In John's account of the storm at sea after the multiplication of the loaves, Jesus restores calm to the sea and his disciples with the same words:

23. Here and in later passages I have adapted the NRSV translation of John's Gospel.

"They saw Jesus walking on the lake and coming near the boat, and they were terrified. But he said to them, 'I AM; do not be afraid'" (Jn 6:19–20). Another significant usage of that phrase strikes terror in the hearts of those who come to arrest Jesus in the Garden of Gethsemane: "Then Jesus, knowing all that was to happen to him, came forward and asked them, 'For whom are you looking?' They answered, 'Jesus of Nazareth.' Jesus replied, 'I AM.' Judas, who betrayed him, was standing with them. When Jesus said to them, 'I AM,' they stepped back and fell to the ground" (Jn 18:4–6).[24]

Those theologians of recent centuries who have wished to de-escalate the New Testament claims for Jesus have difficulties with John's Gospel; there are few clearer presentations in the New Testament of the central paradox of the tenting of the LORD God in the Word made flesh. Let me conclude these remarks with an attempt to translate the last verse in the prologue to John's Gospel "God no one has ever seen," John warns us. And yet, the evangelist insists that "God the Only Begotten, existing inside the Father's breast—He himself has made [God's] meaning clear" (Jn 1:18).[25]

The Most Beautiful Names of God in Islam

The phrase used so often in a Muslim setting, "In the name of God" (*bi-'smi'llahi*), eventually developed into a noun in Arabic, *basmala*,

---

24. In the NRSV the Greek *ego eimi* is here translated as "I am he," losing the point of the reference to the tetragrammation by Jesus. Brown succinctly points out the ambiguity suggested by the use of the words "I AM" in John's Gospel, especially when those words are used without a predicate: "Since the usage goes far beyond ordinary parlance, all recognize that the absolute *ego eimi* has a special revelatory function in John.... Divine theophanies ... often have this formula: Do not be afraid; I am the God of your ancestors" (*Gospel of John*, 1:533–34).

25. This is my own translation. The NRSV renders these words more simply: "No one has ever seen God. It is God the only Son, who is close to the Father's heart, who has made him known." The New American Bible Revised Edition of 2011 renders it thus: "No one has ever seen God. The only Son, God, who is at the Father's side, has revealed him." The one word in Greek translated as "has made him known" by the NRSV and "has revealed him" by the NABRE, *exegesato*, suggests the work of an interpreter, even an exegete. Joseph Ratzinger (later Pope Benedict XVI) suggested just this in an early work: "One could almost say, in reference to the Greek text, that it [the Word made Flesh] has become the 'exegesis' of God for us." See Ratzinger, *Introduction to Christianity*, 54. Hans Urs von Balthasar has even written an article using such imagery in its title: "God is his own exegete," *Communio* 4 (Winter 1986): 280–87. I wish to thank my colleague Joseph T. Lienhard, SJ, for directing my attention to this article of von Balthasar.

designating the very process of so invoking God by name. Many activities performed in a Muslim setting begin with that short phrase: the
eating of meals, the writing of books, the beginning of a journey. Every
sura of the Qur'an but one (Qur'an 9) begins with a more elaborate version of the *basmala*: "In the name of God, the Merciful One Filled with
Mercy" (*bi-'smi'llahi-r-rahmani-r-rahim*).[26]

To speak the name (*ism*) of any human person in Arabic is to address him or her by the single part of longer Arabic nomenclature that
denotes the person as such apart from any relationship to other persons (parents, children) or other realities (ethnicity, profession). The
usual sequence of traditional Arabic nomenclature includes at least
four and sometimes five elements. The first is the *kunya*, which re-
lates the one named to his or her child *Abu* X ("Father of X"), *Umm* Y
("Mother of Y"). Normally a *kunya* is followed by the second element
in nomenclature, a person's own proper name (*ism*). The *ism* is often
the name of some great figure from the past, preferably with a Muslim
historical referent, but not always. The *ism* is sometimes constructed
from the word for servant (*'Abd*) and one of the names of God ('Abd
Allah, 'Abd al-Rahman, and the like). The third element in nomenclature
is the *nasab*, an indication of the person's personal descent: *Ibn* X or
Bint Y (son or daughter of X or Y). Such a descent group can be traced
back many generations and usually names both men and women by
their descent from male ancestors. The fourth element is the *nisba*, the
adjectival indication of the person's clan, geographical, juristic, mystical, or professional connections, for example: *al-Khazraji* (the member of the clan of the Banu Khazraj), *al-Iskandari* (the Alexandrian),
al-Maliki (the adherent of the juristic school of Malik ibn Anas), *al-
Tijani* (the member of the Tijaniyya Sufi confraternity), *al-Khayyati* (the
member of a clan of tailors; if the person so named is actually a tailor,
the long *i* is omitted from the professional *nisba*). The fifth element in
some Muslim nomenclature, the *laqab*, is sometimes called in English
"the nickname." Early Muslim nicknames can be honorific (*al-Rashid*,
"the Just") or mocking (*al-Himar*, "the Jackass"); they sometimes begin

26. Why Qur'an 9 does not begin with the *basmala* is a matter of much speculation.

with the Arabic words *Dhu* (masculine) or *Dhat* (feminine), indicating possession, real or metaphoric, of something. Other popular varieties of *laqab* indicate political importance: *Nizam al-Mulk* (Order of the Realm). Many famous Muslims in past history are best known by their *laqab*.[27]

Although there are traditionally ninety-nine "most beautiful names of God" (*asma' al-husna*), *Allah* is the quintessential name of God. To begin anything "in the name of God," then, does much more than signify a certain authorization by God of what follows. Rather it enables the person praying with the *basmala* to locate himself or herself spiritually *in* God's name, giving them a certain entry into or presence within the reality of God. All of the preliminaries to worship—purifications by ablution, formulation of the intention to worship, response to the call to worship—lead up to positioning of the devotee in the reality of God symbolized by the name of the One to whom prayer is directed.

Allah is a name for God that is not unique to Arab Muslims; it served as the name for God among other Arabic-speaking monotheists, even before the time of Muhammad. In *Allah* the word for a god, *ilah*, is combined with the article *al-* to become *Allah* (*the* god), not unlike the Septuagint and New Testament Greek *ho theos*. Thus the Qur'an states: "Say: As for me, I am only human like you; it has been revealed to me that your god [*ilahukum*] is an only God [*ilahun wahidun*]. Then seek the straight path to God, beg God's forgiveness. Woe to those who ascribe partners to God" (Qur'an 41:6). The pre-Islamic Arabs, however, seem to have included Allah as one among many in a loosely configured pantheon, even ascribing daughters to Allah: al-Lat, al-'Uzza, and Manat (Qur'an 53:19–20). Each of these three goddesses was associated with territories economically and politically important for Muhammad and his first followers. The strict monotheism of the revelation that Muhammad received regarded all cultus directed toward these three goddesses or any other divinities as *shirk*, the sinful ascription of associates to God.

In the Islamic tradition ninety-nine "most beautiful" names of God

27. See Editors, "Ism," *EI2*, 4:179a–181b.

are enumerated, traditionally thought to be mentioned in the text of
the Qur'an: "To God belong the most beautiful names. Call on God with
them; scatter those who blaspheme with God's names" (Qur'an 7:180).
In actual fact, more than ninety-nine names of God can be found in
the Qur'an, and the lists of those names are not consistent. Most writers consider the name *Allah*, which occurs more than 2,500 times in
the Qur'an, to be the first of the ninety-nine, although a few scholars
claim that it is the hundredth name. The names of God in most lists
emphasize the numinous nature of God, God's *jalal* (majesty), as well
as God's *jamal* (beauty). Muslims in celebration or in distress glorify
God in pungent exclamations like the *takbir*, "God is greater [than any-
thing]!" (*Allahu akbar*). The devout hedge every future hope, trivial or
profound, with a wish that it may come to pass "if God allow" (*in sha'
Allah*). Immediately after pronouncing the name of God many Muslims
interject *subhanahu wa ta'ala* ("Praised be God and exalted!").

The first words of revelation, according to much of Islamic tradition, were the initial verses of *Surat al-'alaq* (the Sura of the Blood Clot:
Qur'an 96). These initial verses epitomize in brief the Quranic proclamation about God, as well as its own self-definition as God's Word
made available for recitation by human beings: "Recite: In the name
of your Lord who created, created humankind from a blood-clot—Recite: Your Lord is the most generous, who taught by the pen, taught humankind what it did not know" (Qur'an 96:1–5). In the first two verses
of Qur'an 96 the creative power of God, intimately disclosed to the already monotheistic Muhammad not simply as "the Lord" but as "your
Lord," is particularly concretized in terms of one demonstration of
God's creative power: the conception and birth of a new human being
"from a blood-clot." The basis for some of the ninety-names of God can
be glimpsed even in those five brief verses: God as Creator (*al-Khaliq,
al-Bari'*), God as most generous (*al-Karim, Dhu'l-jalali wa'l-'ikram*), God
as knower and teacher (*al-'Alim, al-Khabir*).

In my somewhat clumsy translation of the *basmala* ("In the name
of God, the Merciful One, Filled with Mercy") and of the two most common of the "most beautiful names" of God enshrined in the *basmala*,

I am striving to grasp the interrelatedness of these two words in Arabic. Both *al-Rahman* and *al-Rahim* derive from the tri-consonantal root R-H-M. The former, *al-Rahman*, seems to have been a name for the supreme god presiding over a hierarchy of lesser gods in pre-Islamic south and central Arabia.[28] This root connoting mercy points imagistically to the womb (*rahim* or *rihm*). To connect the mercy of God with feminine characteristics or connections is to understand God's perfection as including all that is most tender in created reality, including the generative and loving characteristics of mothers. A famous *hadith* attributed to Muhammad narrates that he restrained a companion from engaging in struggle in the path of God (*jihad*) precisely because the companion's mother was still alive. That companion would not attain heaven by a martyr's death, Muhammad averred, but by filial devotion to his mother: "Then stay with her and look after her needs. Your heaven lies under her feet."[29] The male-centeredness of so much contemporary Islamic rigorism loses sight of these very tender elements in the Qur'an and in the Prophet's thought.

Of the great medieval Muslim commentators on the first verse of the opening sura of the Qur'an, Abu Ja'far al-Tabari (d. 923) has the most to say, relying on earlier exegetes of the Qur'an. He quotes the seventh-century Qur'an expert Ibn 'Abbas to the effect that the *basmala* meant, in its original context, "Recite with the invocation of God, your Lord. And stand and sit with the invocation of God."[30] From Ibn 'Abbas he also derives the definition of *Allah* as "He Who possesses the attributes of divinity [*al-uluhiyyah*] and of being worshiped [*al-ma'budiyyah*] with respect to all his creatures."[31] On the names of God as *al-Rahman* and *al-Rahim* al-Tabari concludes with his own judgment that the former name, the one of greater import, is reserved to God alone:

28. See B. Carra de Vaux and Louis Gardet, "Basmala," *EI2*, 1:1084b–1085a.

29. The source of this famous *hadith* (saying of Muhammad) is the tenth-century CE collector of hadith, Ahmad al-Nasa'i. It can be found in his famous *al-Sunan al-kubra*, the "Large Hadith Collection." There are several fond references to this *hadith* on Muslim websites, most notably www .islaam.org.

30. Abu Ja'far Muḥammad b. Jarīr al-Tabari, *The Commentary on the Qur'an*, ed. and trans. J. Cooper (Oxford: Oxford University Press, 1987), 1:54.

31. Ibid., 55.

God speaks of Himself specifically as *al-rahman*: "Say: 'Call upon Allah, or call upon *al-rahman*; whichever you call upon, to him belong the Names Most Beautiful'" ([Qur'an] 17:110), and He has forbidden any of his creatures to be so called, even though there are some among His creatures who deserve to be named with some of its meanings.... Therefore *al-rahman* comes second to His name Allah. However, as for his name *al-rahim*, we have already said that it is permissible to describe someone other than Him by it.... this is why His name Allah come before His name *al-rahman*, and his name *al-rahman* before His name *al-rahim*.[32]

Muslim men as a result can be called 'Abd al-Rahman (Servant of the Merciful One), but never simply Rahman, although I must say I have known some men named 'Abd al-Rahman who are familiarly called "Rahman."

Sufis, the mystics of the Islamic tradition, have often speculated about the names of God and have even asked if there is a "greatest name" of all. The thirteenth-century Egyptian mystic Ibn Ata'ullah of Alexandria sought from God "to make me know by means of Your treasured-up Knowledge, and protect me by means of the mystery of Your well-guarded name."[33] Shaykh Nizam al-din Awliya, a mystic of Delhi in the late thirteenth and early fourteenth century, when asked about "the greatest name" cited a saying of the early Muslim mystic, Ibrahim Adham: "'Yes, I do know it, and I will tell you about it.... First, you should cleanse your stomach of unlawful food, then you should empty your heart of love of this world, and then after that by whatever name you call upon God that is the Greatest Name.'"[34]

At least in places where the puritanical influence of Saudi Arabia's neo-Hanbalism (so-called Wahhabism) has not been intensely felt, the *subha*[35] or "Muslim rosary" is often seen entwined in the fingers of the devout. Some practitioners of this devotion recite the ninety-nine names of God on the ninety-nine beads of such a rosary; more recite

---

32. Ibid., 58–59.

33. Ibn 'Ata'illah, "The Book of Wisdom" (*Kitab al-hikam*), trans. Victor Danner, in *Ibn 'Ata' Allah/Kwaja 'Abdullah Ansari*, ed. Victor Danner and Wheeler Thackston (New York: Paulist Press, 1978), 124.

34. Nizam Ad-Din Awliya, *Morals for the Heart*, trans. Bruce B. Lawrence (New York: Paulist Press, 1992), 193.

35. The beads used are often called *misbaha* or *tasbih*.

three times thirty-three beads, each third concentrating on one or another of the many ejaculatory prayers that serve Muslims as succinct recollections (*adhkar*) of God. The most common form of this devotion entails thirty-three utterances of *Subhan Allah* ("Glory be to God"), followed by thirty-three utterances of *Al-hamdu l'illah* ("Praise be to God"), ending with thirty-three utterances of the most basic expression of praise for God in the Islamic tradition: *Allahu akbar* ("God is greater [than anything]").

The recitation of the names of God and the simpler recitations of *adhkar* with beads bring God close to mortal human beings. A folk tradition, known in many parts of the Islamic world, maintains that the principal lines in a left hand mimic the number eighty-one in Arabic (٨١) and the lines in the right hand mimic the number eighteen in Arabic (١٨). Thus the palms of their two hands, extended before faithful Muslims in prayer, remind them quite simply of both the majesty and the closeness of God. A more literal than usual rendering of the Throne Verse, a Quranic verse replete with names for God, might suggest similar reflections (Qur'an 2:255):

God—there is no god but He, the Living, the Eternal! Neither fatigue nor sleep seizes Him! To Him belong whatever is in heaven or on earth. Who can intercede with Him unless He allows it? He knows what lies in their hands before them and what lies behind their backs. They cannot comprehend anything He knows except by His leave. His Throne encompasses both heaven and earth: His maintaining heaven and earth does not tire Him. He is the Exalted, the Glorious One!

Naming and Gendering God: A Problem

As mentioned above, the name God uttered from the burning bush to Moses ("I AM WHO I AM") has no gender in the Hebrew language, and that name is quite possibly a denial that mere human beings can address God adequately. Greek and Latin renderings of the Hebrew phrase "I AM WHO I AM" tend to give God a masculine gender in order to preserve God's personhood. In modern times, however, the image of a male

dominant God has caused no small discomfort not only for some wom-
en but also for some men.[36]

The Hebrew Bible seems to sense this imagistic problem in some
of its more lyric passages. In the song of Moses toward the end of the
Book of Deuteronomy, God is a solid foundation ("the Rock") as well
as a father for Israel (Dt 32:4–6), but God the Rock and father is also
imaged more maternally, compared to an eagle feeding and protecting
its young (Dt 32:11–14a):

As an eagle stirs up its nest, and hovers over its young; as it spreads its wings,
takes them up, and bears them aloft on its pinions, the LORD alone guided
[Israel]; no foreign god was with him. He set [Israel] upon the heights of the
land, and fed him with produce of the field; he nursed him with honey from the
crags, with oil from flinty rock, curds from the herd, and milk from the flock.

God is never called "She" in the Hebrew Bible; that too easily suggests the mother goddesses of Israel's polytheistic neighbors. But the
prophetic literature sometimes recognizes the limitations of purely
masculine imagery for God. In Hosea we find a direct contrast between
a merciful and loving God and an angry male human being: "I will not
execute the ferocity of my anger nor will I turn back to take revenge on
Ephraim," the LORD says, "for I am God, not a man" [ki-'el anoki we-
lo'ish] (Hos 11:9).[37] There are also several other passages in the Hebrew
Bible that compare God's actions to those of a woman. Thus in Second
Isaiah we hear the LORD shout: "For a long time I have held my peace,
I have kept still and restrained myself; now I will cry out like a woman
in labour, I will gasp and pant" (Is 42:14). Later in Second Isaiah the
LORD insists on the divine fidelity shown to Israel in maternal imagery:
"Can a woman forget her nursing-child, or show no compassion for the
child of her womb? Even these may forget, yet I will not forget you" (Is
49:15).[38] In Third Isaiah the LORD, as it were, has given birth and con-

---

36. On this topic and the problems it poses for liturgical use of scripture, see Richard J. Clifford,
"Inclusive Language in the Lectionary," *Church* (Summer 2000): 21–24.

37. Author's translation, made with the assistance of Richard J. Clifford, SJ.

38. For a very detailed examination of the gender significance of these passages in Isaiah, see
Hanne Leland, *Silent or Salient Gender: The Interpretation of Gendered God-Language in the Hebrew
Bible, Exemplified in Isaiah 42, 46 and 49*, Forschungen zum Alten Testament 2. Reihe (Tübingen:
Mohr Siebeck, 2008), 100–128 and 161–92.

soles weeping Zion: "As a mother comforts her child, so I will comfort you; you shall be comforted in Jerusalem" (Is 66:13).

In the New Testament a hen, a bird less formidable than an eagle, provides Jesus with a model for his own tender feelings for Israel's capital and its inhabitants: "Jerusalem, Jerusalem, the city that kills the prophets and stones those who are sent to it! How often have I desired to gather your children together as a hen gathers her brood under her wings, and you were not willing" (Lk 13:34; see also Mt 23:27). Jesus himself seems to overcome the duality of male and female in his relationship with his followers. Women were major financial supporters of the ministry of Jesus and fellow journeyers with the Twelve. This included women with rather unusual backgrounds like the cured schizophrenic, "Mary, called Magdalene, from whom seven demons had gone out,"[39] as well as the wealthy wife of a Herodian official, "Joanna, the wife of Herod's steward Chuza" (Lk 8:2–3).

Nowhere more clearly than at the Last Supper as narrated by John does Jesus quite deliberately step down from the dignity of his role as "Teacher and Lord" (Jn 13:13), taking off his outer garment and kneeling before his disciples. He washes their feet, just as Mary of Bethany had anointed his own feet a few days earlier with precious nard (Jn 12:3). In Mark's Gospel, the imitation of the nameless woman in Bethany who anointed the head of Jesus with precious ointment—which Jesus interpreted as preparation for burial (Mk 14:8)—is urged on all who would follow Jesus: "'Truly I tell you, wherever the good news is proclaimed in the whole world, what she has done will be told in remembrance of her'" (Mk 14:9). All the Gospels agree that women were the first witnesses of the resurrection of Jesus, the women called "myrrh-bearers" in Byzantine Christian tradition. Those faithful wom-

39. Robert J. Karris, OFM, comments that "the physical well-being of these women, who had been healed of evil spirits and maladies, is visible proof of the power of God's kingdom in Jesus. Jesus' power is especially manifest in the restoration to health of Mary, from the small Galilean town of Magdala, from whom seven (number of totality) demons have been removed." See "The Gospel According to Luke," in *NJBC*, 697b. The confusion of Mary of Magdala in this passage (Lk 8:2) with the woman "who was a sinner" who bathed the feet of Jesus with her tears and dried them with her hair (Lk 7:37–38) arose in the Western Christian tradition and has been the subject of many paintings; the Greek East did not make the same mistake. See J. E. Fallon, "Mary Magdalene, St.," *NCE2*, 9:285–88.

en came to the tomb to complete the "women's work" of embalming begun at Bethany, and in doing so they remind us that Jesus did not disdain "women's work" but urged it on all who would hear and bear witness to the good news.

In the Qur'an, as in the Hebrew Bible and the New Testament, God is never addressed as "She." Although God is sometimes called a father in the Hebrew Bible, that form of address is more common in the New Testament. Any ascription of paternity to God—literal or metaphorical—is simply rejected in the Qur'an: "Say: 'He is God, One! God the Eternally Adamantine, neither begetting nor begotten! There is nothing comparable to God" (Qur'an 112:1–3). The original context of that Quranic denial of divine paternity may be the localized pagan Arab devotion to the so-called daughters of God (Qur'an 53:19–22), but it was also applied to the Trinity as that Christian mystery may have been understood in seventh-century Arabia: "They are surely faithless who claim that God is third of three, while there is of God nothing but one God" (Qur'an 5:73).

A disincarnate tradition of faith, Islam also arose in a historical social setting, pagan Arabia, where women's status was traditionally rather low, but that does not distinguish Islam from many other religious traditions in their origins. That social factor, however, does not mean that God lacks transcendent qualities characterized by words typically associated with women's actions. The *basmala*, the invocation of God's name that starts every sura of the Qur'an but one, as mentioned above, relies on words linguistically related to the womb (*rihm* or *rahim*) to characterize God's merciful nature.

In some of the central Asian developments of the esoteric Isma'ili Shi'a tradition, Fatima, the daughter of Muhammad and the wife of 'Ali, the first Imam, has sometimes become identified with God as *al-Fatir*, the originator.[40] The title of God as *al-Fatir* occurs six times in

40. See Laura Veccia Vaglieri, "Fatima," *EI2*, 2:841b–850a, especially her treatment of creation in one particular strain of central Asian Ismac'ili thought: "God, a being of light ... before the Creation, with five limbs: hearing, sight, the senses of smell and taste, and speech (which on earth were to become Muhammad, 'Ali, Fatima, al-Hasan and Al-Husayn) manifested Himself when the world began in 'Ali, and then in successive theophanies; that of Fatima took place in Paradise after the creation of primordial men as a figure adorned with thousands of colours and seated on a throne with

the Qur'an, most prominently in the first line and title often given to Qur'an 35: "Praise be given to God, Original Source of the heavens and the earth, the Commander of angels as messengers—two-winged, three-winged, four-winged. [God] increases in creation what he wills. Truly God is powerful in every matter." The triliteral root of the Arabic word, *Fatir*, can be taken to suggest a theory of creation as emanation: the overflow of the divine in the finite. Such a theory of emanation differs radically from the usual idea of the created as separate from the Creator. Emanationist imagery is not only known among esoteric Shi'is but also among certain Sunni mystics.[41]

Finally, of course, God is neither he nor she, in any ordinary use of such pronouns, nor is God an impersonal it. Human concepts of gender and person do not apply univocally to the One whose power and presence and love surround us men and women of finite imaginations in ways that we cannot reduce to words.

Conclusion: Wrestling with God

Merely mortal words—Jewish, Christian, or Muslim—can never completely wrestle God to the ground. We cannot force the divine wrestler to reveal to us the ineffable name in any exhaustive sense. Perhaps that is part of what Ludwig Wittgenstein meant when he formulated his famously unexplained seventh proposition: "Whereof one cannot speak, thereof one must be silent."[42] Wittgenstein went through many stages of understanding that proposition. The late philosopher and theologian Paul Ricoeur (d. 2005) notes more positively that in hymns of celebration, supplication, and thanksgiving, "God becomes a 'you' to the human you." Ricoeur goes on to assert that

---

a crown on her head (Muhammad), two ear-rings in her ears (al-Hasan and al-Husayn), and a sword carried in a shoulderbelt ('Ali); all the garden of Paradise shone upon the appearance of this radiant figure" (849a). Also see Louis Massignon, "Der gnostische Kult der Fatima in schiitischen Islam," in *Opera Minora*, ed. Yoakim Moubarac (Paris: Presses universitaires de France, 1969), 1:514–22.

41. See in particular the Tijani mystical prayer called "The Jewel of Perfection" (*Jawharat al-kamal*) in Patrick J. Ryan, SJ, "The Mystical Theology of Tijani Sufism and Its Social Significance in West Africa," *Journal of Religion in Africa* 30, no. 2 (May 2000): 211.

42. *Tractatus Logico-Philosophicus*, trans. C. K. Ogden (London: Routledge and Kegan Paul, 1922), 188–89. The original German is just as succinct: "Wovon man nicht sprechen kann, darüber muss man schweigen."

the word "God" cannot be understood as a philosophical concept, not even "being" in the sense of medieval philosophy or in Heidegger's sense. The word "God" says more than the word "being" because it presupposes the entire context of narratives, prophecies, laws, wisdom writings, psalms, and so on. The referent "God" is thus intended by the convergence of all these partial discourses. It expresses the circulation of meaning among all the forms of discourse wherein God is named.[43]

Preachers on television who babble on about God so confidently, as well as teenagers who text each other with the acronym OMG!: both populations could imbibe wisdom by contemplating the history of the naming or non-naming of God in the monotheistic traditions that trace their historical origins to the Middle East. Whether we avoid pronouncing the ineffable name of God, or bow our heads at the personal name of the Word of God made flesh, or follow the mention of God's name with the exclamation *subhanahu wa ta'ala* ("Praised be He and exalted!"), we who put our faith in one God recognize deep down the mystery with which we are forced to deal so tentatively. Words may elude us.[44] Still, in the words of T. S. Eliot:

> Words, after speech, reach
> Into the silence.[45]

But perhaps we can and must do more than keep silence. Silence about God seems too gloomy a conclusion to my reflections. We must, like Jacob, struggle with the nameless divine wrestler by night. Other verses from Eliot may help to illuminate the darkness of that wrestling:

> I said to my soul, be still, and let the dark come upon you
> Which will be the darkness of God.[46]

43. "Naming God," in Paul Ricoeur, *Figuring the Sacred: Religion, Narrative and the Imagination*, ed. Mark I. Wallace, trans. David Pellauer (Minneapolis, Minn.: Fortress Press, 1995), 227–28.
44. On the theological theme of divine incomprehensibility, see Elizabeth A. Johnson, *She Who Is: The Mystery of God in Feminist Theological Discourse* (New York: Crossroad, 1992), 104–12.
45. Eliot, *Collected Poems*, 180.
46. Ibid., 186.

A Long Letter Ended

D., I said these meditations on aspects of faith are for you, but they are also for me. Like you, I also have to face up to the final test for each one of us: the hour of death. The Our Father in the usual translation used in English concludes with these words: "Lead us not into temptation, but deliver us from evil" (Mt 6:13). More accurately it should be rendered as "Keep us from the final testing and deliver us from the Evil One." For many modern people that is too mythic, since we have reduced the Evil One to a figure of children's comedy and the idea of eschatological battle has been trivialized by science fiction. But those of us closer to death realize that there is a final testing for each one of us: the challenge that comes from hopelessness and despair, especially as we look back at what we might have done but did not. The Evil One stands in defiant opposition to the God who calls us from before birth: into being, into doing, into self-surrender.

Let me return to the Epistle to the Hebrews. After evoking those images of faith as the reality that undergirds our hopes and the argument that convinces us about realities we do not see, the author enumerates a long list of heroes and heroines of faith in Israel's past, among them Abel, Enoch, Noah, Abraham, Sarah, Isaac, Jacob, Joseph, Moses, Rahab, Gideon, Barak, Samson, Jephthah, David, Samuel, and the prophets. What the author says about these saints of old strikes me as quite significant (Heb 11:13–16):

All of these died in faith without having received the promises, but from a distance they saw and greeted them. They confessed that they were strangers and foreigners on the earth, for people who speak in this way make it clear that they are seeking a homeland. If they had been thinking of the land that they had left behind, they would have had opportunity to return. But as it is, they desire a better country, that is, a heavenly one. Therefore God is not ashamed to be called their God; indeed, he has prepared a city for them.

Of all the biblical models of faith cited by the author of the Epistle to the Hebrews, I feel the most empathy for the one whom the pious would consider the most disreputable, Rahab, the prostitute of Jericho. The Book of Joshua tells her story in some detail. Joshua sent two spies into the land of Canaan shortly after he had led the Israelites across the Jordan. When they came to the Canaanite fortress of Jericho they were welcomed for a night's lodging by a prostitute, Rahab. When the ruler of Jericho heard of their arrival, he demanded that the prostitute "bring out the men who have come to you" (Jos 2:3), but Rahab lied and claimed that they had left her establishment. In the presence of the Israelite spies she professed her faith in the God of Israel, the God as well of the whole universe: "The LORD your God is indeed God in heaven above and on earth below" (Jos 2:11). In turn she asked the spies for an assurance that when Jericho would be conquered they would "spare my father and mother, my brothers and sisters, and all who belong to them, and deliver our lives from death" (Jos 2:13).

The spies swore their fidelity to that covenant with Rahab and they also gave Rahab "a crimson cord" (Jos 2:18) to tie in her window to mark her house as the only one in Jericho not to be destroyed when the armies of Israel conquered. When Jericho was eventually taken by the Israelites and subjected to total destruction, Joshua decreed that "Only Rahab the prostitute and all who are with her in her house shall live because she hid the messengers we sent" (Jos 6:17). The Epistle to the Hebrews sees in this story a great model of faith. "By faith the walls of Jericho fell after they have been encircled for seven days. By faith Rahab the prostitute did not perish with those who were disobedient, because she had received the spies in peace" (Heb 11:30–31). Neither the Book of Joshua nor the Epistle to the Hebrews makes anything of Rahab's disreputable profession. She was "justified by faith apart from works prescribed by the law," as Paul would contend (Rom 3:28). The Epistle of James, on the contrary, insists that "Rahab the prostitute [was] justified by works when she welcomed the messengers and sent them out by another road" (Jas 2:25). Matthew's Gospel names Rahab among the ancestors of Jesus, married to Salmon, the great-great-grandfather of King David (Mt 1:5–6). Rahab had expatriated herself and her family from Jericho, her native city. If chroniclers of ancient Jericho could have told her story, they would have called her a traitor. But Rahab saw larger horizons.

Jewish *midrashim* from the early centuries CE, inventive meditations on the Hebrew scriptures, consider Rahab a model Gentile convert to Judaism, listing her among the four most beautiful women in history along with Sarah, Abigail, and Esther. In these Jewish traditions she marries Joshua and both priests and prophets are numbered among her descendants.[1] Clement, probably the third successor of Peter as head of the Roman Christian community, wrote a letter to the disputatious Christian community at Corinth in the last years of the first century. In that letter Clement cites Rahab as an exemplar of faith, hospitality and even prophecy: "Thus they [the spies who gave her the crimson cord] made it clear beforehand that it is through the blood of the Lord that there is redemption for all who keep faith and place their hope in God. See then, beloved, that not only faith but also prophecy came to birth in this woman."[2] Two centuries later the theologian Origen also saw in the crimson cord in Rahab's window a symbol of the cleansing blood of Jesus: "She received from those explorers the strongest sign of salvation, the crimson cord. For it is through the blood of Christ that the universal

---

1. See Tamar Kadari, "Rahab: Midrash and Aggadah," *Jewish Women's Archive*, available at jwa.org/encyclopedia/article/rahab-midrash-and-aggadah.

2. See "First Letter of Clement," 12.7–8, in *The Apostolic Fathers*, ed. and trans. Bart D. Ehrman, Loeb Classical Library 24 (Cambridge, Mass.: Harvard University Press, 2003), 56. The translation from the Greek is my own.

Church is saved, in Jesus Christ our Lord. To him be glory and power for ever and ever. Amen."[3]

D., why does this story of Rahab remind me of you? You expatriated yourself and your family, giving up comfort in Europe five decades ago to take up an arduous career in situations of poverty where you insisted, unlike so many of your colleagues, that you and your family live simply, as "strangers and foreigners on the earth," among those you were trying to assist. I don't think you did this because "you desired a better country, that is, a heavenly one." You would never lay claim to such piety. But you were then, and remain today, the most deeply moral human being I have ever met. You are ten years older than I, and as they used to say in the old gangster movies, none of us is getting out of here alive. Thank you for all you were able to do for poor people. Thank you for being a living patron saint for me. May God reward you for a life given for others, a life of faith expressed in practical love for humankind, love for the image and likeness of the God with whom, finally, you always kept faith. Remember above all else the famous words of St. Paul: "And now faith, hope and love abide, these three; but the greatest of these is love" (1 Cor 13:13).

I conclude, D., with an account of two suffering people whose last "Amen" I was privileged to witness.

My sister—my only sibling—died while I was bringing this book to its conclusion. After some years of declining health, she suffered a stroke and was hospitalized not far from where she had lived most of her married life, where she and her husband had raised their three children. Many members of the family gathered at her bedside over the last two weeks of her life. I wanted to bring my sister Communion in the hospital, but feeding and oxygen tubes made it impossible to give her the host. I decided to administer the sacrament of the sick, anointing her forehead and her hands. I was struck by the slight movement of her lips when I recited the Lord's Prayer. But I also noticed at the end of every prayer in the ritual how her lips indicated that she was saying "Amen." The faith with which she had lived all her life remained wholehearted in those concluding days of her earthly existence.

3. The Greek of Origen is missing; this is the author's translation from the Latin in *Patrologia Graeca*, ed. J.-P. Migne (Paris: Imprimerie Catholique, 1854–66), 12:856. For a different English rendering translation of this passage, see Origen, *Homilies on Joshua*, ed. Cynthia White, trans. Barbara J. Bruce, FOTC 105 (Washington, D.C.: The Catholic University of America Press, 2002), 73.

Many years earlier, at a time of civil unrest and evening curfews in Ghana, a man I did not know arrived at the door of the house where I lived in a remote corner of the campus of the University of Ghana. It was well after midnight and it seemed that the man had been walking all over the campus looking for the lecturer who was also the Catholic chaplain—me. In the process he roused from sleep the Methodist, Presbyterian, and Anglican chaplains. "My brother is dying in the university hospital," he shouted to me through the glass door. Despite warnings from the old man who cooked for me, a protective guardian who lived at the other end of my small bungalow, I dressed, took the oil for the anointing of the sick and drove to the sick man's bedside. As was the situation with my sister many years later, the man's mouth was filled with tubes and he seemed only semi-conscious.

"I brought the priest," his brother fairly shouted at the dying man. I did not recognize him, but he was a hall porter in one of the student residences who seemed not to have been active as a Catholic for some years. Before I started the rite I decided to begin with a brief penance service, given the fragility of the man's condition. I asked him to squeeze my hand if he was sorry for his sins. Instead, he raised his head, his eyes still closed, and nodded vigorously.

"O.K.," I said, "nod your head if you are sorry for your sins." He did so again, quite as vigorously. There was no mistaking his penitence as well as his faith, the nodded "Amen" that was his deep-down "Yes" to God. I absolved him. Then, still holding his feverish hand, I began the reading from the Epistle of James (Jas 5:14–16):

Are any among you sick? They should call for the elders of the church and have them pray over them, anointing them with oil in the name of the Lord. The prayer of faith will save the sick, and the Lord will raise them up; and anyone who has committed sins will be forgiven. Therefore confess your sins to one another, and pray for one another, so that you may be healed. The prayer of the righteous is powerful and effective.

Halfway through the reading, and about a minute after I had absolved the dying man, I realized that his hand was growing cooler: he was dead. I finished the ritual and turned to his brother, who had not yet realized what had happened. When I told him that his brother had died, he burst into tears and clung to me. Nurses entered the room, removed the tubes and covered the corpse with a sheet. "You are a hero," I told the man's brother. "You walked all around the campus in the dark for hours looking for my house. You were able to bring your brother what he wanted more deeply than anything else, the final chance to affirm his faith in God. Because of you he was able to nod his head, to signify his final 'Amen.'"

I will never forget the name of the man who died that night, Edward Nutsugah. I pray he will be there in turn when I am dying and help me to nod the "Amen" of my faith in God.

SELECTED BIBLIOGRAPHY

Abrahams, Israel, Jacob Haberman, and Charles Manekin. "Belief." *EJ2*.

Ahmad, Aziz. "Din-i Ilahi." *EI2*.

Ahmad, S. Maqbul. "Djughrafiya." *EI2*.

Ahmed, Shahab. "Satanic Verses." *EQ*.

Allman, Jean, and John Parker. *Tongnaab: the History of an African God*. Bloomington: Indiana University Press, 2005.

Ancient Christian Commentary on Scripture: Old Testament III: Exodus, Leviticus, Numbers, Deuteronomy. Edited by Joseph T. Lienhard, SJ, in collaboration with Ronnie J. Rombs. Downers Grove, Ill.: InterVarsity Press, 2001.

Anderson, Lisa. "Qaddafi's Islam." In *Voices of Resurgent Islam*, edited by John L. Esposito, 134–49. Oxford: Oxford University Press, 1983.

Andrae, Tor. *Mohammed: The Man and His Faith*. Revised, edited, and translated by Theophil Menzel. San Francisco: Harper Torchbooks, 1960.

"Apocalypse of Abraham." Translated and edited by R. Rubinkiewicz, in *The Old Testament Pseudepigrapha*, edited by James H. Charlesworth. Garden City, N.Y.: Doubleday, 1983.

Aquinas, Thomas. *Summa Theologiae, Pars Prima*. Edited by Peter Caramello. Turin: Marietti, 1950.

Aristotle. *Nicomachean Ethics*. Translated by C. D. C. Reeve. Indianapolis, Ind.: Hackett, 2014.

Arkoun, Mohammed. *Rethinking Islam: Common Questions, Uncommon Answers*. Translated and edited by Robert D. Lee. Boulder, Colo.: Westview Press, 1994.

———. *Islam: To Reform or To Subvert*. London: Saqi Essentials, 2006.

Arnaldez, Roger. "Ibn Rushd." *EI2*.

Augustine. *Confessions*. Translated by Henry Chadwick. Oxford: Oxford University Press, 1992.

———. *Confessionum libri tredecim*. Library of Latin Texts. Available at clt.brepolis .net/llta/pages/Toc.aspx.

———. *Enarrationes in Psalmos*. PL 36. Available at www.augustinus.it/latino/ esposizioni_salmi/index2.htm.

The Babylonian Talmud. Seder Nezikin. Translated and edited by H. M. Lazarus. London: The Soncino Press, 1935.

The Babylonian Talmud. Seder Zera'im. Translated and edited by Maurice Simon. London: The Soncino Press, 1958.

"Balfour Declaration 1917." *The Avalon Project: Documents in Law, History and Diplomacy*. Available at avalon.law.yale.edu/20th_century/balfour.asp.

Balthasar, Hans Urs von. "God is his own exegete." *Communio* 4 (Winter 1986): 280–87.

Bausani, Alessandro. "Bab" and "Babis." *EI2*.

———. "Baha' Allah" and "Baha'is." *EI2*.

Becker, Adam H., and Annette Yoshiko Reed, eds. *The Ways That Never Parted: Jews and Christians in Late Antiquity and the Early Middle Ages*. Minneapolis, Minn.: Fortress Press, 2007.

Benedict XVI, Pope. "General Audience of December 6, 2006: Apostolic Journey to Turkey." Available at www.vatican.va.

———. "Pilgrimage to the Holy Land: Meeting with Muslim religious leaders, members of the Diplomatic Corps and Rectors of universities in Jordan in front of the mosque al-Hussein bin Talal in Amman (May 9, 2009)." Available at www.vatican.va.

———. *Jesus of Nazareth: The Infancy Narratives*. New York: Image, 2012.

Benedict XVI, Pope, Michael B. McGarry, and Deborah Weissman. *Pope Benedict XVI in the Holy Land*. New York: Paulist Press, 2011.

Bergoglio, Jorge Mario, and Abraham Skorka. *On Heaven and Earth*. Translated by Alejandro Bermudez and Howard Goodman. New York: Image, 2013.

———. *Sobre el cielo y la tierra*. New York: Vintage Español, 2013.

The Book of the Cave of Treasures. Translated by E. A. Wallis Budge. London: Religious Tract Society, 1927.

Bosworth, C. E. "al-Sham." *EI2*.

Böwering, Gerhard, SJ. "Covenant." *EQ*.

Bretton-Granatoor, Rabbi Gary. "After 100 Days, It's Clear That New Pope Is A Friend of the Jews." Anti-Defamation League. Available at www.adl.org/news/op-ed/after–100-days-its-clear-that-new-pope-is-a-friend-of-the-jews.

Brock, Sebastian. "Jacob of Serugh's Poem on the Sleepers of Ephesus." In *I Sowed Fruits into Hearts. Odes Sol. 17:13: Festschrift for Professor Michael Lattke*, edited by P. Allen, M. Franzmann, and R. Strelan. Early Christian Studies 12. Strathfield: St. Paul's Publications, 2007.

Brown, Raymond E., SS. *The Gospel According to John (I–XII)*. The Anchor Bible 29. Garden City, N.Y.: Doubleday, 1966.

———. "Not Jewish Christianity and Gentile Christianity but Types of Jewish/Gentile Christianity." *Catholic Biblical Quarterly* 45 (1983): 74–79.

Buber, Martin. *I and Thou*. Translated by Ronald Gregor Smith. Second edition. New York: Charles Scribner's Sons, 1958.

———. *Werke*. Munich / Heidelberg: Kösel-Verlag / Verlag Lambert Schneider, 1963.

———. *A Land of Two Peoples*. Edited by Paul Mendes-Flohr. Chicago: University of Chicago Press, 2005.

Buber, Martin, and Franz Rosenzweig. *Scripture and Translation*. Translated by Lawrence Rosenwald with Everett Fox. Bloomington: Indiana University Press, 1994.

Burton, John. "Naskh." *EI2*.

Byrne, Máire. *The Names of God in Judaism, Christianity, and Islam: A Basis for Interfaith Dialogue*. London: Continuum, 2011.

Cahen, Claude. "Amin." *EI2*.

Carra de Vaux, B., and Louis Gardet. "Basmala." *EI2*.

Carter, Stephen. *Civility: Manners, Morals, and the Etiquette of Democracy*. New York: Basic Books, 1998.

Catechism of the Catholic Church. Second edition. Rome: Libreria Editrice Vaticana, 2007.

Chabbi, Jacqueline. "Zamzam." *EI2*.

"Church Manual." Available at www.adventist.org/en/information/church-manual/.

Cicero. *De re publica, De legibus, Cato maior de senectute, Laelius de amicitia*. Edited by J. G. F. Powell. Oxford: Clarendon, 2006.

Clarke, Catherine Goddard. *The Loyolas and the Cabots: The Story of the Crusade of Saint Benedict Center 1940–1950*. Richmond, N.H.: Saint Benedict Center, 1950.

Clifford, Richard. "Inclusive Language in the Lectionary." *Church* (Summer 2000): 21–24.

Clifford, Richard, and Roland Murphy. "Genesis." In *NJBC*, 2.

The Code of Canon Law: A Text and Commentary. Edited by James A. Corriden, Thomas J. Green, and Donald E. Heintschel. New York: Paulist Press, 1985.

Cole, Juan. *Engaging the Muslim World*. New York: Palgrave Macmillan, 2009.

Comas, Juan. "Historical Reality and the Detractors of Father Las Casas." In *Bartolomé de las Casa in History: Towards and Understanding of the Man and his Work*, edited by Juan Friede and Benjamin Keen, 487–539. DeKalb: Northern Illinois University Press, 1971.

"A Common Word Between Us and You." Jordan: The Royal Aal al-Bayt Institute for Islamic Thought, 2009. Available at www.acommonword.com.

The Complete Jewish Bible With Rashi Commentary. Available at www.chabad.org/library/bible_cdo/aid/9864/jewish/Chapter-3.htm.

Concise Oxford Companion to the English Language. Edited by Tom McArthur. New York: Oxford University Press, 1998.

Congar, Yves, OP. *Challenge to the Church: The Case of Archbishop Lefebvre*. Translated by Paul Inwood. Huntington, Ind.: Our Sunday Visitor, 1976.

Cornford, Francis MacDonald. *Plato and Parmenides: Parmenides' Way of Truth and Plato's Parmenides*. New York: Bobbs-Merrill, 1951.

Cowdrey, H. E. J. "The Genesis of the Crusades." In *The Holy War*, edited by T. P. Murphy. Columbus: Ohio State University Press, 1976.

Cross, Frank Moore. *From Epic to Canon: History and Literature in Ancient Israel*. Baltimore, Md.: The Johns Hopkins University Press, 1998.

Crouzel, H. "Origen and Origenism." *NCE2*.

Cyril of Jerusalem. *The Works of Saint Cyril of Jerusalem*. Translated by Leo P. McCauley, SJ, and Anthony A. Stephenson. FOTC 64. Washington, D.C.: The Catholic University of America Press, 1970.

Day, Dorothy. *By Little and By Little: The Selected Writings of Dorothy Day*. Edited by Robert Ellsberg. New York: Alfred A. Knopf, 1983. Reprinted as *Dorothy Day: Selected Writings*, edited by Robert Ellsberg. Maryknoll, N.Y.: Orbis Books, 1992.

———. *The Long Loneliness*. San Francisco: HarperSanFrancisco, 1997.

"Declaration of Principles: 1885 Pittsburgh Conference." Available at ccarnet.org/rabbis-speak/platforms/declaration-principles/.

The Didache or The Teaching of the Lord to the Gentiles by the Twelve Apostles. Translated and edited by J. B. Lightfoot. Available at www.annomundi.com/bible/didache.pdf.

Duffy, Eamon. *Faith of Our Fathers: Reflections on Catholic Tradition*. London: Continuum, 2004.

Dulles, Avery, SJ. *The Assurance of Things Hoped For: A Theology of Christian Faith*. Oxford: Oxford University Press, 1994.

———. "Covenant and Mission." *America* 187 (October 21, 2002): 8–11.

———. "Leonard Feeney: In Memoriam." *America* 138 (February 25, 1978): 135–37.

Dupuis, Jacques, SJ, and Josef Neuner. *The Christian Faith in the Doctrinal Documents of the Catholic Church*. Revised edition. New York: Alba House, 1982.

Editors of *EI2*. "Djahiliyya." *EI2*.

———. "Ism." *EI2*.

———. "Rukn." *EI2*.

Eliot, T. S. *Collected Poems, 1909–1962*. New York: Harcourt, Brace and World, 1963.

Enchiridion Symbolorum Definitionum et Declarationum de Rebus Fidei et Morum. Edited by H. Denzinger and A. Schönmetzer, SJ. Thirty-second edition. Freiburg im Breisgau: Herder, 1963.

Encyclopaedia Judaica. Revised edition. Detroit: Macmillan Reference USA / Keter Publishing House Ltd., 2007.

The Encyclopaedia of Islam: New Edition. Edited by Hamilton Gibb et al. Leiden: Brill, 1960–2009.

Encyclopaedia of the Qur'an. Edited by Jane Dammen McAuliffe. Leiden: Brill, 2001.

Eusebius of Caesarea. *The Ecclesiastical History*. Loeb Classical Library 153. Cambridge, Mass.: Harvard University Press, 1926.

————. *Vie de Constantin*. Sources chrétiennes 559. Paris: Les Éditions du Cerf, 2013.

Fahd, Toufic. "Sa'y." *EI2*.

————. "Talbiya." *EI2*.

al-Farabi. *Alfarabi: Philosophy of Plato and Aristotle*. Translated by Muhsin Mahdi. Ithaca, N.Y.: Cornell University Press, 2001.

Feiler, Bruce. *Abraham: A Journey to the Heart of Three Faiths*. New York: Harper-Collins, 2002.

"First Letter of Clement." In *The Apostolic Fathers*, translated and edited by Bart D. Ehrman. 2 vols. Loeb Classical Library 24. Cambridge, Mass.: Harvard University Press, 2003.

Fitzmyer, Joseph A., SJ. *The Gospel According to Luke (I–IX)*. The Anchor Bible 28. Garden City, N.Y.: Doubleday, 1981.

Francis, Pope. "'Visit to the Grand Mufti of Jerusalem: Address of Pope Francis, Building of the Great Council on the Esplanade of the Mosques. Jerusalem, Monday, 26 May 2014." Available at www.vatican.va.

"Gesta Francorum." In *The First Crusade: The Accounts of Eyewitnesses and Participants*, translated by A. C. Krey. Princeton, N.J.: Princeton University Press, 1921. Available at sourcebooks.fordham.edu/halsall/source/gesta-cde.asp.

al-Ghazali. *Deliverance from Error: An Annotated Translation of* al-Munqidh min al Dalal *and Other Relevant Works of al-Ghazali*. Translated by Richard Joseph McCarthy, SJ. Louisville, Ky.: Fons Vitae, 1999.

————. *The Remembrance of Death and the Afterlife* [*Kitab dhikr al-mawt wa-ma ba'dahu*]. Book XL of *The Revival of the Religious Sciences* [*Ihya' 'ulum al-din*]. Translated and edited by T. J. Winter. Cambridge: Islamic Texts Society, 1989.

Gibbs, Gabriel, OSB, and Owen J. Murphy, Jr. *Harvard to Harvard*. Still River, Mass.: Ravengate Press, 2006.

Glatzer, Nahum. "Introduction." In *The Essential Philo*, edited by Nahum N. Glatzer, translated by C. D. Yonge. New York: Schocken Books, 1971.

Glueck, Nelson. *Hesed in the Bible*. Cincinnati, Ohio: Hebrew Union College Press, 1967.

Grabar, Oleg. *The Dome of the Rock*. Cambridge, Mass.: Belknap Press of Harvard University Press, 2006.

Gregory, David L. "Dorothy Day, Workers' Rights and Catholic Authenticity." *Fordham Urban Law Journal* 26 (1998): 1371–92.

Griffith, Sidney. "Christian Lore and the Arabic Qur'an: The 'Companions of the Cave' in *Surat al-Kahf* and in Syriac Christian Tradition." In *The Qur'an in its Historical Context*, edited by Gabriel Said Reynolds. London: Routledge, 2008.

The HarperCollins Study Bible (New Revised Standard Version of 1989). Edited by Harold W. Attridge. San Francisco: HarperOne, 2006.

Harrington, Daniel J., SJ. "The Gospel of Mark." In *NJBC*, 41.

Hartmann, Louis, and S. David Sperling, "God, names of." *EJ2*.

Hastings, Adrian. *The Church in Africa 1450–1950*. Oxford: Clarendon Press, 1994.

A Hebrew and English Lexicon of the Old Testament with an Appendix Containing the Biblical Aramaic based on the Lexicon of William Gesenius. Translated by Edward Robinson. Edited by Francis Brown, S. R. Driver, and Charles A. Briggs. Boston: Houghton Mifflin, 1907.

Hebrew-English TANAKH. Philadelphia: Jewish Publication Society, 1991; new edition, 2003.

Heilman, Samuel C. *Defenders of the Faith: Inside Ultra-Orthodox Jewry*. New York: Schocken, 1992.

————. *Sliding to the Right: The Contest for the Future of American Jewish Orthodoxy*. Berkeley: University of California Press, 2006.

Heilman, Samuel C., and Fred Skolnik. "Haredim." *EJ2*.

Heilpern, John. "Minister of Finance." *Vanity Fair* (April 2010): 80.

Henriques, Diana. *The Wizard of Lies: Bernie Madoff and the Death of Trust*. New York: Henry Holt, 2011.

Heschel, Abraham Joshua. *Moral Grandeur and Spiritual Audacity: Essays*. Edited by Susannah Heschel. New York: Farrar, Straus and Giroux, 1996.

Heschel, Abraham J., and Morris M. Faierstein. *Prophetic Inspiration After the Prophets: Maimonides and Other Medieval Authorities*. Hoboken, N.J.: Ktav, 1996.

Hildegard of Bingen. *Scivias*. Translated by Mother Columba Hart and Jane Bishop. New York: Paulist Press, 1990.

Hilkert, Mary Catherine. *Speaking with Authority: Catherine of Siena and the Voices of Women Today*. New York: Paulist Press, 2001.

Hodgson, Marshall G. S. *The Venture of Islam: Conscience and History in a World Civilization*. 3 vols. Chicago: University of Chicago Press, 1974.

Holt, P. M. *The Age of the Crusades: The Near East from the Eleventh Century to 1517*. London: Longman, 1986.

Holwerda, David E. *Jesus and Israel: One Covenant or Two?* Grand Rapids, Mich.: Eerdmans, 1995.

The Holy Qur'an. Translated by A. Yusuf Ali. Second edition. Plainfield, Ind.: American Trust Publications, 1977.

Homer. *The Odyssey*. Translated by Robert Fagles. New York: Viking Penguin, 1996.

Horner, Tom. *Jonathan Loved David: Homosexuality in Biblical Times*. Philadelphia: Westminster, 1978.

Howard, George. "On the 'Faith of Christ.'" *Harvard Theological Review* 60 (1967): 459–65.

Ibn al-'Arabi. *Ibn al'Arabi: The Bezels of Wisdom*. Translated by R. W. J. Austin. New York: Paulist Press, 1980.

Ibn 'Ata' Allah. "The Book of Wisdom" (*Kitab al-hikam*). Translated by Victor Danner in *Ibn 'Ata' Allah/Kwaja 'Abdullah Ansari*, edited by Victor Danner and Wheeler Thackston. New York: Paulist Press, 1978.

Ibn Ishaq. *The Life of Muhammad*: A Translation of Sirat Rasul Allah. Translated by Alfred Guillaume. Second edition. Lahore: Pakistan Branch of Oxford University Press, 1968.

Ignatius Loyola. *Saint Ignatius Loyola: Personal Writings*. Edited by Joseph A. Munitiz and Philip Endean. London: Penguin Books, 1996.

Ivereigh, Austen. *The Great Reformer: Francis and the Making of a Radical Pope*. New York: Henry Holt and Company, 2014.

Jansen, J. J. G. "Sayyid Kutb." *EI2*.

Jaspers, Karl. *The Origin and Goal of History*. Translated by Michael Bullock. New Haven, Conn.: Yale University Press, 1953.

The Jewish Annotated New Testament: New Revised Standard Version. Edited by Amy-Jill Levine and Marc Zvi Brettler. Oxford: Oxford University Press, 2011.

John of the Cross. *The Collected Works of John of the Cross*. Translated by Kieran Kavanaugh, OCD, and Otilio Rodriguez, OCD. Washington, D.C.: Institute of Carmelite Studies, 1979.

John Paul II, Pope. *John Paul II in the Holy Land–in his own words: with Christian and Jewish perspectives*. Mahwah, N.J.: Paulist Press, 2005.

Johnson, Elizabeth A. *She Who Is: The Mystery of God in Feminist Theological Discourse*. New York: Crossroad, 1992.

Johnson, Luke Timothy. "Rom 3:21–26 and the Faith of Jesus." *Catholic Biblical Quarterly* 44 (1982): 77–90.

Jones, Kathleen. *Women Saints: Lives of Faith and Courage*. Maryknoll, N.Y.: Orbis, 1999.

Just, Felix, SJ. "Amen, Amen Sayings in the Fourth Gospel." Available at catholic-resources.org/John/Themes-Amen.htm.

Kadari, Tamar. "Rahab: Midrash and Aggadah." Available at jwa.org/encyclopedia/article/rahab-midrash-and-aggadah.

Kaplan, Mordecai M. *The Meaning of God in Modern Jewish Religion*. Detroit: Wayne State University Press, 1994.

Kassis, Hanna E. *A Concordance of the Qur'an*. Berkeley: University of California Press, 1983.

Kennedy, Edward M. *True Compass: A Memoir*. New York: Twelve, 2009.

Kershner, Isabel. "Israel to Phase Out Religious Exemptions." *New York Times*. March 13, 2014. Available at www.nytimes.com/2014/03/13/world/middleeast/israel-restricts-exemptions-from-military-service.html.

Kierkegaard, Søren. *Fear and Trembling*. Translated by Walter Lowrie. Princeton, N.J.: Princeton University Press, 1941.

Korn, Eugene. "Covenantal Possibilities in a Post-Polemical Age: A Jewish View." In *Studies in Christian-Jewish Relations* 6 (2011): 1–13. Available at ejournals.bc.edu/ojs/index.php/scjr.

Korn, Eugene, and John T. Pawlikowski. *Two Faiths, One Covenant? Jewish and*

Christian Identity in the Presence of the Other. Lanham, Md.: Rowman and Littlefield, 2005.

Kraut, Benny. *From Reform Judaism to Ethical Culture: the Religious Evolution of Felix Adler*. Cincinnati, Ohio: Hebrew Union College Press, 1979.

Krokus, Christian S. *The Theology of Louis Massignon: Islam, Christ, and the Church*. Washington, D.C.: The Catholic University of America Press, 2017.

Laoust, Henri. "Ibn 'Abd al-Wahhab." *EI2*.

———. "Ibn Taymiyya." *EI2*.

Lerner, Ralph. *Maimonides' Empire of Light: Popular Enlightenment in an Age of Belief*. Chicago: University of Chicago Press, 2000.

Levenson, Jon D. *Inheriting Abraham: The Legacy of the Patriarch in Judaism, Christianity, and Islam*. Princeton, N.J.: Princeton University Press, 2012.

Levtzion, Nehemia, and J. F. P. Hopkins, eds. *Corpus of Early Sources for West African History*. Translated by J. F. P. Hopkins. Cambridge: Cambridge University Press, 1981.

Levush, Ruth. "Israel: Supreme Court Decision Invalidating the Law on Haredi Military Draft Postponement." Law Library of Congress. Available at www.loc.gov/law/help/haredi-military-draft.php.

Lewy, Hans, Alexander Altmann, and Isaak Heinemann. *Three Jewish Philosophers*. Third edition. New Milford, Conn.: Toby Press, 2006.

Liber Devotionum ad Usum Scholasticorum Societatis Jesu. Fifth edition. Chicago: Loyola Press, 1947.

Madelung, W., and E. Tyan. "'Isma.'" *EI2*.

Mahoney, John. *The Making of Moral Theology: A Study of the Roman Catholic Tradition*. Oxford: Clarendon Press, 1987.

Maimonides, Moses. *Book of Knowledge: From the Mishneh Torah of Maimonides*. Translated by H. M. Russell and Rabbi J. Weinberg. New York: Ktav, 1983.

———. "13 Foundations of Judaism." Translated by Marc Mermelstein. Available at www.mesora.org/13principles.html.

———. "Treatise on the Resurrection." Translated by Hillel G. Fradkin. In Ralph Lerner, *Maimonides' Empire of Light: Popular Enlightenment in an Age of Belief*. Chicago: University of Chicago Press, 2000.

Malcolm X. *The Autobiography of Malcolm X*, with the assistance of Alex Haley. New York: Grove Press, 1965.

Martin, Maurice, and Rose Marie Massad. "'Al-Takfir wal-Hijrah': A Study in Sectarian Protest." In *Arab Culture 1977: Religious Identity and Radical Perspectives*. C.E.M.A.M. Reports 5. Beirut: Dar al-Mashreq, 1980.

Martin, Richard C. "Pilgrimage: Muslim Pilgrimage." *EJ2*.

Massignon, Louis. *Opera Minora*. Edited by Youakim Moubarac. Paris: Presses universitaires de France, 1969.

————. *The Passion of al-Hallaj: Mystic and Martyr of Islam*. Translated by Herbert Mason. Princeton, N.J.: Princeton University Press, 1982.

————. "The Three Prayers of Abraham." In *Testimonies and Reflections: Essays of Louis Massignon*, edited by Herbert Mason. Notre Dame, Ind.: University of Notre Dame Press, 1989.

Mawdudi, Sayyid Abu'l Al'a. *Let Us Be Muslims*. Edited by Khurram Murad. Leicester: Islamic Foundation, 1982.

McKenzie, John L. "Aspects of Old Testament Thought." In *NJBC*, 77.

Meddeb, Abdelwahab. *The Malady of Islam*. Translated by Pierre Joris and Ann Reid. New York: Basic Books, 2002.

————. *Islam and the Challenge of Civilization*. Translated by Jane Kuntz. New York: Fordham University Press, 2013.

Meier, John P. "Jesus." In *NJBC*, 1321b.

————. *A Marginal Jew*, vol. 2: *Mentor, Message, and Miracles*. Garden City, N.Y.: Doubleday, 1994.

Mendelssohn, Moses. *Gesammelte Schriften Jubiläumsausgabe*. Stuttgart-Bad Cannstatt: Frommann-Holzboog, 1971.

————. *Jerusalem or On Religious Power and Judaism*. Translated by Allan Arkush. London: University of New England Press for Brandeis University Press, 1983.

Mendenhall, George E. "Faith and Covenant in Israel and the Ancient Middle East." *The Biblical Archaeologist* 17, no. 2 (May 1954); no. 3 (September 1954): 49–76.

Metcalf, Barbara Daly. *Islamic Revival in British India: Deoband, 1860–1900*. Princeton, N.J.: Princeton University Press, 1982.

Meyer, Donald. *The Positive Thinkers: Popular Religious Psychology from Mary Baker Eddy to Norman Vincent Peale to Ronald Reagan*. Middletown, Conn.: Wesleyan University Press, 1988.

Midrash Rabbah. Translated by Rabbi Dr. H. Freedman and Maurice Simon. London: Soncino Press, 1939.

Miller, William D. *Dorothy Day: A Biography*. New York: Harper, 1982.

Molnar, Thomas. "Charles Maurras, Shaper of an Age." *Modern Age* 41, no. 4 (1999): 337–92.

Morgan, Ted. "L'Affaire Touvier: Opening Old Wounds." *New York Times* Sunday Magazine. October 1, 1989. Available at www.nytimes.com/1989/10/01/magazine/l-affaire-touvier-opening-old-wounds.html.

"Morning Service for Week-Days." In *The Union Prayer Book for Jewish Worship*. New York: The Central Conference of American Rabbis, 1940.

Nasser, Gamal Abdel. *The Philosophy of the Revolution*. Buffalo, N.Y.: Economica Books, 1959.

Nelson, Eric. *The Jesuits and the Monarchy: Catholic Reform and Political Authority in France. 1590–1615*. Aldershot: Ashgate Publishing Company for the Institutum Historicum Societatis Jesu, 2005.

Neusner, Jacob. *Torah from Our Sages: A New American Translation and Explana-tion: Pirke Avot*. Dallas: Rossel Books, 1984.

The New Catholic Encyclopedia. Second edition. Edited by Thomas Carson. Detroit: Thomson, Gale, 2002.

The New Jerome Biblical Commentary. Edited by Raymond E. Brown, SS, Joseph A. Fitzmyer, SJ, Roland E. Murphy, O. Carm. Englewood Cliffs, N.J.: Prentice Hall, 1990.

Newman, John Henry Cardinal. *An Essay on the Development of Christian Doctrine*. London: Longmans, Green, and Co., 1909.

Niebuhr, H. Richard. *Christ and Culture*. Revised edition. San Francisco: Harper-Collins, 2001.

Nizam Ad-Din Awliya. *Morals for the Heart*. Translated by Bruce B. Lawrence. New York: Paulist Press, 1992.

Norris, H. T. *The Pilgrimage of Ahmad Son of the Little Bird of Paradise*. Warminster: Aris and Phillips, 1977.

O'Brien, Michael. *John F. Kennedy: A Biography*. New York: St. Martin's Press, 2005.

O'Connor, Cardinal John. "Dorothy Day's Sainthood Cause Begins." *Catholic New York*. March 16, 2000. Available at www.catholicworker.org/dorothyday/canonizationtext.cfm?Number=82.

Origen. *Homilies on Joshua*. In *Patrologia Graeca*, edited by J.-P. Migne, vol. 12. Paris: Imprimerie Catholique, 1854–66.

———. *On First Principles*. Translated by G. W. Butterworth. New York: Harper and Row, 1966.

The Oxford Dictionary of the Christian Church. Edited by F. L. Cross. London: Oxford University Press, 1961.

The Oxford Study Bible: Revised English Bible with the Apocrypha. Edited by M. Jack Suggs et al. New York: Oxford University Press, 1992.

Oxtoby, Willard G., ed. *World Religions: Western Traditions*. Oxford: Oxford University Press, 1996.

Padwick, Constance. *Muslim Devotions: A Study of Prayer-Manuals in Common Use*. London: SPCK, 1961.

Pannenberg, Wolfhart. "The Revelation of God in Jesus of Nazareth." In *Theology as History. New Frontiers in Theology: Discussions Among Continental and American Theologians*, edited by James M. Robinson and John B. Cobb, Jr. New York: Harper and Row, 1967.

———. "Dogmatic Theses on the Doctrine of Revelation." In *Revelation as History*, edited by Wolfhart Pannenberg, translated by David Granskou. London: Macmillan, 1968.

Peale, Norman Vincent. *The Power of Positive Thinking: Special 35th Anniversary Edition*. New York: Simon and Schuster, 1987.

Pedersen, J. "Amin." *EI2*.

Pepper, George B. *The Boston Heresy Case in View of the Secularization of Religion: A Case Study in the Sociology of Religion*. Lewiston, N.Y.: Edwin Mellen Press, 1988.

Peres, Shimon. "Address of His Excellency Shimon Peres, the President of Israel, Vatican Gardens, Sunday, 8 June 2014." Available at www.vatican.va.

Perkins, Pheme. "The Gospel According to John." In *NJBC*, 61.

Philo. *Philo IV*. Translated by F. H. Coulson and G. H. Whitaker. Loeb Classical Library 261. Cambridge, Mass.: Harvard University Press, 1932.

———. *Philo VI*. Translated by F. H. Coulson. Loeb Classical Library 289. Cambridge, Mass.: Harvard University Press, 1984.

Qutb, Sayyid. *Milestones*. Damascus: Dar al-Ilm, n.d.

Rahman, Fazlur. *Islam*. Second edition. Chicago: University of Chicago Press, 1979.

Rahner, Karl. *Foundations of Christian Faith: an Introduction to the Idea of Christianity*. Translated by William V. Dych, SJ. New York: Crossroad, 1982.

Rattray, Robert Sutherland. *Religion and Art in Ashanti*. Oxford: Clarendon, 1927.

———. *The Tribes of the Ashanti Hinterland*. Oxford: Clarendon Press, 1932.

Ratzinger, Joseph Cardinal. *Einführung in das Christentum*. Munich: Kösel-Verlag, 1968.

———. *The Spirit of the Liturgy*. Translated by John Saward. San Francisco: Ignatius Press, 2000.

———. "The Heritage of Abraham: The Gift of Christmas." *L'Osservatore Romano*. December 29, 2000.

———. *Introduction to Christianity*. Translated by J. R. Foster. San Francisco: Ignatius Press, 2004.

Ricoeur, Paul. *Figuring the Sacred: Religion, Narrative and the Imagination*. Translated by David Pellauer. Edited by Mark I. Wallace. Minneapolis, Minn.: Fortress Press, 1995.

Riley-Smith, Jonathan. *The First Crusade and the Idea of Crusading*. Second edition. London: Continuum, 2012.

Robinson, F. C. R. "Mawdudi." *EI2*.

Rosenzweig, Franz. *Ninety-Two Poems and Hymns of Yehuda Halevi*. Translated by Thomas Kovach, Eva Jospe, and Gilya Gerda Schmidt. Edited by Richard Cohen. Albany: State University of New York Press, 2000.

Rudoren, Jodi. "Ten Jewish Men Detained at Temple Mount." *New York Times*. October 14, 2013.

Ryan, Patrick J. "The 'Catholic Muslim': The Conversion of Louis Massignon." *Commonweal* 140 (January 25, 2013): 15–18.

Sacks, Jonathan. *To Heal a Fractured World: the Ethics of Responsibility*. New York: Schocken Books, 2005.

Sanneh, Lamin. *Abolitionists Abroad: American Blacks and the Making of Modern West Africa*. Cambridge, Mass.: Harvard University Press, 1999.

Sarna, Nahum M., Baruch A. Levine, Jacob Milgrom, and Jeffrey H. Tigay. *The JPS*

Torah Commentary: The Traditional Hebrew text with the new JPS Translation Commentary. New York: Jewish Publication Society, 1991.

Scheindlin, Raymond. *The Song of the Distant Dove: Judah Halevi's Pilgrimage.* New York: Oxford University Press, 2008.

Schimmel, Annemarie. *Mystical Dimensions of Islam.* Chapel Hill: University of North Carolina Press, 1975.

Schwarzfuchs, Simon R. "Crusades." *EJ2.*

Sells, Michael A., ed. and trans. *Early Islamic mysticism: Sufi, Qur'an, Miraj, Poetic and Theological Writings.* New York: Paulist Press, 1996.

Setzer, Claudia. *Resurrection of the Body in Early Judaism and Early Christianity: Doctrine, Community and Self-Definition.* Leiden: Brill, 2004.

Simpson, J. A., and E. S. C. Weiner. *The Oxford English Dictionary.* Oxford: Clarendon Press, 1989.

Singer, Isaac Bashevis. *A Friend of Kafka and Other Stories.* New York: Farrar, Straus and Giroux, 1970.

Skehan, Patrick W. "Septuagint." *New Catholic Encyclopedia: Supplement* (2009), 920b.

Smith, Jane I. "Faith." *EQ.*

Smith, Wilfred Cantwell. *Modern Islam in India: A Social Analysis.* Second edition. Lahore: Sh. Muhammad Ashraf, 1963.

———. *The Faith of Other Men.* New York: New American Library, 1965.

———. *Islam in Modern History.* Princeton, N.J.: Princeton University Press, 1957.

Sorensen, Theodore C. *Kennedy.* New York: Harper and Row, 1965.

TaHa, Mahmud M. *The Second Message of Islam.* Translated by Abdullahi Ahmed an-Na'im. Syracuse, N.Y.: Syracuse University Press, 1987.

al-Tabari, Abu Ja'far Muḥammad b. Jarīr. *The Commentary on the Qur'an.* Edited and translated by J. Cooper. Oxford: Oxford University Press, 1987.

Tafsir Ibn Kathir. Available at www.qtafsir.com/index.php?option=com_ content&task=view&id=3000.

The Talmud: Selected Writings. Translated by Ben Zion Bokser. Mahwah, N.J.: Paulist Press, 1989.

Teresa of Avila. *The Life of Teresa of Jesus: the Autobiography of Teresa of Avila.* Translated and edited by E. Allison Peers. New York: Image Books, 1991.

"Universal Prayer: Day for Pardon." Available at www.vatican.va.

Updike, John. *Pigeon Feathers and Other Stories.* New York: Knopf, 1962.

Vaglieri, Laura Veccia. "Fatima." *EI2.*

Vatican Council II. *Lumen Gentium.* November 21, 1964. Available at www.vatican.va.

———. *Nostra Aetate.* October 28, 1965. Available at www.vatican.va.

Vincent of Lerins. *Commonitorium.* Available at www.documentacatholicaomnia .eu/04z/z_0370–0450Vincentius_Lirinensis_Commonitorium_Primum_ [ex_Editione_Baluziana]_MLT.pdf.html.

Vollbrecht, Judith A. *Structure and Communitas in an Ashanti Village: The Role of Funerals*. Ann Arbor, Mich.: University Microfilms, 1979.

Walker, J. Brent. "Should American Flags be in Church Sanctuaries?" Baptist Joint Committee for Religious Liberty. Available at bjconline.org/should-american -flags-be-in-church-sanctuaries/.

Washington, Margaret. *Sojourner Truth's America*. Chicago: University of Illinois Press, 2009.

Watt, W. Montgomery. *Muhammad at Mecca*. Oxford: Clarendon Press, 1953.

———. *Muhammad at Medina*. Oxford: Clarendon Press, 1956.

———. *Muslim Intellectual: A Study of al-Ghazali*. Edinburgh: University of Edinburgh Press, 1963.

———. *The Formative Period of Islamic Thought*. Edinburgh: University of Edinburgh Press, 1973.

Wehr, Hans. *A Dictionary of Modern Written Arabic*. Edited by J. Milton Cowan. Ithaca, N.Y.: Cornell University Press, 1966.

Weinfeld, Moshe. "What Makes the Ten Commandments Different?" *Bible Review* 7, no. 2 (April 1991): 29–36.

Wensinck, A. J. "Kibla." *EI2*.

Wensinck, A. J., J. Jomier, and B. Lewis. "Hadjdj." *EI2*.

"'Whistleblower' label for St. Mary MacKillop called innaccurate and wrong." Catholic News Agency, Rome. October 28, 2010. Available at www.catholic newsagency.com/news/whistleblower-label-for-st.-mary-mackillop-called -innaccurate-and-wrong/.

Wills, Garry. *Inventing America: Jefferson's Declaration of Independence*. Boston: Houghton Mifflin, 2002.

Wills, Lawrence. "The Gospel According to Mark." In *The Jewish Annotated New Testament: New Revised Standard Version*, edited by Amy-Jill Levine and Marc Zvi Brettler. Oxford: Oxford University Press, 2011.

Wine, Sherwin T. *Judaism beyond God: A Radical New Way to be Jewish*. Farmington Hills, Mich.: Society for Humanistic Judaism, 1985.

Wittgenstein, Ludwig. *Tractatus Logico-Philosophicus*. Translated by C. K. Ogden. London: Routledge and Kegan Paul, 1922.

Young, Richard. *The Rise of Lakewood Church and Joel Osteen*. New Kensington, Penn.: Whitaker House, 2007.

Zornberg, Avivah Gottlieb. *The Particulars of Rapture: Reflections on Exodus*. New York: Image, 2000.

INDEX

Abba, 215–16

Abbas, Mahmoud, 46

Abboud, Shaykh 'Omar, 112

'Abd Allah II (king of Jordan), 113

abolition, 136–37

Abraham: and "Abrahamic religions," 46–47, 52; in Benedict XVI, 47; and call of patriarch, 54–57, 61–62, 64; covenant with, 43, 54–57; culture and, 117–19; faith and, 60–65, 74–77; in Feiler, 53; in Francis, 46–47; in Galatians, 61–62, 68; in Genesis, 51, 53–57; Hagar and, 70–72; *hajj* and, 196–97; in Hebrews, 74–75; henotheism of, 68–69; in Ibn 'Arabi, 69–70; Isaac and, 65, 75–77; in Isaiah, 76; Islam and, 35, 50–52, 66–70, 72–73; in James, 74–75; in John Paul II, 47; Judaism and, 53–60, 66–67, 76; in Kierkegaard, 77; in Levenson, 52–54; in *Lumen Gentium,* 49; Mecca in, 67; monotheism and, 53, 66–70; in New Testament, 60, 66–69, 74–76; in *Nostra Aetate,* 49–50; in Paul, 60–65; in Philo, 57–58; pilgrimage and, 183–84, 196–97; plurality and, 68; and prayer for Isaac, 51; and prayer for Ishmael, 51–52; and prayer for Sodom, 51; in Priestly source of Genesis, 56–57; problems with, 70–73; as progenitor of Israel, 54–60; in Qur'an, 35, 66–69, 72–73, 75; repentance and, 136; in Wisdom, 76

Abraham's Path, 52–53

Abu Bakr, 147

Action Française, 85

Acts of the Apostles, 63–64, 165–66, 191

Addison, Joseph, 79

Adler, Felix, 96

Adonai, 55, 208, 211–12, 217–18

Afghanistan, 90–91, 115

afterlife. *See* life after death

'ahd, 23, 34–35

Akbar (Mughal emperor), 116

'Alawi, 101

Albania, 102

'Ali, 89, 228

'Ali al-Rida, 201

aliya, 182–88, 192

Allah, 36n34, 69, 221–25

al-Rahim, 223–24

al-Rahman, 223–24

āmana, 33, 35–36

Amaziah, 184

Amen: faith and, 27; of Jesus Christ, xv, 30–31; in Paul, 31–32

American flag, 99–100

Amin, xv, xv–xvi

Amos, 184

Amos, Book of, 184

An-Na'im, 'Abdullahi Ahmed, 150

Antiochus IV Epiphanes (Seleucid ruler), 93, 160

Aquinas, Thomas, 11, 174

Arabic naming conventions, 220–21

Arinze, Francis, 123–24, 212n16

Arkoun, Mohammed, 114–16

Arkush, Alan, 94n46

Asherah, 126

Ashkenazi Jews, 82–83

Atatürk, Mustafa Kemal, 102

Augustine, 9–10

Averroes. *See* Ibn Rushd

Axial Period, 128–29

Baal, 126
bara'atun, 34n32
Barimah, Agyei, 156–58, 176
Barth, Karl, 92
Bartholomew (ecumenical patriarch), 45–46
basmala, 219–20, 222–23, 228
Bedouin, 57, 71
Beer-sheba, 183
Ben Hanina, Jose, 130, 134
Ben Sirach, Jesus, 31
Ben Zakkai, Yohanan, 134
Benedict XVI (pope), 3, 47, 84, 88, 109–11, 124, 138–39, 192–93. *See also* Ratzinger, Joseph
Berakot, 130, 211
Bereshit Rabbah, 58–59, 62–63
Bergoglio, Jorge Mario, 111–12. *See also* Francis (pope)
Bethel, 183–84
Billot, Louis, 85
bin Laden, 'Usama, 91
blasphemy, 64, 205–6, 222
Boston, 8, 120
brotherhood, 20–21
Bruno, Giordano, 122
Buber, Martin, 4, 16, 41, 105–7, 208n6
bullroarer, 5n4
Bunyan, John, 180–82

Canaan, 55–57, 67, 196, 232
Carter, Stephen, 107–8
Cassidy, Edward, 123
Catherine of Siena, 137
Catholic Worker community, 140–41
Cave of Treasures, The (Ephrem), 65
Christ and Culture (Niebuhr), 80–81, 91–92, 96–97
Cicero, 22
civil rights movement, 132–33
Claudel, Paul, 3
Clement, 233
Common Word initiative, 110–14
Confederacy of the Virtuous, 143
Confessions (Augustine), 9
Constantine, 191–92
Coton, Pierre, 205–6

"Covenant and Mission" (Dulles), 42n47
covenants: and Abraham, 43, 54–57; between equals, 20–23; faith and, 28–38; with God, 39–42; Judaism and, 42–43; as marriage, 39–40; in New Testament, 28–33; in Qur'an, 23, 33–38; suzerainty, 23–27; in Torah, 23–25, 29
Crusades, 193–94
Cultural Zionism, 105–7
culture: Christ and, 81; defined, 79–80; faith integrating, 104–16; faith rejecting, 81–91; Islam and, 88–91, 100–104, 112–16; Judaism and, 81–84, 92–96, 105–9
Culture-Protestantism, 92
Cushing Richard, 86n20
Cyril (bishop of Jerusalem), 192

Daniel, Book of, 129n6, 161, 185
Dar al-'Ulum, 90–91
David, 20–22, 183, 215
Day, Dorothy, 139–42
Day of Pardon, 121–25
death. *See* life after death
Deborah, 137
Decius (Roman emperor), 169
"Declaration on the Relation of the Church to Non-Christian Religions," 49–50
de las Casas, Bartolomé, 137
Deuteronomist author of Genesis, 208
Deuteronomy, Book of, 24, 27, 127, 164, 164n12, 183, 226
discipleship, 29
"Dogmatic Constitution on the Church," 48–49
Dreyfus Affair, 85
Duffy, Eamon, 17–18
Dulles, Avery, 28–30, 42n47, 87n12

Ecclesiasticus, 31, 154
Edict of Milan, 191–92
Ego eimi ho-ōn, 209
Egypt, 28, 56–57, 71, 73, 90–91, 93, 159, 161, 192, 210, 224
Ehyeh-Asher-Ehyeh, 208–10
El, 206
elengchos, 6

Eliot, George (Mary Ann Evans), 79
Eloah, 207
Elohim, 206–8, 212, 217
Elohist author of Genesis, 55–56, 71, 208
Enlightenment Jew, 4
Ephrem, 65
Erdogan, Recep Tayyip, 102
Etchegaray, Roger, 123
Ethical Culture movement, 96
Ethiopia, 136, 143, 146
Eusebius, 191n15, 192n16
Exodus, Book of, 25–26, 126–27, 182–83, 208, 210–11, 213
Ezekiel, Book of, 127–31, 160

faith: Abraham and, 60–65, 74–77; accommodating culture, 91–104; Amen and, 27; as attachment, 26–27; bilateral nature of, 23; as connection, 26–27; covenant and, 28–38; crisis of, 11–13; in Epistle to Hebrews, 2–3, 6; future and, 3–4; integrating culture, 104–16; in Islam, 11–13; in John, 32; in Judaism, 26–27; justification by, 60–65; in Mark, 29–30; in New Testament, 28–33; in Qur'an, 33–38; rejecting culture, 81–91; in Revelation, 32–33; suzerainty covenants and, 23–27
Faith of Our Fathers (Duffy), 17–18
falsafa, 100–101, 173
Farabi, Abu Nasr al-, 101
Fatima, 201, 228–29
Fear and Trembling (Kierkegaard), 77
Feast of Christ the King, 48–49
Feast of First-Fruits, 182
Feast of Passover, 182, 189, 190
Feast of Tabernacles, 182–83
Feast of Weeks, 182
Feeney, Leonard, 86–88
Feeneyites, 86–88
Feiler, Bruce, 53
1 Corinthians, 32, 41, 64, 165–67, 214
1 Kings, 134, 183
1 Maccabees, 93
1 Samuel, 21
1 Thessalonians, 167n16
First Vatican Council, 86

Flanagan, Bernard, 88
Floch, Henri le, 85
Fourth Lateran Council, 10n7
France, 85, 205; language of, 205–6
Francis (pope), 45–47, 50, 88, 111–12, 124. *See also* Bergoglio, Jorge Mario
"Friend of Kafka, A" (Singer), 16–17
friendship, 20–23, 40–41, 121
funerals, 175–76. *See also* life after death
future, faith and, 3–4

Galatians, Epistle to, 31, 61–64, 68, 72, 134–35, 165, 216
Galileo Galilei, 122
Gantin, Bernardin, 122
gendering God, 225–29
Genesis, Book of, 26, 51–59, 62–67, 70–77, 183–84, 206, 208, 212
Genesis Rabbah, 212, 217
Germany, 79, 86, 131–32
Ghana, 5, 19, 78, 156–57, 175, 178, 235
Ghazali, Abu Hamid al-, 11–13, 101–2, 173–75
Gnostics, 92, 152, 228n63
God: as *Abba*, 215–16; as *Adonai*, 211–12; as *Allah*, 221–22; as *al-Rahim*, 223–24; as *al-Rahman*, 223–24; in Aquinas, 11, 11n8; in *basmala*, 219–20, 222–23; in Buber, 41; covenant with, 39–42; as *Ego eimi ho-ōn*, 209; as *Ehyeh-Asher-Ehyeh*, 208–10; as *Eloah*, 207; as *Elohim*, 206–8, 212, 217; in Elohist author of Genesis, 55–56; as Father, 215; fidelity with, 22–23; gendering, 225–29; in Humanistic Judaism, 96; as *Kyrios*, 218; in *Lumen Gentium*, 50; in *Nostra Aetate*, 50; in Qur'an, 36–37, 40–41; in Song of Solomon, 39; suzerainty covenants and, 25; transcendence of, 10; in Yahwistic author of Genesis, 55
God, naming of: Christ and, 213–19; gendering and, 225–29; in Islam, 219–25, 228–29; in Judaism, 206–13
Goliath, 21
graciousness, 3–4, 25, 34
Grand Mufti, 46–47
grave goods, 159
Green Book, The (Qaddafi), 103

Hagar, 54, 56–57, 70–73, 136, 196
Haggai, 185
Haggai, Book of, 82, 130, 185
hajj, 72, 144, 182, 195–200
Halevi, Judah, 185–86
Hallaj, Al-Husayn ibn Mansur al-, 148–49
Hamao, Stephen Fumio, 123
hanif, 66, 145
Hanukkah, 93, 109, 189n12
haredim, 81–84
Harissa, 201
Harvard University, 86
ha-Shem, 214–17. *See also* tetragrammaton
Haskala, 94
Hebrews, Epistle to, 1–3, 6, 41–42, 74–75, 117, 143, 231–33
Hebron, 183
Hellenization, 92–93, 100–102, 160
henotheism, 68, 207–8
Henri IV (king of France), 205–6
Herod the Great, 185
Heschel, Abraham Joshua, 130–33
hesed, 108
Hildegard of Bingen, 137
hityavnut, 92–93
Hobbes, Thomas, 79
Hodgson, Marshall, 101n61
Holocaust, 42n47, 83, 110–12, 123, 163
Holwerda, David E., 43n48
Hopkins, Gerard Manley, 7–9
Huldah, 137
hypostasis, 2–3

Ibadiyyah, 89n26
Iblis, 148–49
Ibn 'Abd al-Wahhab, 90
Ibn 'Arabi, 69–70, 116
Ibn 'Ata'illah, 224n33
Ibn Haylan, Yuhanna, 101
Ibn Ibrahim, Yahya, 199–200
Ibn Ishaq, Muhammad, 73, 143, 146–47
Ibn Kathir, 144
Ibn Rushd (Averroes), 101
Ibn Talal, Ghazi ibn Muhammad, 113
Ibn Taymiyya, 89–90
Ibn Umm Maktum, 'Abd Allah, 144
idolatry, 48, 69, 126–27, 184

Incoherence of the Philosophers, The (Ghazali), 101, 174
Ireland, 100, 201–2
Isaac, 51, 54, 56–57, 59, 65, 71, 75–77, 136, 165, 183–84
Isaiah, Book of, 26, 63–64, 68, 76, 82, 110, 159, 207–8, 215, 218, 226–27
Ishmael, 51–52, 71–73
Islam: Abraham and, 35, 50–52, 66–70, 72–73; *Common Word* initiative and, 112–14; culture and, 100–104, 112–16; faith in, 11–13; faith rejecting culture in, 88–91; Hagar in, 73; Hellenization and, 100–102; Ishmael and, 51–52; in Libya, 102–4; life after death in, 170–75; in *Lumen Gentium*, 49–50; in Massignon, 51–52; and naming of God, 219–25, 228–29; nature in, 38; neo-Hanbalism and, 224–25; in *Nostra Aetate*, 49–50; pilgrimage and, 195–201; plurality and, 152; polytheism and, 69; in prayer for Feast of Christ the King, 48; repentance and, 142–50; Sufism in, 12, 116, 220, 224; in Turkey, 102; Wahhabism and, 224–25. *See also* Qur'an
Islamism, 48
Israel, 46–47, 83–84, 95, 106–7
Itzhaki, Shlomo. *See* Rashi

Jacob, 183
Jacob of Serugh, 168–70, 172
jahiliyya, 89–90
James, Epistle of, 74–75, 235–36
Jaspers, Karl, 128–29
Jefferson, Thomas, 97
Jeremiah, Book of, 4, 28, 41, 127, 133–34
Jeroboam (ruler of Northern Kingdom), 184
Jerusalem; or, On Religious Power and Judaism (Mendelssohn), 94
Jesus Christ: "Amen" of, xv, 30–31; culture and, 81; at Last Supper, 227; and naming of God, 213–19; pilgrimage and, 187–91; and sacrifice of Isaac, 65
Job, Book of, 17–18, 207
John, Gospel of, xv, 30–32, 60, 81, 166–67, 189–90, 217–19

John of Damascus, 44–45
John of the Cross, 39–40
John Paul II (pope), 47, 88, 121–22, 124–25, 151
Johnson, Samuel, 79
John the Baptist, 60
Johst, Hanns, 79–80
Jonathan, 20–22
Joshua, Book of, 24, 232–33
Josiah, 127
Jubilees, Book of, 68–69
Judah, 26–27
Judaism: Abraham and, 53–60, 66–67, 76; Ashkenazi, 82; civil rights movement and, 132–33; covenant and, 42–43; culture and, 81–84, 92–96, 105–9; Ethical Culture movement, 96; faith in, 26–27; *haredim* in, 81–84; Hellenization and, 92–93, 160; Holocaust and, 42n47, 83, 110–12, 123, 163; Humanistic, 95–96; Israel and, 83–84; life after death in, 159–64; Mizrahi in, 82; naming of God in, 206–13; pilgrimage and, 182–87, 200; in prayer for Feast of Christ the King, 48–49; Reconstructionist, 95; Reform, 95, 163; repentance and, 126–33; Second Temple, 31, 108–9; Sephardi in, 82; Shoah and, 42n47, 83, 110–12, 123, 163; Zionism and, 105–7. *See also* Talmud; Torah
Judges, Book of, 137
justification: by faith, 60–65
Justinian (Byzantine emperor), 168n19

Ka'ba, 67, 69, 145, 195–97
Kaplan, Mordecai, 95
Karris, Robert J., 227n39
Kennedy, John Fitzgerald, 98
Kennedy, Joseph P., 86n20
Kennedy, Robert, 86n20
Kennedy family, 86
Kestenbaum, Sara, 107–8
Khadija, 33
Kharijites, 89–90
Kierkegaard, Søren, 77
Korn, Eugene, 42n47, 43n49
kufr, 89–90
Kyrios, 217–18

Lakewood Church (Houston), 98–99
Last Supper, 227
Lefebvre, Marcel, 84–85, 88
Leo XIII (pope), 140
Levenson, Jon D., 52–54, 61
Libya, 102–4
life after death: in Christianity, 164–70; in Islam, 170–75; in Judaism, 159–64. *See also* funerals; resurrection
Loyola, Ignatius, 194–95
Luke, 28n13
Luke, Gospel of, 41, 63, 137, 164–65, 167, 188–89, 214n20, 227
Lumen Gentium, 48–49
Lutheran Reformation, 123

MacKillop, Mary, 138–39
Maimonides, Moses, 94, 162–63, 200
Makkot, 130
Manasseh, 126–28
Mark, Gospel of, 29–30, 64, 94n45, 113, 164, 189–90, 215, 227
marriage: covenantal relationship as, 39–40
Mary, 72–73, 187, 201
Mary Magdalene, 167, 227
Massignon, Louis, 50–52, 149n48, 228–29n40
Matthew, Gospel of, 31, 134, 164, 167, 189, 213–14, 216–17
Maurin, Peter, 140–42
Maurras, Charles, 85
Mawdudi, Mawlana, 90–91
Mecca, 12, 35, 67, 69, 72, 73, 91, 103, 143–50, 195–200. *See also* hajj
Meddeb, Abdelwahab, 115–16
Melchizedek, 65, 184
Melito of Sardis, 191n15
Mendelssohn, Moses, 94–95
Mendenhall, George E., 24
mercy, 25, 31, 36, 42, 48, 112, 161, 175, 199, 212–13, 217, 220–23
Middlemarch (Eliot), 79
Miriam, 137
Mishneh Torah (Maimonides), 162–63
mithaq, 23, 34–35
Mizrahi Jews, 82

monotheism, 41, 47, 52–53, 58, 66–70, 75, 104–5, 145–47, 151, 188, 197–98, 221–22, 230

More, Thomas, 79

Moriah, 74, 183–84, 196

Mount 'Arafat, 199, 202

Muhammad: as al-Amin, 33; hajj and, 197–98; polytheism and, 69; repentance and, 143–48. See also Islam

Muslims. See Islam; Qur'an

Nana Tongo, 5

Nasa'i, Ahmad al-, 223n29

Nasser, Gamal Abdel, 102

National Conference of Citizens for Religious Freedom, 98

nature, 38

Nazism, 110, 112, 131–32

neo-Hanbalism, 224–25

Newman, John Henry, 153–55

New Testament: Abraham in, 60, 66–69, 74–76; Amen in, xvi; covenant in, 23, 28–33; culture and, 91–92; faith in, 28–33, 36; naming of God in, 214, 216–17, 221, 228; repentance in, 121, 133–34; Trinity and, 214. See also specific books

Nguyen Van Thuan, François Xavier, 124

Niebuhr, Richard, 80–81, 91–92, 96–97

Nixon, Richard Milhous, 98

Nizam al-din Awliya, Shaykh, 224

Nizam al-Mulk, 11–12, 221

Nostra Aetate, 49–50, 109, 123

Numbers, Book of, 162, 184, 211

Nusayri, 101

Nutsugah, Edward, 236

O'Connor, John, 140

Office of the Dead, 15–18

Origen, 168

Origenists, 168–69

Osteen, Joel, 98–99

Palestine, 46–47, 57–58, 106

Pannenberg, Wolfhart, 167–68

Passover. See Feast of Passover

patriarch, call of, 54–57, 61–62, 64

Paul, 31–32, 42, 53–54, 60–65, 72, 134–37, 165–67, 214–18

Paul VI (pope), 88

Pawlikowski, John T., 43n49

Peale, Norman Vincent, 97–98

Peres, Shimon, 46

Peter, 135

Pharisees, 161, 165, 169, 190

Philippians, Epistle to, 63, 218

Philo, 57–58, 60, 62

Pico della Mirandola, Giovanni, 79

"Pigeon Feathers" (Updike), 176

pilgrimage: Christ and, 187–91; Christianity and, 187–95, 200–201; Islam and, 195–201; Judaism and, 182–87, 200

Pilgrim's Progress, The (Bunyan), 180–81

Pirke Avot, 20n1

Pittsburgh Platform, 163

Pius X (pope), 85

Pius XI (pope), 48, 52, 85

plurality, 67n40, 68, 152

polytheism, 69, 146, 198

Pontifical Council on Religious Relations with Jews, 42n47

positive thinking, 97–99

Power of Positive Thinking, The (Peale), 97–98

Priestly source, of Genesis, 56–57, 208

"Profession of Faith" (Lefebvre), 84

Prosperity Gospel, 98–99

Proverbs, Book of, 32n29, 58, 108

Psalms, xv, 10, 20, 159, 182, 184, 207

Qaddafi, Mu'ammar, 102–4

Qur'an, xv–xvi; Abraham in, 35, 66–69, 72–73, 75; Amin in, xv; covenant in, 23, 33–38; culture and, 88–91; faith in, 33–38; God in, 36–37, 40–41; Hagar in, 72–73; Iblis in, 148–49; Isaac in, 75; Mary in, 72–73; plurality in, 68; resurrection in, 170–72. See also Islam

Qutb, Sayyid, 90, 91

Rabi'a al-'Adawiyya, 40–41

Rahab, 232–34

Rahman, Fazlur, 148n45

Rahner, Karl, 10

Rashi (Shlomo Itzhaki), 61, 131, 134, 210–11
Rattray, Robert Sutherland, 5n4, 158n1
Ratzinger, Joseph, 3–4, 109–10, 122, 219.
    See also Benedict XVI (pope)
Realistic Zionism, 107
"Reflections on Covenant and Mission,"
    42n47
repentance: and Day of Pardon, 121–25;
    and development of Christian tradition,
    133–42; in Greek, 121; in Hebrew, 121;
    Islam and, 142–50; in John Paul II,
    121–22; Judaism and, 126–33; in Mark,
    29; in New Testament, 133–34; self-
    criticism and, 151–55
Rerum Novarum, 140
resurrection, 159–60, 163–64, 168n19,
    170–71, 227–28. See also life after death
Revelation, Book of, 32–33, 191
"Revival of the Disciplines of Piety, The"
    (Ghazali), 11–12
Revival of the Religious Sciences, The
    (Ghazali), 174–75
rhombus, 5n4
Ricoeur, Paul, 229–30
Romans, Epistle to, 42, 61

Sacks, Jonathan, 105–9
Sadat, Anwar al-, 90–91
Sadducees, 161–62, 164
Sarah, 54, 56, 70–72, 117–19, 136
Satin Slipper, The (Claudel), 3
Saul, 21, 63
Schimmel, Annemarie, 37
Schlageter (Johst), 79–80
Schweitzer, Albert, 167
2 Chronicles, 69, 127, 137, 184
2 Corinthians, xv, 31
2 Kings, 126–27, 134, 137
2 Maccabees, 160–61
2 Samuel, 21–22
Second Temple Judaism, 31, 108, 162,
    185–91
Second Vatican Council. See Vatican II
Segal, Alan, 151n52
self-criticism, 151–55
Sephardi Jews, 82
Septuagint, xvi, 208–9, 217, 221

Serratelli, Arthur, 212n16
Shechem, 24, 183
Shoah, 42n47, 83, 110–12, 123, 163
Singer, Isaac Bashevis, 16–17
Sirach, Book of, 31, 76
Sirat Rasul Allah (Ibn Ishaq), 73
Skorka, Abraham, 46, 111–12
slavery, 72, 136–37
Sleepers of Ephesus, 168–72
Smith, Wilfred Cantwell, 36, 90n34,
    102n66, 163
Sodom, 51, 118
Solomon, 83, 128, 183–84
Song of Solomon, 22, 39
Spellman, Francis, 140
"Spiritual Canticle, The" (John of the
    Cross), 39–40
Stephen, 64
Stevenson, Adlai, 98
Strauss, Viktor von, 129n6
subha, 224–25
Sufism, 12, 116, 220, 224
Summa Theologiae (Aquinas), 11n8
supersessionism, 42n47
Surah of the Banquet, 34

Tabari, Abu Ja'far al-, 223–24
TaHa, Mahmud Muhammad, 149–50
Takfir wa'l-Hijra, 90–91
Talmud: anti-Zionism and, 83; and nam-
    ing of God, 217; repentance and, 130;
    resurrection in, 162
Ten Commandments, 25–26, 134
Teresa of Avila, 138
Tertullian, 81
tetragrammaton, 211–18. See also ha-Shem
Thatcher, Margaret, 180–81
Theodosius II (Byzantine emperor), 169–70
Thérèse of Lisieux, 138
Thomas, 167, 217
Tiberias, 200
To Heal a Fractured World (Sacks), 107–8
Tolstoy, Leo, 81
Tongnaab, 5
Torah: Abraham and, 57–58; Amen and,
    31; Bereshit Rabbah and, 58–59; cove-
    nant in, 23–25, 29; Hagar and, 72;

Torah (cont.)
  haredim and, 83; name of God in, 208, 212–13; pilgrimage and, 182; resurrection in, 164
Tractate Sanhedrin, 162, 164
transcendence, of God, 10
Trinity, 10n7, 214, 216, 228
Truth, Sojourner, 137
Turkey, 102, 110

Ugarit, 206
Updike, John, 176

Vaglieri, Laura Veccia, 228n40
Vatican II, 48–50, 84–86
Vichy France, 85
Vietnam War, 133
Vincent of Lérins, 152–53

Wahhabism, 224–25
wakes, 175–76
Whyte, Francis, 85n18
Williams, Delores S., 72
Wills, Garry, 97
"Windhover, The" (Hopkins), 7–9
Wine, Sherwin, 96
Wisdom, Book of, 76, 154
Wittgenstein, Ludwig, 229
women, 3, 72–73, 137, 142, 227–28, 233
Woods, Julian Tenison, 138–39
World War I, 139
World War II, 131–32

Yahwistic author of Genesis, 55, 70, 208, 212
Yawm Alastu, 37–38
Yitzhak, Levi, 4

Zionism, 83, 105–7, 187, 200

Amen: Jews, Christians, and Muslims Keep Faith with God was designed in Meta Serif with Meta display type and composed by Kachergis Book Design of Pittsboro, North Carolina. It was printed on 60-pound House Natural Smooth and bound by Sheridan Books of Chelsea, Michigan.